Praise for *Dead Wh*

"*Dead White Guys* is both one father's letter to his daughter and one part intellectual guide to our times. Candid, personal, and wide-ranging, it is unpretentious and wise, and would make a perfect gift for many a young person."

—Gish Jen,
author of *World and Town*

"This heartfelt book is intimate yet universal. A brilliant exploration of the Great Books of the Western World and the wisdom to be found within."

—Dinty W. Moore,
author of *Between Panic and Desire*

"This is an extraordinary book. Though Mr. Burriesci wrote it to his daughter, Violet, every one of us needs to sit down and read this exploration of what it means to read a meaningful book; every one of us needs to sit down and ponder its message that the great old books matter, today, here, now."

—Bret Lott,
author of *Letters and Life*

"In case you're not sure who those great guys are, here is a great way to begin your study. So they won't have died in vain."

—Alan Cheuse,
author, professor, book critic for NPR's *All Things Considered*

"As parents, we all feel the need to convey to our children the wisdom that we have accumulated in life, however modest it may be. Matt Burriesci takes this universal impulse further—bringing to life for his beloved daughter Violet the great books of the Western canon. In the process, he shares the challenges of his own life, and how literature served him in the most difficult of times. This is more than a memoir: it is a rich testimony to the power and value of literature in the individual life."

—Jon Parrish Peede,
National Endowment for the Arts, 2007-2011

"Aside from being a touching, funny, and tender memoir, Matt Burriesci's *Dead White Guys* is sure to generate substantial discussion (and perhaps a little controversy) inside the national literary community, especially with the tens of thousands of motivated book buyers inside the MFA community. Matt spent years helping build the largest literary conference in the United States, building the national literary infrastructure, and forging relationships with hundreds of writing programs, literary conferences, and publishers across the country. Literary leaders recognize Matt as a leading advocate for the importance of humanities in our society, and this book shows us why. An essential book for the 21st century."

—Christian Teresi,
Association of Writers and Writing Programs

"How fortunate is Matt Burriesci's daughter to have her father's reflections on the great works in Western thought and it's the lucky reader who is privy to them. Burriesci might have waited until Violet was older before writing these essays, but they may not have been lit as they are with the miracle of birth and the enlarging tenderness of being a new parent. Burriesci's human context gives these seminal ideas new clarity and fresh urgency."

—Stephen Young,
The Poetry Foundation

"*Dead White Guys* manages to be intensely personal and universal at once. This book about the importance of literature and philosophy is an education in itself. Lucky Violet, lucky us."

—Hilma Wolitzer,
author of *An Available Man*

"In Matt Burriesci's deeply moving book, a blithely disguised time-capsule letter to his daughter Violet—not to be opened until the year 2028—he does what Hemingway invoked all writers to do. He writes true sentences. One true sentence at a time. These sentences are beautifully wrought but they also have a purpose, which is to provide her with a bookshelf full of life lessons that he has gathered from his humorously labeled 'Dead White Guys,' a passel of great thinkers from Plato to Montaigne, Shakespeare to Marx. 'You will desperately need their counsel,' he writes, but not as academic calisthenics. His real gift to her and to his readers is the much-needed reminder that there is a difference between the acquisition of knowledge and the love of wisdom. His advice to her for a well-lived life is to be skeptical of authority and to ask questions. 'Life will test you,' he writes, 'it will try to strip your soul, but I know you will prevail.' No doubt, you too, dear reader, will benefit and prevail as you read this propulsive journey through the pages of his gleaned wisdom."

—Phil Cousineau,
author of *The Art of Pilgrimage*

DEAD WHITE GUYS

GUYS

A FATHER, HIS DAUGHTER AND THE
GREAT BOOKS OF THE WESTERN WORLD

BY MATT BURRIESCI

Published in the United States by Viva Editions, an imprint of Start Midnight, LLC, 375 Hudson Street, Twelfth Floor, New York, New York 10014.

Printed in the United States.
Cover design: Scott Idleman/Blink Design
Cover illustration: iStockphoto
Text design: Frank Wiedemann
First Edition.
10 9 8 7 6 5 4 3 2 1

Trade paper ISBN: 978-1-63228-017-6
E-book ISBN: 978-1-63228-026-8

Library of Congress Cataloging-in-Publication Data is available.

CONTENTS

April 8, 2015
To be read September 1, 2028

———————

Dear Violet,

When you were born I promised you a book. I didn't have much money, my job was uncertain, and the world was crazy, but I thought I could at least write you a book.

I'd like to say I was simply born with a talent to write, but it's not true. I came to writing because I was small, like you. When I was a boy, writing was an activity that didn't care how tall you were, or how strong, or how fast. I got some attention for it early on. People encouraged me. I pursued it. But I'm not in the same solar system as the writers included in this book.

So wherever this book is deficient, the fault is entirely mine, and where my inadequacy does injustice to these authors, I am sorry, both to you, and to them. Each of the works in this book demands more time and attention, and smart people disagree over what they mean. I encourage you to read them yourself. If you're looking for advice, I'll give you the best piece of advice anyone ever gave me, which came from your great-grandmother when she was 90 years old. Upon learning that I'd landed my first job, she said, "Keep your zipper zipped, your mouth shut, and if you go out in the rain, you'll get wet." I thought she'd lost her marbles. Now I think she was the wisest person I ever knew.

I wanted you to have this book for many reasons. Obviously, *The Great Books of the Western World* mean a great deal to me personally, and I wanted to share them with you. More important, I know you will not encounter them much in your education, which will be focused on teaching you—well, pretty much the opposite of everything you will find in *The Great Books of the Western World*.

Many of these books will be kept from you, or you will be scared away from them. People will tell you these books are too difficult, or they are worthless, or obsolete, or even that they are degenerate—that they are racist, sexist, or morally offensive. I called it *Dead White Guys* for a reason. As someone who worked in the humanities for decades, I know *The Great Books of the Western World* were the object of considerable criticism and even contempt. Even inside its own narrow confines, the 54-volume set, first produced by Encyclopedia Britannica in 1952 under the leadership of Robert Maynard Hutchins and Mortimer Adler, does have some rather mystifying absences (Cicero, Ovid, Voltaire, and others). And of course there is also the rather glaring lack of women, as well as the absence of any writers of color. Future editions of the set did try, rather cloyingly and unsuccessfully, to address these deficiencies. There's room for criticism.

I'm sure this is not what Adler and Hutchins intended, but eventually, the "established canon" so exemplified in *The Great Books of the Western World* became viewed as "just a bunch of dead white guys." To read them was to perpetuate systemic oppression orchestrated by white European males. So the term "dead white guys" became something I heard again and again, first as an English student, and later as the leader of a national association representing the humanities in higher education. By then it had truly become a term of derision—a term that separated the world into two opposing camps: those who were "for" diversity and inclusion, and those who were "against" it.

There exists, however, another reason for the criticism and contempt. *The Great Books of the Western World* are not interested in promoting our illusions, and they do not care about authority. They are neither gentle nor polite. They teach you how to see through illusions, and they demand that you question both yourself and your masters. Some people are afraid of that, and with good reason. And I should warn you, Violet: these books will challenge *your* illusions, too. At times you will be uncomfortable with what you find here.

But I am reminded of Flannery O'Connor's remark: "The truth does not change according to our ability to stomach it."

As for the identity politics of who is and who isn't included here—well, these are not the only books available to read, nor should they be. Yes, this set has faults. That doesn't mean you should skip Plato. Yes, you should challenge these authors, and even disagree with them. But that is the very essence of their tradition. As for diversity, the authors that are included come from different millennia, from different national, religious, political, economic, scientific, and cultural assumptions. They spoke different languages, they lived in different states, some in political entities we would not recognize as nations or states. And they certainly don't share the same point of view.

The one thing these writers do share is that they seem to be primarily concerned with our lives as *human beings*, and not merely as units of states, religions, economies, or political parties. They may consider those systems, and how best to organize them, but they are trying to make things *better*—and usually at the great expense of the prevailing ruling class of their respective ages, which is why many of them were ostracized and punished—even tortured or put to death. They possessed the ability to step outside the illusions of their eras, and to examine the human condition with courage, honesty, compassion, and logic.

These writers can teach you *how* to think, not *what* to think.

This is what I set out to give you.

By the time you read this, I believe *The Great Books of the Western World* will be more important than at any point in human history. You will desperately need their counsel, but your education will have been geared toward utility and function. You will learn to build wings. You will learn to adapt, to use technology, to become its master. You will learn to be a 21st-century worker. That is fine, even necessary. After all, you *will* be a 21st-century worker. You will also be an American. You may identify yourself as a Democrat, Republican, or an Independent. You'll probably be Christian and capitalist. At college, you will be a major, and then one day you will define yourself by your career.

But before you were any of those things, you were a human being with a soul. And I believe that we have souls, Violet; I believe that there is something inside us that is not merely the shadow of chemical and biological reactions. Plato believed this as well, but a lot of smart people disagree, including Aristotle. Aristotle believed the soul was merely an effect produced by the body. Before you arrived in my life, I was firmly in Aristotle's camp, but now I am convinced that Plato was correct. You arrived in this world without any knowledge, without fully functioning lungs, without any ability to care for yourself—and yet from the first moments of your fragile existence, you were animated by something beyond data and chemistry.

You had spirit, Violet. Man, did you have spirit.

You were fortunate to be born a citizen of one of history's greatest empires—one that had mastered the material world. But in our rise to global dominance, our empire (as all empires before it) forgot about the immaterial world, even ridiculed it as silly, or as lacking utility or value—and we have now begun to suffer the consequences of that neglect. Those consequences were on vivid display in 2010, the year you arrived in this world: financial ruin, disastrous wars, a broken and corrupt political system—they are all connected. And they are not unique to the modern era.

Perhaps things will have changed by the time you read this, but today in America, *value* has increasingly come to mean "monetary value." In 2010, Georgetown University's Center on Education set out to determine the "value" of various college degrees by measuring lifetime earnings of graduates. Not surprisingly, median annual earnings for English and humanities majors were much lower than median earnings for engineering and science majors.

"I don't want to slight Shakespeare," said one of the authors of the study. "But this study slights Shakespeare."

This is how *you* will be taught to measure value, Violet. Because America has always been an economic and technological culture, we demand empirical metrics from everything. As capitalists, we insist that everything intrinsically possesses some sort of *return on investment*. If I spend $X studying Shakespeare, then I should reap $X+1 from my labor, or else the enterprise has somehow been deficient.

I have some experience with Mr. Shakespeare. In my first job out of college, I worked for the Chicago Shakespeare Theater. I managed databases for them, and I orchestrated direct mail campaigns. Although widely used in other industries, these were relatively new tools for the theater world, and they demanded some minor administrative changes in the way the theater conducted its affairs.

But when the theater produced *Hamlet*, nobody changed the lines.

Why didn't we? A primitive man like Shakespeare could not speak to our technological age, with our higher standard of living, our computers and our Internet, our brain scans, our airplanes, and our thermonuclear devices. We could do better than Shakespeare now.

Maybe I could improve upon Shakespeare, possessing an education that was far superior to Shakespeare's own. Shakespeare didn't know what I did. He didn't know about atoms, evolution, or gravity. He certainly didn't know how disease was transmitted. The man seldom bathed himself, and he likely tossed his excrement out the window into the street. He didn't know how to build a database, or even why one would ever need such a thing. He'd never traveled around the world. He barely understood there were other continents across the ocean. He clearly had problems with the geography and history of his own country. His writing is filled with monsters, faeries, and ghosts. What a silly, dirty, ignorant man he was!

And what was the point of yet another production of *Hamlet*? The play had been produced millions of times. Surely everyone had seen it already. The audience knew everything that was going to happen. Wouldn't they be bored? There was nothing new in *Hamlet*. *Hamlet* wasn't even new when Shakespeare wrote it. He ripped off the plot and characters from another guy's play, and that guy probably stole the plot from somebody else. The basic plot structure goes all the way back to Ancient Greece, to Aeschylus, who invented the plot structure in the *Oresteia*. Guy's dad is killed. Guy agonizes over what to do. Guy avenges his dad's murder. Guy goes bonkers.

And hadn't we, as a technologically advanced civilization, answered Prince Hamlet's questions by now? Can we ask the questions of *Hamlet* of our search engines, the way we find directions or get a stock quote?

> *How are we to behave in an immoral world?*
> *How do we know the truth?*
> *What is reality?*
> *What is justice?*
> *What happens to us when we die?*
> *Do we have control over our own lives, or are we*
> *destined to do the things we do?*
> *Why do bad things happen?*
> *Does God exist?*

If God exists, does God care what happens to me?
What do I owe the state?
What do I owe my family?
What do I owe myself?
When should I use force?
When should I break the law?
Why do I want what I cannot have?
Why do the wicked seem to prosper, while the good seem
to suffer?
Why do I feel so alone?
What is courage?
Why am I here?
Why is anyone here?
Am I just a machine, or do I have a soul?

By the time you read this, you will be 18, and despite your superior education and your access to near-miraculous technology, you will probably still be asking the same questions I did when I was your age, which are the same questions Shakespeare asked 400 years ago, and the same ones Aeschylus posed 2,500 years before you were born. Maybe you think you have some answers. I hope you do. But as you get older you will find these questions more and more difficult. When I was your age, I thought I had answers. I knew right from wrong. I was in control of my own destiny. I knew the truth when I saw it. I knew the wicked would never prosper, and that the good would always prevail. I was certain there was no god, and even more certain that I was on this earth to become rich and famous.

Now that I'm older, all my answers seem absurd. I've seen the wicked prosper and the good punished. And what I once thought was evil now sometimes seems good. It's hard to tell right from wrong anymore. I'm highly skeptical of anything purporting to be the truth, yet I do believe in God, even though I can't understand that God, and God's existence defies logical proof. And I don't think I'm here for fame and fortune.

I think one of the reasons I'm here is so I could know you. That's been one of the greatest gifts of my life. Just knowing you. Seeing you grow up. Watching you learn to do things, witnessing your stubbornness. Admiring it. You were always so tough, so hilarious, and so radiant, Violet. You changed my life, and all I have to give you in return are words, words, words.

Today you're all grown up, and I hope this letter finds you on an adventure of your choosing, someplace far away from your mom and me. But once, a long time ago, back in fall 2012, we walked together to the park in Alexandria, Virginia. I always loved walking with you when you were little. You would hold my hand for a bit, and when you got tired, you'd ride on my shoulders. You were just beginning to speak in full sentences then, and that day you suddenly became aware that there were other daddies and other children at the park. You knew we were like them somehow—we weren't exactly them, but we were all similar in some ways. We took a break, and we sat on a park bench, you with a juice box in your hand. You saw another father putting his daughter in a swing, and you pointed to him and said, "He's a daddy, and you're a daddy."

I was impressed by your realization, by your ability to categorize things in the world. I marveled at how purely Aristotelian your thinking was. You were creating that space in your brain that identified the shared characteristics of daddies. *Daddies took you to the park. Daddies put you on their shoulders. Daddies helped you get in the swing.*

I said, "That's right, Violet. He's a daddy, and I'm a daddy. But what are you?"

You thought about this for a minute, your little eyes searching for an answer. Processing. Processing. Then you smiled and pointed to yourself.

"I'm a Violet!" you said.

You are more than a machine, Violet. There are things in life that can't fit inside little boxes. There is a value that can't be measured in dollars.

There are more things in heaven and earth than are dreamt of in your philosophy.

Love,
Dad

Desiring therefore to present myself to your Magnificence with some testimony of my devotion toward you, I have not found among my possessions anything that I hold more dear than, or value so much as, the knowledge of the actions of great men, acquired by long experience in contemporary affairs, and a continual study of antiquity; which, having reflected upon it with great and prolonged diligence, I now send, digested into a little volume, to your Magnificence.

And although I may consider this work unworthy of your countenance, nevertheless I trust much to your benignity that it may be acceptable, seeing that it is not possible for me to make a better gift than to offer you the opportunity of understanding in the shortest time all that I have learnt in so many years, and with so many troubles and dangers; which work I have not embellished with swelling or magnificent words, nor stuffed with rounded periods, nor with any extrinsic allurements or adornments whatever, with which so many are accustomed to load and embellish their works; for I have wished either that no honor should be given it, or else that the truth of the matter and the weightiness of the theme shall make it acceptable ....

Take then, your Magnificence, this little gift in the spirit in which I send it; wherein, if it be diligently read and considered by you, you will learn my extreme desire that you should attain that greatness which fortune and your other attributes promise.

—Niccolò Machiavelli, *The Prince*

CHAPTER 1

WHAT DO I KNOW?

PLATO

Apology

———— ⚬⚬⚬ ————

Y our mom thought something was wrong. She said she couldn't "feel" you.

I could feel you just fine. I put my hand on your mom's stomach and you kicked. Three days ago we saw you on the ultrasound sucking your thumb. We listened to your heartbeat. The doctor told us you had the hiccups.

Your mom *always* thought something was wrong. We'd been to the doctor a dozen times now, and every time they said you were fine. *Here we go,* I thought, rolling my eyes. *Another false alarm.*

I told her to lie down and wait 15 minutes. You're paranoid, I said. I joked with the guys at work about my "crazy pregnant wife." You weren't due for another two months. It said so right on my calendar: MAY 19th, 9:00 AM VIOLET, right next to my accounting meeting.

But your mom insisted.

Didn't she know how busy I was? I didn't have time for pregnancy scares every week. I had important work to do! I was a CEO. The head honcho. I had the corner office and the private bathroom. In just three days, I was leaving for the most important meeting of my life. My assistant reserved me a fancy hotel suite in Denver. When I arrived in Denver, a limousine driver would meet me at baggage claim, holding a sign with my name on it. When I checked into the hotel, the general manager of the hotel would greet me at the door. "Welcome to Denver, Mr. Burriesci," he'd say, extending his hand. He'd even pronounce my name correctly. I imagine that someone took great care to spell my name phonetically for him. Then he'd hand me a special pin to wear on my lapel. The pin would be shaped like a pineapple. The pineapple pin conveyed a message to the rest of the hotel staff for the duration of my stay: *do whatever this man asks you to do.* A chilled six-pack of my favorite beer would await me in the Presidential Suite, along with a handwritten note from the national sales manager.

"I'm serious," she said. "I really think something's wrong."

So I sighed, I left an important meeting about my important meeting, and we drove to the doctor for more tests. The doctor assured us, again, that there was no cause for concern.

"Don't be such a demanding, overachieving mom," the doctor said, playfully swatting your mom's arm with the clipboard.

"See?" I told your mom, patting her hand. "Everything's fine."

Six days later, your mom almost bled to death while I delivered my important speech on the other side of the country. The doctors cut your mom open and pulled you out. She was in labor for only 20 minutes before you were born, all three pounds, 13 ounces of you.

"It's possible we might've missed something," the doctor conceded.

The first time I saw you, the flight attendant was telling me to turn off my phone. Your grandpa emailed me a picture. There you were, on your back, unconscious, with your little hands outstretched, and semiclenched. You were in pain, lying in a clear plastic box. A giant tube covered your entire face, and there were wires everywhere. A feeding tube in your belly button. Some kind of glowing monitor snapped onto your foot. It looked like evil scientists were trying to give you superpowers, except your lungs weren't working and you might die. We could not hold you. We could not feed you. Upstairs from the NICU, your mom was recovering from major surgery.

"You have to think of it like a car crash," the doctors told me while you both slept. "It's like they've both been in car crashes."

Your digestive system wasn't up to speed, so they gave you an IV. You were jaundiced, so they put you under the heat lamp. Your lungs hadn't fully developed, so they inserted a breathing tube. It was possible your brain had been starved of oxygen, a condition called *hypoxia*. They'd know better tomorrow. When tomorrow came, they'd know better tomorrow. I needed to sign more forms.

There were other infants in the ward with you, other parents sitting by their sides. We would nod at each other, but we never spoke. We didn't talk to the other parents in the NICU, and they did not talk to us. Some babies left that ward. Others did not.

You spent the first month of your life in an incubator. Within a few days you were lying in that thing with your arms outstretched as though you were sunbathing. This, to me, has always summed up your natural spirit, Violet. You always bore adversity well. You were cheerful and tough from the start.

I do not handle adversity well. I sure wasn't cheerful. I'd stopped sleeping normally months ago. I usually slept less than four hours a night. The night before you were born, I didn't sleep at all, even in my fancy suite in Denver. It had nothing to do with you. I couldn't sleep because I was filled with anxiety and dread about my "important" job.

I was about to lose that job, and I knew it.

I didn't know what I would do if I lost my job. 2010 was the height of the Great Recession, and jobs were scarce. I also had a geography problem. I received offers, but all of them were in Washington, DC, a 90-minute commute each way. But we couldn't move, because we couldn't sell our house. At the peak of the housing crash, our home lost half its value. We owed the bank more than the house was worth. Even if we could find a buyer, we couldn't afford to sell, and we couldn't even rent it out for the cost of the mortgage payment. Like many people at that time, we were stuck.

It would be months before your mom recovered, and you weighed less than four pounds. We needed to feed you every hour. Your mom couldn't possibly go back to teaching, at least not for another year. She couldn't even walk upstairs. We had some savings, but only enough to last us a few months. How would I provide for us? What would we do?

I fixated on the worst-case scenario. I was certain I would remain unemployed, burn through our savings, and lose the house. Even before you were born, I was unhinged from lack of sleep and anxiety, and the stress manifested physically. I lost 20 pounds in three months. The skin on my hands and feet broke out in deep and painful sores. I had to cover them with huge gauze bandages and

3

medical tape. I looked like the invisible man.

As you and your mom recovered in the hospital, and all this fear churned in my gut, I went home at nights to prepare the nursery. One night, I removed several tall bookshelves from the room. I started packing up a 54-volume set of *The Great Books of the Western World*. They'd served as décor in my various abodes since I purchased them at a flea market for $50. I liked having those books around. I even read some of them in college. But mostly I kept them around to make myself feel smart.

I took a break from cleaning, and I opened the first book, which I believed to be a glorified table of contents. The editors had assembled a reading list, *10 Years of Reading*. The first book on the list was Plato's *Apology*.

In Greek, *apologia* doesn't mean "apology" like we understand it. It means "defense speech." In the context of ancient Athenian trials, the accused would make an *apologia*, the way a defendant might speak in his own defense today.

Plato's *Apology* is the defense speech of the philosopher Socrates, who was put on trial in Athens in 399 BCE, on charges that he was an atheist, and that he'd corrupted the youth of Athens. Socrates was convicted of these charges and sentenced to death. He accepted his sentence and drank poison. Cheerfully.

Socrates was an actual historical figure, but he himself never wrote anything down (or if he did, it's lost to us). After he was executed, his student Plato used Socrates as a kind of lead character. Our historical notion of Socrates—as the doomed yet noble philosopher who annoys everyone—comes to us almost entirely from Plato's version of him. It may be that Plato was trying to honor Socrates, and record his teachings faithfully and to the best of his ability. It may be that Plato simply used Socrates as a character, to advance Plato's own ideas. It could be a bit of both. It doesn't really matter. The Socratic Dialogues are so engrained in our Western way of thinking that it's difficult to imagine the world that preceded them.

As original a creature as you may be, Violet, what you think, and the way you think about it, was shaped by Plato. In some sense, we are all Platonists. The same is true of all the authors in this book.

4

Many respond to Plato directly, even thousands of years after his death. As Macedonia is rising, Aristotle responds first, and in quite a contrary manner, disagreeing with Plato almost comprehensively. Centuries later, under the Roman Empire, Augustine will embrace Christianity with help from Plato. In the renaissance, Machiavelli will argue that Plato's ideas don't stand up to real-world scrutiny. After the industrial revolution, Karl Marx will claim that Plato's notions have simply been used as a tool of oppression.

So Plato isn't just another dude on a list, Violet. The list exists because of Plato. And the hero of Plato's dialogues is Socrates. Socrates loved wisdom. He did not seek riches, power, glory, or honor, though he seemed to acquire enough of those things to get by. He spent his entire life pursuing wisdom, and at the end of that life, he freely admitted that he possessed no wisdom whatsoever.

In response to the charges leveled against him, Socrates explains that he is not an atheist, and he has not corrupted the youth. These are trumped-up charges. He claims that the most pernicious charge leveled against him is unspoken: that certain Athenians want to punish him, because they claim that Socrates believes himself to be a wise man.

Socrates explains to the court how he obtained this reputation as a wise man. A long time ago, he and a friend visited the Oracle at Delphi. The friend decided to ask the Oracle if anyone in the world was wiser than Socrates.

My friend asked the oracle to tell him whether anyone was wiser than I was, and the Pythian prophetess answered, that there was no man wiser.

Socrates didn't know what the Oracle could possibly mean by this.

I said to myself, what can the god mean? And what is the interpretation of this riddle? For I know that I have no wisdom, small or great. What then can he mean when he says that I am the wisest of men? And yet he is a god, and cannot lie; that would be against his nature.

Socrates decides to test the Oracle. He visits all the people that he believes must be wiser: the politicians, the poets, and the craftsmen.

5

First Socrates visits a politician renowned for his wisdom. This particular politician had great power and responsibility. Surely, Socrates could quickly dispatch the Oracle by proving that this ruler was wiser. But Socrates is surprised after speaking with the ruler.

When I began to talk with him, I could not help thinking that he was not really wise, although he was thought wise by many, and still wiser by himself.

Even though the politician knows how to pass legislation, wage war, and navigate various factions, he doesn't possess any actual wisdom. He just knows how to do some stuff. But he *thinks* that this knowledge makes him wise. Socrates must admit that, though he himself is not wiser than the politician, at least he knows that he doesn't know.

I suppose I am better off than he is, for he knows nothing, and thinks that he knows. I neither know nor think I know. In this latter particular, then, I seem to have slightly the advantage on him.

Then Socrates decides to visit the great poets. Surely they have to be wise! They produce beautiful art that inspires people. They can recite the great poems of antiquity. But again, Socrates is disappointed.

There is hardly a man here who would not have talked better about their poetry than the poets did themselves.

Socrates concludes that the poets act from divine inspiration. Just because they possess talent doesn't mean they possess any wisdom. But like the politician, they, too, thought that they were wise.

All right, Socrates said: *I'll go talk to the craftsmen. They have to be wiser than I am. They produce useful and necessary things for society.* But again, he finds that all the tradesmen think that they're wise because they can manage money, build a boat, or make a horseshoe. Socrates leaves them the same way he left the others, thinking, *Well, they aren't wise, either, but they still think that they are.*

So now Socrates has pissed off everyone: the politicians, the poets, and the tradesmen, because he's told them all that their knowledge amounts to doodley squat. This, says Socrates, is why he's really on trial, and not this business about atheism or corrupting the youth, which is nonsense. And then he explains what the Oracle actually meant.

> *But the truth is, O men of Athens, that God only is wise; and by his answer he intends to show that the wisdom of men is worth little or nothing; he is not speaking of Socrates, he is only using my name by way of illustration, as if he said, "He, O Men, is the wisest, who, like Socrates, knows that his wisdom is in truth worth nothing."*

I thought my job was so important. I thought *I* was so important. Suddenly you were here, and I didn't know if you would ever leave the hospital. I didn't know how to take care of you, or even if I *could* take care of you. I didn't even know who I was, or what I wanted, or what was important in life. But it certainly wasn't my job, my ambition, or the value of my home. I wasn't an executive. I was just some guy at the hospital asking a bunch of questions nobody could answer. I had no idea what was going to happen, and I couldn't control a thing. Neither could the doctors. Nobody knew a damned thing—not in the hospital, not at work, and not in life.

You concentrated on the necessary things in life: You breathed. You ate. You slept. And while you may have been frail, helpless, and ignorant, you were also pure, honest, and innocent. For the moment, you were free from the cynicism and desperation I had begun to embrace as a responsible adult. Yes, I would clothe you, feed you, and care for you. None of that was as important as my true obligation to you, which was pretty simple: just don't ruin you. Don't pollute your spirit with my faults, my bad habits, and my bad ideas about the real world.

For the first time, I finally began to examine my own ambition, my own ego, and the whole system I was caught up in, largely because *you* knew none of it. You didn't come with a résumé and a credit score, Violet. You weren't a Democrat or a Republican. You weren't a capitalist, or a Christian, or even an American. You were a little girl just trying to survive in nature.

Your way was the *real* truth. We're *all* just trying to survive in nature. All these economic and political mechanisms we're obsessed with, and which drive our decisions, and fill us with fear, anxiety, and rage—they don't really exist. We invented all of them to help us survive. There is no such thing as "America," no such thing as the dollar, no such thing as Goldman Sachs, or a credit default swap, a mortgage, or a "median income." In the long run, all these contrivances vanish, only to be replaced by other fictions.

Not so long ago, the Roman Empire occupied more than a million square miles. Rome controlled a vast and global trade network previously administered by the Carthaginians, the Athenians, and the Minoans—all vanished empires themselves. Rome commanded unparalleled military, economic, and cultural power. The Roman imperial structure endured for 1,500 years (in one form or another), succeeding 500 years of the Roman Republic, and several centuries of Roman monarchy. For many centuries, the primacy of Rome was simply a fact of life; it was the way things were. Rome was permanent and indestructible. Everybody knew that.

Remember what you knew when you were born, and listen to Socrates: only the gods know.

The rest of us may act important and wise. We may dress up in fancy suits, stick pineapple pins on our lapels, make a bunch of money, run our little political schemes, wage our wars, or even read a bunch of old books. We delude ourselves that our titles, our property, and our tiny accomplishments in life grant us wisdom we don't actually possess. And the more money we make, the more power we acquire, the harder it becomes to utter three little words: *I don't know.*

And oh, Violet, how those words can help you in your life! Don't be like me, and be ashamed of your ignorance, or pretend that you know it all. Don't ever be scared to admit when you don't know something.

Socrates didn't know, either. But at least he *knew* he didn't know. I didn't even know that much before you came into my life. I thought I knew things because some hotel staff in Denver did what I told them. You would arrive on May 19th. It was on my calendar. Your mom was fine. You were fine. I would lose my job, and it would plunge our family into ruin. I didn't know anything, and I was terrified to admit it.

So what can I possibly teach you? Simply that *nobody* knows, Violet. The chairman of the Federal Reserve doesn't know. The president of the United States doesn't know. Your priest doesn't know. Your boss doesn't know. *I* don't know. At best, we're using all the available evidence to make prudent judgments. At worst, we're proceeding carelessly from complete ignorance, or deliberately ignoring crucial information. And most of the time, we're operating as best we can, given that we can't possibly know all the variables at play.

That is why you must approach the world with a great deal of skepticism. You can't simply take things at face value, especially when they're coming from authority figures, and *especially* when those authority figures lay claim to absolute certainty. One may have power and authority and also know nothing. It's actually quite common. So be like Socrates, and question *everything*.

We come equipped with natural skepticism as children, but it's yanked out of us like a bad tooth. "But why?" was once your favorite question. *Why* to everything—*Why do I have to wear my pants? Why do I have to brush my teeth? Why doesn't the cat want a hug?*

And what was my response to you? *Why? Because I said so, that's why. Because everyone wears pants. Brush your teeth or they'll turn black. Hug the cat and he'll bite you.*

You live in a democracy.
All men are created equal.
Religion is God.
Violence never solves a thing.
You have rights that can never be taken away.
The Invisible Hand of the Market will solve problems.
Our primitive enemies hate us for our freedoms.
We must invade this country or we're all doomed.
We must bail these banks out.
Stop asking why. Trust me. Just do what you're told.

Well, don't trust me, Violet, and don't just do what you're told. Question everything and everyone.

(Well. Except your mother.)

CHAPTER 2

WHEN IS IT RIGHT
TO DO THE WRONG THING?

PLATO
Crito

When you were two I took you swimming in Florida. Your grandpa gave you a plastic scoop and some cups, and you sat on the steps of the pool and scooped water into the cups. You set the cups down for just a moment, and a bigger kid ran up and snatched them from you. The kid's parents witnessed this but did nothing. They laughed.

You looked at me confused.

"Take turns?" you asked.

Some people don't take turns, Violet. Some people are just assholes.

Two years before you were born, a bunch of bank executives ran up and stole everybody's cups. I hope you don't have to live through something like the Great Recession, but unfortunately, I'm certain that at some point you will, seeing as how the United States has lurched from one financial crisis to the next for as long as I've been alive. Each one seems worse than the last, and every crisis ends the same way: the greedy, corrupt, and incompetent criminals are rewarded, while all their victims pay the price. I confess that the Rube Goldberg device that led to the financial collapse of 2008 is too absurd for me to comprehend fully, but I do understand this much: there was incompetence, fraud, and manipulation atop the major financial institutions. Millions of innocent people lost their jobs, their life savings, and their homes. Not a single bank executive went to prison. The biggest offenders became multimillionaires or even billionaires.

In my own life, I've seen other people do horrible things, and they just seem to get away with it. Nobody holds them accountable. Nobody cares if they break the rules. And when I look around, I see all these Other People doing so much better than me. They don't worry about their job security, or about money. They go to the best schools, they live in the best homes, they have every opportunity—why shouldn't I be like them?

In a world like this, it is always tempting to ask: Why should I play by the rules? What is the benefit of acting fairly, and according to principles, when others act so atrociously?

When is it right to do the wrong thing?

———

Crito is about Socrates in jail. Despite his reasoned defense, he's just been convicted of atheism and corrupting the youth, and he's been sentenced to death. He's innocent, the trial was a farce, and the sentence was incredibly harsh. On top of all that, Socrates has a wife and children who depend upon him. What will they do when he is dead?

And yet when *Crito* begins, Socrates is sleeping peacefully in his jail cell. His good friend Crito has come to convince Socrates to bust out of the joint, to go with him to Thessaly, where he'll be received warmly, and where he can spend the rest of his days eating like a king and boozing to his heart's content. It'll be wine, women, and song, and the sweetest little piece of paradise you ever saw—or Socrates could stay and drink poison, and die alone in his prison cell.

Crito makes a lot of compelling arguments for Socrates to bust out of jail. First of all, there's a strong chance of success. Crito says it can all be arranged very easily. Socrates has plenty of supporters. Even some of the people who convicted him don't want to see him executed. Socrates has every reason to ignore the unjust ruling against him. The trial was a sham, and he's clearly an innocent man. He's a hero, in fact. Why give these jerks the satisfaction? And what will his family do when he is dead? Who will take care of them? Isn't it wrong for Socrates to abandon them by accepting his fate? Isn't it, in fact, his moral obligation to break out of jail and go with Crito to Thessaly?

Socrates nods and smiles. "Maybe you're right, Crito. Let's discuss."

Socrates admits that it's true he's been treated unjustly. And this was an evil. Then he asks Crito: Is injustice always an evil?

Socrates. Are we to say that we never intentionally do wrong, or that in one way we ought and in another we ought not do wrong, or is doing wrong always evil and dishonorable ... in spite of the opinion of the many, and in spite of the consequences whether better or worse, shall we insist on the truth of what I have said before, that injustice is always an evil and dishonor to him who acts unjustly? Shall we say so, or not?

Crito. Yes.

Socrates. Then we must do no wrong?

Crito. Certainly not.

Socrates. Nor when injured injure in return, as the many imagine, for we must injure no one at all?

Crito. Clearly not.

Socrates. Again, Crito, may we do evil?

Crito. Surely not, Socrates.

Socrates. And what of doing evil in return for evil, which is the morality of the many. Is that just or not?

Crito. Not just.

Socrates. For doing evil to another is the same as injuring him?

Crito. Very true.

> *Socrates. Then we ought not to retaliate or render evil for evil to any one, whatever evil we may have suffered from him.*

But okay, Crito says, that's all well and good in *theory*, but we're talking about the *real world*, here, Socrates! You're going to die! Think of your *family*, think of your own life! You're going to die!

Socrates basically answers, "So what?" After all, how do I know that death's a bad thing? Nobody knows that. Maybe death's the best thing that could ever happen to me. You ever think of that, Crito? The way I see it, there are basically two possibilities about death. The first is that there's nothing on the other side. Life ends, and then there's total oblivion. How great would that be! In that case, death would be an end to all my worldly cares, like a nice nap that lasts forever. I don't have to worry about making a living, or engaging in these silly politics, or defending myself against absurd charges. Everything will just stop and there will be peace and quiet. On the other hand, maybe there *is* an afterlife, and if so, then I've done no wrong, and my soul will go to paradise. Or maybe someplace else. Who knows? I don't. But I'd like to find out!

And yes, Crito, you are right that I have been falsely accused. I am innocent. But if I go with you, and ignore the legal ruling against me, then wouldn't I make myself guilty? Wouldn't I prove all these people right about me, all these people who claim that I'm a lawbreaker? Right now, I'm an innocent man with a clear conscience, but if I go to Thessaly with you, won't they be able to say, *"You see, we were right about Socrates! He's a criminal."* Won't I become what I've sworn I was not?

After all this injustice, the truth is, nobody forced me to live in Athens. I made that decision myself. I could've gone to Crete or Sparta. But instead I stayed here. And you know why I stayed here? I liked it. It was a great place to live. Think about all the good things Athens has done for me. I was born here. My own marriage was consecrated under the law of Athens. Athens has great laws. At any time in my life, I could've taken all my property and left. That was perfectly legal, because that's how good the law of Athens is.

And let's talk about the law in general. My whole life, haven't I talked about how important it is to follow the law, and haven't I used the laws of Athens for all sorts of things? If I break the law now, am I not proving myself an ungrateful hypocrite? Am I not *mocking* the law? Am I not saying, "Do what I say, not what I do?"

Now Crito, you tell me that we can go to Thessaly, and it will be a paradise. And if I go to Thessaly, yes, I might have a few more days of life in me, but what will that life be like? First of all, no one will take me seriously. They'll say, "Well, here's Socrates—tell us all about how important the law is, Socrates, when you yourself have ignored it." I'll be a fugitive and a laughingstock! And besides that, I'll be *completely* dependent on other men. How does that help my family? If I stay here and die, you and all my other friends will look after them, but if I go to Thessaly, I truly will be abandoning them, because Thessaly is a lawless, ugly place, like Tijuana, and my family will have to come with me, and they won't be able to live in this glorious city of Athens.

So thanks, Crito, but no thanks. I'm touched by your jailbreak scheme. But I'd rather stay here and die, so I'll be able to live with myself. And who knows? It might just be the best thing that ever happened to me.

⚊ ⚊

Other People would've jumped at the chance to escape with Crito. But Socrates doesn't care what Other People would do. He doesn't care about "the morality of the many." Socrates is true to himself, and he tries to live up to his own standards, regardless of the consequences.

When you were born, I certainly cared about Other People. Actually, I was obsessed with Other People. When I was starting out as a writer, whenever anyone had any success, instead of feeling happy for that person, I felt angry, jealous, and resentful. I thought of success as some sort of finite resource, and if someone had some, that meant there was less for me. When my friends began to publish their first books, I'd think, I have to catch up to them, or They're so far ahead of me.

It was the same in my professional life. Whenever one of my peers got a promotion, or began making more money than me, or moved ahead in any way, I would measure my situation against theirs, however incomparable those situations might be.

We do this as a country, too. Every week there's a headline about how some country reported higher scores on math and science tests, or some country has built some new stealth doohicky that's faster than our stealth doohicky, or some country's economy is growing faster than ours.

All of that is as irrelevant as the kind of car your neighbor drives. It took me a long time to learn that there's only one person you should measure yourself against: yourself. It doesn't matter what Other People do or don't do. It doesn't even matter if they act atrociously, crash the economy, or steal your cups. What matters is how you live your own life. That's all you can control, anyway, Violet— and often even that's a tall order.

So don't worry about Other People, Violet. Don't do things you'll regret later, even if you feel like you're justified at the time.

Guard your integrity with your life, and don't be an asshole.

CHAPTER 3

HAVE WE BECOME GODS?

ARISTOPHANES
The Clouds

———⊃◦◦⊂———

L ast year scientists produced a comprehensive, three-dimensional map of the human brain. This atlas—as well as the increasingly sophisticated ones sure to follow in the coming years—will allow scientists to understand how the brain works, and eventually, to create artificial intelligence.

This is going to happen, Violet, and probably in your lifetime. One day, not so far in the future, someone will produce the Human Brain 2.0. Imagine a machine smarter than the smartest person on earth. It is not simply good at math. It is the greatest economist, doctor, and military mind in all of human history. It creates new knowledge. It absorbs information instantaneously from everywhere, augments itself constantly, and manufactures anything it wants. It requires no sleep, no water, and no food. It may derive its power from the sun, or perhaps it develops and creates a new source of renewable energy. Every second it acquires and assimilates more data. Every second it becomes faster, better, and smarter.

It doesn't have to be a box or a machine. It may simply be a series of mathematical codes—an enormously complex (or even surprisingly simple) software program that can duplicate itself instantly, or embed itself around the world. It can take command of factories and three-dimensional printers, and produce its own mechanical or biological components. But it need not do any of this in order to exist. It can move about effortlessly between physical bodies, or be present in multiple locations at the same time. It can duplicate itself, or it can produce lower-level models that function as completely obedient slaves, which are nevertheless infinitely more capable than any human being. It can survive in outer space. By human standards, it's practically immortal. No one can fathom its intentions. No one can understand it—not even the scientists who created it.

Have we become gods?

Socrates theorized that the physical world could not be trusted, and that the universe could ultimately only be understood abstractly, through mathematics. It was (and remains) a radical idea: that the physical world we interact with is not the real world, but merely a shadow of true reality; a pale reflection of cosmic, unknowable, and absolute laws and forms.

In an apt metaphor provided by Plato in Book VII of *Republic*, Socrates imagines how the world responds to radical ideas. I paraphrase it for you here.

Plato: The Allegory of the Cave
Imagine there are prisoners chained in a cave. They have spent their whole lives in this cave, and they are chained in such a way so that they can only see the cave wall directly in front of them.

Behind them there is a fire, and every day, people and animals walk in front of the fire, casting shadows on the cave wall in front of the prisoners. The prisoners believe that the shadows themselves are real things. They start to name the shadows. They see a shadow of a rabbit, and they call it a rabbit. They see a shadow of a horse, and they call it a horse. And so on.

This goes on their whole lives, until one day, one of the prisoners escapes from the cave. He staggers out into the world, and there he sees a real rabbit, and a real horse, and he looks up, and he sees the blinding light of the sun.

Suddenly he realizes that all the things he saw in the cave were merely shadows, pale reflections of the actual, true

forms of nature. He descends back into the cave to try to
educate the other prisoners, but they will not listen to him.
They think he's crazy, and they try to kill him.

We don't like it when people question our shadows. Our shadows become more real than actual reality. We inhabit a world filled with artificial constructs and structures, and we call those shadows "the real world." We submerge ourselves in our careers, our systems of barter and exchange, and the interests of our nation-states. We spend our adult lives preparing our children to enter this real world, when really what we're doing is teaching them bizarre rules of incredibly intricate schemes, and training them to operate the levers that make this real world function. *"Fridays are business casual!"*

And as Socrates discovered, those who question these shadows are punished routinely, and severely.

But though Socrates was a skeptic, he was not an atheist. He was a believer—a *devout* believer—in the gods. After he drank poison, he remembered that he had failed to sacrifice a chicken to the god Apollo, and as he lay in his cell, dying from poison, he asked his friends to do so for him, so he would not neglect his duties to the god. How could Socrates believe in the gods and *also* believe that the universe could only be understood through rational inquiry?

◆～◆

One of the reasons Socrates enjoyed a poor reputation among the Athenians was because of his portrayal by Aristophanes, who presented a caricature of him in his play *The Clouds*.

Aristophanes lived in the fifth–fourth century BCE. Before playwrights like Aristophanes, the most popular form of comedy was the satyr play. A satyr was a mythological creature that was half goat and half man. Satyr plays were incredibly obscene and sexual—the "fart-joke" comedies of the ancient world, in which the players ran around the stage with enormous erections, mostly harassing women.

Aristophanes took that and turned it into something new. The actors in the plays of Aristophanes still wore enormous strap-on phalluses, which would grow or contract depending on the events onstage, but now the plays weren't just about sex and toilet humor.

The comedic plays of Aristophanes became social commentary. Suddenly the theater took on war, religion, and politics. Plays that were once harmlessly obscene become dangerously subversive and offensive to powerful people. Nothing, and no one, was off-limits.

The Clouds is about a degenerate gambler named Strepsiades and his loafer son Pheidippides. In an effort to escape his debts, Strepsiades tries to enroll himself in the "Thinkery," a proto-college run by Socrates. Strepsiades hopes that Socrates can teach him how to lawyer his way out of his gambling debts. But Socrates decides that Strepsiades is too stupid to appreciate his wisdom, so Strepsiades sends his son Pheidippides to the Thinkery instead.

The son proves a much better student than his father. He emerges from the Thinkery a changed and "learned" man, and he promptly beats his own father, using the logic he's learned at the Thinkery to justify his behavior. As the son beats his father (a heinous and awful taboo in Greek culture) he argues logically that it's perfectly natural for a son to beat his father. After all, doesn't a father beat his son to correct the child's bad behavior? If the old man needs correcting, shouldn't the son beat the father? He cites numerous examples from nature to justify the beating, and then suggests that when he's done correcting his father, he's going to go and beat his mother, too.

Enraged, the old man burns down the Thinkery with Socrates and all his students inside.

Aristophanes presents Socrates as a pompous, double-talking fool. When we first meet Aristophanes's version of Socrates onstage, the philosopher is suspended in a basket, studying the heavens. The students of the academy inform Strepsiades of the incredible intellectual pursuits occurring within Socrates's Thinkery.

Strepsiades. I'm come to be a student in your thinking house!

Student. Come then. But they're high mysteries, remember. Socrates was asking Chaerephon how many feet of its own a flea could jump.

Strepsiades. How did he measure this?

Student. Most cleverly. He warmed some wax, and then he

caught the flea, and dipped its feet into the wax he melted, then let it cool, and there were Persian slippers! These he took off, and so he found the distance.

Strepsiades. O Zeus and King, what subtle intellects!

Student. Well, how about this? Why, Chaerephon was asking him in turn, which theory did he sanction: that the gnats hummed through their mouth, or backwards through their tail?

Strepsiades. Aye, and what said your Master of the Gnat?

Student. He answered thus: the entrail of the gnat is small, and through the narrow pipe the wind rushes with violence straight towards the tail. There, close against the pipe, the hollow rump receives the wind, and whistles to the blast.

Strepsiades. So then the rump is trumpet to the gnats! O happy, happy in your entrail-learning!

Socrates informs Strepsiades that the clouds are actually the true gods, and that all the natural phenomena are the result of interactions between them. This version of Socrates elevates reason above religion or faith, which he suggests is merely the superstitious nonsense of the ignorant. Suddenly, a Chorus of Clouds reveals itself to both men.

Chorus of Clouds
*Our welcome to thee, old man [Strepsiades],
who wouldst see the marvels
that science can show;
And thou, the high priest of this subtlety feast [Socrates],
Say what would you have us bestow?*

Strepsiades
*O Earth! What a sound, how august and profound!
It fills me with wonder and awe.*

Socrates
These, these then alone, for true Deities own,
The rest are all Godships of straw.

Strepsiades
Let Zeus be left out; he's a god beyond doubt;
Come, that you can scarcely deny.

Socrates
Zeus indeed! There's no Zeus; don't you be so
obtuse.

Strepsiades
No Zeus up aloft in the sky!
Then you first must explain, who it is who sends the rain
Or really I must think you are wrong.

Socrates
Well, then, be it known, these send it alone;
I can prove it by arguments strong.
Was there ever a shower seen to fall in an hour
When the sky was all cloudless and blue?
Yet on a fine day the Clouds are away
He might send one, according to you.

This is followed by a load of toilet humor, about how thunder is caused when the clouds bump into each other, and how lightning bolts are the clouds pooping, etc. Aristophanes's Socrates is urging the public to abandon their worship of the gods—even calling it stupid—in favor of rationalizing everything.

The teachings of Socrates upend the social order, and a son feels intellectually empowered to beat his own parents. Then Strepsiades burns down the Thinkery, with Socrates still inside.

Strepsiades
For with what aim did ye insult the Gods.
And pry around the dwelling of the moon?
Strike, smite them, spare them not, for many reasons,
But most because they have blasphemed the Gods!

We cringe at the notion of a learned man being burned alive for pursuing rational inquiry, especially in the name of protecting superstitious ideas. But that's not really the point of *The Clouds*. The point is that we shouldn't take the gods lightly, and we shouldn't presume to know more than they do. But because we are mere mortals, we will continue to make both of these mistakes. And when we do, we invite our own destruction.

We shouldn't pretend to be gods. That's good advice, Violet. It's advice Socrates would've actually embraced, and it's said that when the play was first presented in Athens, Socrates not only attended, but gave it a rousing ovation. The man had a sense of humor. As smart as Socrates was, he knew he could've spent his life contemplating how fleas fart, for all the gods care. That's why it's funny.

On the day you were born, I apologized to the almighty—whatever it is—and I thanked it profusely. Prior to your arrival, I thought myself above such superstitious nonsense. But I became convinced of God that day—and it's not because you're a precious little snowflake, Violet. It's because your arrival into this world defied reason.

First of all, scientific error saved your life. Your mom knew something was wrong, but even after all the ultrasounds, blood tests, monitoring, and probing, nobody found a thing. And thank God they didn't, because if the doctors had discovered the problem prior to your birth, you probably wouldn't be here. Your mom would've been placed on bedrest. She would've stopped working and stayed at home. We lived in the DC area at the time, and we could only afford a house on the outskirts of the suburbs, very far west. It took a good 40 minutes to get from our house to the hospital, and that was in ideal traffic.

A week after all those tests at the doctor's office, your mom suffered a placental abruption. When that occurred, you had minutes to live. Had your mom been at home, you would not have survived the time it took for an ambulance to get to our home and convey you to the hospital. You would've suffocated. Your mom might've died, too. She easily could've bled to death in the back of an ambulance, stuck in traffic on I-66. But that didn't happen. Instead, your mom continued teaching at a school five minutes from the hospital.

Stranger still, when your mom arrived at the hospital, it just so happened that her doctor was there, and she was not busy delivering another baby. That doctor didn't have an office there. It was pure coincidence. Because of the tests she'd performed on your mom just the week before, she could deliver you quickly. From the time your mom entered the hospital to the time you were born, less than 20 minutes elapsed. You can't get a sandwich in Washington, DC, in 20 minutes.

You weren't out of the woods yet. You were still very sick, and you would need to be hospitalized for several weeks. Another stroke of good fortune: the hospital just happened to have one of the best NICUs in the country.

It can all be explained rationally. But maybe events are connected in some way that we don't understand. Maybe you were meant to be here, Violet, against all reasonable odds. I believe that, even if I can't prove it.

I also believe in the immortal soul, because from the start, you were animated by something more than mere biology. In the first days of your life, your biology was the problem. Your *spirit* sustained you. You were stubborn, tough, and cheerful from the moment you were born. You had no earthly reason to possess these qualities. You were tiny, weak, and tired, you could barely breathe, and you were very sick—yet you came preequipped with the *exact traits* you required. Some would argue that your environment simply brought out these traits, or that I mistook instinctive behavior for expressions of personality. I don't think so. I think you were that person *before* you were alive. I think you came here from somewhere else, and that your spirit simply inhabits a frail physical shell.

I have faith, *and* I believe in reason.

Socrates understood that reason and faith are not incompatible. You don't have to pick one, Violet. Yes, given our limitations as human beings, science and rational inquiry are our only pathways to understanding the universe. Our perceptions are flawed and primitive, and they cannot be trusted. The universe may indeed be mathematical. Socrates believed all of this.

But he also believed in an infinite and immortal soul. He believed in something *beyond* the physical world, and perhaps beyond the mathematical one: an animating force of good in the universe that man could never hope to see or understand. We could only perceive its effects indirectly in the universe—the "shadows" its light cast.

24

There might be truths that we simply cannot comprehend, given our limitations as human beings. That doesn't mean we should stop trying to find them.

Look at what all that trying has brought us: longer lives, agriculture, atomic power, new economic and political systems, beer, and Scrabble. For all that, we can't even get along with one another. We kill each other like savage animals. We can't feed our hungry. We can't even balance our checkbooks. And we are trapped, like desperate islanders on a tiny, dying rock, floating in an infinite sea of empty space.

One day we may create an entity more capable than a man, and we will jump up and down and congratulate ourselves on our big achievement.

"Whoop-te-doo," the gods will say, and laugh. "The humans finally figured out how fleas fart."

CHAPTER 4

IS THERE ANY JUSTICE
IN THE WORLD?

PLATO

Republic

━━━━◦◦◦◦━━━━

At Oxford I encountered the British class system. As a 20-some-thing American, the idea of social class repelled me. One night, after a few pints at the Oxford Union, I had a lively debate with a British student about the relative merits of the American and British political systems. At one point I became frustrated and blurted out, "Everything here depends on class." The British student replied quickly, "At least we admit the fact of social class."

I didn't believe America had a class system until the year after you were born, Violet. I thought this was the land where class didn't exist, where one could move up the ladder at will, with a little elbow grease and a can-do attitude!

Years later, when I was in charge of an arts organization, I received a phone call from a wealthy board member. He'd sent me a $1,000 donation, and I'd recognized the gift with a form letter. I sent them to everyone who made donations, handwriting a little note in the corner. The board member was mad.

"Don't waste postage to recognize a lousy $1,000," he barked. "People like me don't care about $1,000. I'm in a different caste than you."

He said this so offhandedly, as if stating a simple fact. He was. This man inherited his enormous wealth. He was worth a staggering amount of money, probably in the neighborhood of $100 million.

And he did not even consider himself rich. He reserved that appellation for far wealthier board members.

He did not intend to insult me. He was actually trying to *help* me. Other board members would've been aghast at his bluntness, but in a way he was more genuine than they, since, as I came to discover, many other board members privately believed exactly the same thing. They just pretended they didn't.

But at that point in my life I understood the truth of American class: namely, that there actually *is* a ruling class in America, that it is a self-perpetuating closed system, and that its values are not the same as those practiced by the vast majority of the country.

I was at the height of my cynicism. What I'd seen in my career led me to believe that power had been concentrated in the hands of an elite class of people whose only goal was to preserve their own power. They were not interested in helping the poor, or advancing the national interest, though they cloaked themselves in that rhetoric. They only *pretended* to do good works—they attended each other's fundraisers, donated money to various charitable causes, including mine—but it was all for show. Worse, they *knew* it was a show. They were only interested in bizarre social schemes I did not understand: getting their picture in the right paper, standing next to the right person at the right function, sitting at the best table. Everything was about appearance. And when megamillionaires weren't donating a lousy thousand bucks to each other's pet causes, they were out screwing everybody blind. They were ruthless, and they were even proud of their ruthlessness. They joked about it with one another. Money and power were the only things that really mattered. Morality was for the poor.

There was no justice in the world.

—•—

Justice is the central pursuit of *Republic*. A lot of people will tell you it's about political science. And there is a lot of political science. But all of that is employed to try to answer a very simple question: Does justice exist at all, and if so, is it preferable to injustice?

When the book begins, Socrates is down at the port of Athens to witness a festival for a new god. On his way back up from the port, men stop Socrates and ask the philosopher to accompany them. They want to talk about justice. The men walk to an elderly man's home, and Socrates says that if we want to talk about justice, we need a definition first.

We quickly discover that *justice* is hard to define. What does the word mean, actually?

Okay, how about this: Justice is telling the truth and keeping your promises.

This sounds pretty good. But Socrates wonders: Is this really a comprehensive definition of justice? After all, aren't there times when telling the truth is wrong, and when keeping your promises is a bad thing? What about in times of war? If you're captured by the enemy during wartime, is it just to tell your enemy the truth, or is it just to lie to them, to deceive them, to send them off in the wrong direction? As for keeping your promises, well—what about that time when your buddy gave you his car keys and you promised to give them back? Then he went and got rip-roaring drunk. Is it just to keep your promise, and give him back his car keys?

Okay, how about this, the other men offer: Justice is doing good to your friends, and doing harm to your enemies.

Socrates finds fault with this definition, too. Aren't there times when you don't really know who your friends and enemies are? Can't you make a mistake? What if you accidentally do good to your enemies and harm your friends because you don't know the difference?

Everyone is starting to get frustrated with Socrates, and a man named Thrasymachus offers a very powerful definition:

"Justice is simply what the strong say it is. Justice is whatever is in the interest of the stronger."

Well, maybe, Socrates says. But don't the strong sometimes mistake their own interests? Let's say your boss orders you to do something that will bankrupt the company. Is it just to do what your boss wants? Is following the boss's orders really in the boss's interest? Is that justice?

But this third definition is a little more powerful than the others. This is something we think Machiavelli might've said: that "might makes right." But if you believe that justice is simply what the strong say it is, then you also believe that there really is no such thing as justice. Justice is simply defined by the people in charge; it changes from state to state. Everything is circumstantial—we live in a world of *situational ethics*, in which right and wrong cannot be defined absolutely. If that's true, then there *is* no such thing as right or wrong. There's no such thing as "justice."

This is *precisely* what I believed when you were born, Violet. There was no such thing as right and wrong or good and evil, let alone justice. The only way you could count on any justice was to acquire power and money. And I had a sign up in my office that reflected my jaundiced view of the world. This is what it said:

> *Power is the only morality.*
> *Force is the only truth.*

So I *believed* it, Violet, and I espoused it. And I doubted that Socrates would convince me otherwise. My own eyes and my own experience led me to believe that justice didn't even exist. The poor and the needy played by one set of rules, while the rich and powerful played by quite another. We were all tricked into this morality business for the benefit of the elite. We pay our debts, keep our word, and play by the rules—they default without penalty, lie without consequence, and break every rule for the sake of personal gain. And gain they do, over and over again. If you were smart, you acted like them, and proceeded without a care in the world about what constituted justice.

Socrates's companions take things one step further: Not only is injustice *preferable* to justice, but it is actually ideal to *pretend* to be just while you're secretly *unjust*. The unjust always use their veneer of respectability to abuse and exploit the weak. It's still important to appear just, because you have to control the poor and weak, who vastly outnumber you. But to *actually* be just is a *defect* of character. The strong tell the weak to follow principles that they themselves would never follow, and in this way, they maintain and expand their power.

So one must ask: Is justice even preferable to injustice? What's good about justice?

Well, what do you mean by "good"? Socrates asks.

The Classes of Good
Socrates's companions offer three categories of good:
1. *That which is good independent of consequences, like a nice flower; something rather harmless, a delight, or a pleasure.*
2. *That which is good, like health, which is desirable for itself, but also for its benefits, which is that we can live well and protect ourselves.*
3. *That which is undesirable, but which does us good; like exercise.*

Socrates agrees that all these classes of good exist.

Well, if that's the case, then it's even *more* obvious: the best thing to be in life is to be *unjust*, but to *appear* to be just. How else do you get the good things in life? Look at the politicians, talking about helping the people, while secretly taking bribes from merchants and screwing everyone. They have the right idea! The unjust man actually has it much better than the truly honest man. After all, the unjust man is usually rich, healthy, and prosperous, while the just man is usually poor, sick, and wretched.

One of Socrates's companions then provides a perfect example of man's true nature by telling the story of a man named Gyges. One day, as Gyges was walking around, the earth split open. In the crevasse that opened up, he found a dead, semidivine dude in some kind of bronze horse with doors. The dead man was wearing a ring, which Gyges promptly climbed down and stole. Then Gyges discovered that if he twisted the ring, it would make him invisible, so he used this power to sleep with the queen, kill the king, and seize power for himself. Because he was invisible, Gyges had no reason to be honest or just, since he could never be caught. From this story, one of the men with Socrates concludes that it is only the fear of punishment that makes us behave in a just fashion.

Think about that, Violet: if *you* could be invisible, and there was no chance you would be caught doing something evil, what would you do? Would you be a nice, law-abiding person if you knew that you would *never* be punished for anything you did? Would you rob a bank if you knew for certain that you'd get away with it?

Maybe you wouldn't rob a bank because you feared punishment in the afterlife? Yeah, that's bullshit, argue Socrates's companions.

The unjust don't fear the afterlife. It doesn't matter what sins they commit—after all, the unjust can simply buy forgiveness from the gods. Whenever a priest wants to build a temple to the gods, whom does he turn to? The unjust, of course! As fast as he can, the priest goes to the industrialists, the moneylenders, and the sinners. The wicked can simply purchase their salvation. The priests exalt the unjust man in public, they pray for his forgiveness, and they use their influence with the gods to pardon his sins.

All this assumes that there even is an afterlife. We might've cooked up the afterlife just to keep the poor in line. If there isn't an afterlife, well, then, all the more reason to be corrupt from the get-go! If we're *never* going to be punished, then why shouldn't we simply lie, cheat, and steal all the time? The just man is merely a rube to the unjust man. This "justice" business is all a big scam to keep people oppressed. In fact, the only reason we have justice at all is to protect rich people's property. Let's prove it!

A. Left to their own devices, people are shit; they'll do whatever they can, take whatever they can, steal, kill, rob—they'll do anything to benefit themselves.

B. But this is no good. If everyone behaves in this wicked way, then nothing ever gets done, and we actually have less chance of survival as individuals. We need to cooperate with each other in order to survive.

C. We decide then, to enter into a *social contract* with one another. We give up the freedom to do as we please, and in exchange, we receive the safety of society; that is, all laws are, in a way, established to punish and/or deter bad behavior. It's the threat of that punishment that keeps us in line, not any innate desire to be just.

D. So people are only just because they fear punishment. But if they can escape punishment, or elude the appearance of doing something wrong, they will act unjustly every time.

The evidence is overwhelming, Socrates!

Well, okay, Socrates says, at this point it might be helpful to examine justice in a context larger than the individual. We have to have a big example so we can see things clearly. Let's "blow it up," as it were. If we can define justice in a big context, we can define it down for the individual, and we can ascertain whether justice or injustice is the preferable path in life. And what better example can we use than the city?

So let us create a "perfectly just" city.

The "Perfectly Just" City

Now Socrates defines the perfectly just city, and we will discover that it is a city with the following (rather surprising) attributes:

It is a tyranny.

It is based on lies.

It is a warlike state.

There is rampant censorship.

There is strict separation of the classes.

The free flow of ideas is forbidden.

Sex is controlled, selective breeding is practiced, and there are no families.

Religion is under state control, and traditional religious values are not permitted.

At first blush, this seems to vindicate Plato's critics, who claim that *Republic* is an argument for totalitarianism. But there is one crucial distinction in the conception of the perfectly just republic, which Socrates himself makes sure to point out: it is *unhealthy*.

To Socrates and everyone else, health seems to be a *perfect good*. Even the people claiming that injustice is preferable conceded that health is good for its own sake, and it is good for the benefits it bestows. To be healthy means you can ward off hunger, you can defend yourself, you can think clearly, and you live longer.

So how can an unhealthy state be a perfectly just state?

Because it is the perfect state—*for that state which exceeds its needs.*

Socrates *first* defines a very different "perfectly just" state. As he's building his imaginary city, he argues that in order to have a state at all, first we need some people. People are different. Some are suited to be carpenters, some farmers, etc. So in the state there should be a **division of labor** that is natural according to everyone's talents. And everyone agrees.

All right, Socrates says—so now our state will have everything it needs. It will have merchants and farmers and shoemakers and carpenters. And...

Will they not produce corn, and wine, and clothes, and shoes, and build houses for themselves? And when they are housed, they will work, in summer, commonly, stripped in barefoot, but in winter substantially clothed and shod. They will feed on barley-meal and flour of wheat, baking and kneading them, making noble cakes and loaves. Those they will serve up on a mat of clean leaves, themselves reclining the while upon beds strewn with yew or myrtle. And they and their children will feast, drinking of the wine which they have made, wearing garlands on their heads, and hymning the praises of the gods, in happy converse with one another. And they will take care that their families do not exceed their means; having an eye to poverty or war.

This is the "first state" that Socrates describes as "perfectly just": a happy state where pious, peaceful people live in a community together. All their needs are met, and they are all happy to talk to each other as equals. They live in a state of harmony, both with nature and one another. There is no conflict. There is freedom. The state is perfectly just.

"Okay, sound good?" asks Socrates. "There's your perfectly just state."

Not so fast, say the other men. It seems Socrates has forgotten something.

"I did?" asks Socrates. "But won't people have everything they want?"

They will have salt and cheese, and olives, and figs, and for dessert they can have peas and beans, and myrtle berries, and roast acorns. And everyone will drink in moderation, and with such a diet, they can be expected to live to a ripe old age, and give their children a long and happy life.

Isn't that enough for a happy life?

The other men don't think that myrtle berries and roast acorns are going to cut it. People like convenience. They like the finer things in life. They want to sleep on cushy beds, eat candy and bacon, and they want to have jewelry and iPads and all sorts of stuff they don't need.

"Ah," says Socrates.

Yes, now I understand: the question you would have me consider is, not only how a State, but how a luxurious state is created; and possibly there is no harm in this, for in such a state we shall be more likely to see how justice and injustice originate. In my opinion, the true and healthy constitution of the State is the one I have just described. But if you wish to see a state at fever-heat, I have no objection. For I suspect that many will not be satisfied with the simpler way of life. They will be for adding sofas and tables, and other furniture, also dainties, and perfumes, and incense, and courtesans, and cakes, all of these not of one sort only, but in every variety; we must go beyond the necessaries of which I was at first speaking.

Okay, Socrates says, if you want your fancy things, here's that state that can provide them:

It is a tyranny.

It is based on lies.

It is a warlike state.

There is rampant censorship.

There is strict separation of the classes.

The free flow of ideas is forbidden.

Sex is controlled, eugenics is practiced, and there are no families.

Religion is under state control, and traditional religious values are not permitted.

Here's why:

If you want things you don't *need* in your city, then you're going to have to have more land. You're not content to survive off of what you've got, so you require *more*—more land for grazing, more land for huge McMansions, more resources—more land, more land. So where are you going to get all that land? Well, you're going to have to take it from your neighbor. You're going to have to create inequality. And how do you do that?

You get yourself an army. And here's a radical idea: States don't keep large standing armies for self-defense. Large armies are required for the state's expansion, in order to seize resources from others. Now, about this army—weren't we saying before about how some individuals are better suited to certain jobs than others? Isn't the same true of soldiers? Isn't war a craft, or an art, just like making shoes, or building houses? If that's true, then we need a whole class of people to be the military. We don't just need an army, we need a *professional military*. What kind of qualities would our professional soldiers possess? Well, first these people would have to have *spirit*. They would be aggressive, they would enjoy conflict, and they would be competitive by nature. And wouldn't they also have to be physically strong, and very fast?

The others concede that yes, all this is true.

Hmm. Well, then, now we have a big problem, don't we? Because this class of people—the **guardian class**—seems extraordinarily dangerous. If one is competitive by nature, and enjoys conflict, and is also strong and fast, why wouldn't this person just attack the citizens of our state?

Socrates has the answer: We'll educate our guardians. We'll train them like dogs not to bite their masters. And of course our education will require certain modifications to the current system, starting with all the bad examples in religion. Think about all those crazy stories that say that Cronos slew his father, and Zeus runs around turning into swans and raping women. What kind of examples are these? God can't be like that, or else people will be like that. We have to make sure that our gods never do *anything* bad. The gods have to be perfectly good, and they can't be the authors of any evils. So the first thing is, we'll have to go over our religion and take out all that stuff that makes people think. Then we'll also have to start getting rid of some literature. Especially Homer. Let's face it, fellows, all this stuff in the *Iliad* has got to go.

"It does?" ask the others, horrified. "Why?"

Well, because it's full of the fear of death, that's why! Look at this part of the *Iliad*, when Achilles's friend dies, and Achilles cries like a little baby. Why should he grieve? He's a soldier. Soldiers die. That's the point of their existence. Nobody should grieve for the dead, and especially not a soldier. It implies that death is a bad thing. We want these people to think death is a *good* thing—and not just a good thing, but the *very best* thing that could possibly happen to you. Otherwise, why would they ever fight in our wars? We have to *glorify* death; we have to make it noble and honorable to be a military man. Our guardians must live to die gloriously.

Of course not everyone will be cut out to be a guardian. The vast majority of people are ignorant, weak, and ruled by their dumb desires. They'll be on the bottom of our state. They'll be useful as farmers and merchants, but they shouldn't aspire to anything greater. The guardian class will keep them in line, but we can't put the guardians in charge, either—they're way too dangerous. What we need is a very small group of wise leaders on top of everyone.

Now we have a nice clean division of the classes, and everyone needs to be content with where they are. They shouldn't be interbreeding with one another, either. That's how people get ideas. Everybody should know his or her place. So as soon as you're born, we'll tell everyone a little lie. We'll tell people that they've been born with one of three kinds of souls: a gold soul (the ruling class), a silver soul (the guardian class), and a bronze soul (everyone else). But it will be a **noble lie**, because it's for everyone's benefit. Right?

Now—about that ruling class—the people with gold souls. Who should these people be? Socrates delivers his best joke. He argues that there's really only one kind of person who could logically run our "perfectly just" city: and surprise, it's someone exactly like Socrates. A philosopher.

There. Now we have our luxurious state, just like everyone wanted.

But do we really want to live in such a state? Socrates himself would despise such a state. How could Socrates love a city that he defines as sick; a city that does not encourage the free exchange of ideas, a city that does not engage in the pursuit of wisdom at all, that has no joy, no art, and no freedom? The city is only concerned with acquiring *more* for its citizens—more land, more resources, more, more, more.

Socrates doesn't want this state. He's kidding. He's making a point.

In a luxurious state, greed, and not justice, is the motivating factor. And inevitably, that greed will lead to the odious state he describes.

Democracy in the *Republic*

Socrates unleashes a brutal critique of democracy in the *Republic*. Democracy has a load of problems, not the least of which is its tendency to devolve into **tyranny**, which is the absolute worst form of government.

We also must consider what "democracy" really is, Violet, because *you don't live in a democracy*. You live in a *republic*. It's not a semantic distinction. The United States has never been a democracy, and it never will be. Ancient Athens was actually a true democracy, in which everyone (well, at least all the propertied men) voted on everything. If Athens wanted to go to war, everybody voted. Ancient Spartans thought the Athenians were nuts for doing everything this way, and so did the founders of our country. Our founders were extremely *anti*-democratic, and mostly for the reasons that Plato gives: chief among them is the concern that democracy tends to devolve into tyranny. Because what happens in a democracy is that inevitably, a *demagogue*, or a "man of the people," emerges, and that demagogue follows a very specific pattern of behavior:

1. He claims to be working for the "little people."

2. He gets his own bodyguard, because he fears for his life from the rich and powerful.

3. He gets a taste of blood. He executes one of his enemies, and, at least as far as this first crime is concerned, the demagogue has perfectly good reasons for it: *"This person was rich, they were an enemy of the people, they were going to kill me..."*

4. On gaining power, the demagogue appears to help the people—at first. He forgives the debts of the poor, and he even distributes land to the people. This increases the demagogue's power immensely. The people are now with him. And the demagogue is all-powerful. He has become a tyrant.

5. Now the tyrant is obsessed only with the maintenance and expansion of power.

6. The tyrant starts a war, but only to consolidate his power. The people rally around the tyrant.

7. The tyrant continues to eliminate all of his enemies.

8. When he runs out of enemies, the tyrant goes after their friends.

Why? Because his allies are dangerous. You can't have people with any kind of power threatening you.

9. By killing anyone who is capable, the tyrant deprives the state of its best citizens: its merchants, its thinkers, its innovators, and its military leaders. In this way, the tyrant impoverishes the people by creating an incompetent state completely dependent on the tyrant.

10. The tyrant continues to enrich himself, directing public monies to private interests.

11. But now the tyrant lives in a state of constant fear. He cannot travel, he cannot trust anyone, he is surrounded by sycophants, idiots, and liars, and everyone wants to kill him. He must sleep in a different bed every night, and his rest is never peaceful.

In his *Histories*, Herodotus recounts the tale of the wise Athenian Solon, who once said, "Count no man happy until the end is known." And there is a remarkably similar end to the lives of perfectly unjust men like the tyrant described by Socrates. Adolf Hitler, Saddam Hussein, Osama bin Laden, and Muammar Gaddafi lived their final days like animals in holes, hiding from the very people they claimed to be liberating. They could not trust anyone, even their own families. They were universally despised. In the end, each of these men was brutally executed. Their bodies were defiled, and their names will be disgraced for eternity.

These figures once terrified the world, but in the end, they were all pathetic, and their names died with them. In the end, they were not powerful at all. And even at the height of their power, they were prisoners of their own lust for power. Friendless, hunted, and despised, their very *lives* became their punishment.

And suddenly Socrates, almost through sleight of hand, has proven something truly amazing:

Justice exists, and it is preferable to injustice.

After all, in our tyrant, haven't we found the "perfectly unjust man who pretends to be just"? And yet, in the end, who would want to live that life? Who would want Mussolini's power, only to be dragged through the streets, bludgeoned to death, with your face literally kicked off your skull, and your body hung up on a meat hook in the public square next to your wife? Did it end well for him?

Or for Hitler? For Saddam Hussein? For bin Laden?

That is the end of injustice writ large, Violet, and moreover, it *always* ends this way. Even before the horrible end, the unjust life is its own punishment. The unjust man has no real friends. Nobody loves him. Everyone wants to kill him, even his own family. He is paranoid and alone, and he can't even enjoy all the power and money he's stolen. It is a life devoid of joy—until it ends badly.

The same principle holds true in smaller cases. Remember that we are looking at a big example—the "perfectly unjust man." The punishment awaiting the "lesser unjust" is similar, just proportional. The lesser unjust may not be dragged through the streets and executed, but eventually, people tend to get what they deserve. Even if they're never held responsible for their crimes, it doesn't matter. Their very lives are punishment enough. They're miserable human beings. It may take time, and you might not even see it, but eventually, justice always prevails.

There is justice in the world, Violet.

CHAPTER 5

WHAT IS HAPPINESS?

ARISTOTLE
Nicomachean Ethics, Book I

At various points in my life I imagined a time when I would be happy. I'd be happy when I got published. I'd be happy when I got the girl of my dreams. I'd be happy when I got that office, that promotion, or that car.

Well, I got published. I got the girl of my dreams. I got that office, that promotion, and that car. "Look at all the things I've got!" I'd say, even as I felt miserable and unfulfilled. Then I felt guilty for feeling unhappy. I reminded myself of all those people who were less fortunate. I kept telling myself, *You should be happy. Why aren't you happy?!*

Even when you came along I felt unhappy. Actually, in the first year of your life, I was more miserable than I'd ever been in my life, and the fact that I was unhappy made me even more miserable. It had absolutely nothing to do with you. You were the best, most radiant part of my life. Like almost everyone else in the world, I just had some problems at work, which also coincided with some financial anxiety. At the time, these problems seemed insurmountable, and I couldn't seem to catch a break. Things seemed to keep going from bad to worse, and I felt it was all extremely unfair. I felt sorry for myself, I dwelled on all the "wrongs" done against me, and I sublimated my rage, directing it at all the wrong targets.

I didn't want you to feel my depression, so I hid it from you as best I could—but I'm certain you were aware of it somewhere in your heart. Yet you were so naturally happy. Sometimes I felt like you were happy for the both of us, and even, at times, as if you were trying to cheer me up.

You always brightened up your surroundings. On Saturdays, when you weren't yet two years old, I used to take you to the sandwich shop up the block, and the people behind the counter would always give me free stuff when you were around—a bag of chips, lemonade, occasionally a cookie. Even though we didn't go there that often, they remembered you. They knew your name. It didn't matter who was working that day. They'd cut your sandwich into quarters without asking, so you could manage a piece in your tiny hands.

Often when I took you there, I was really just trying to get out of the house. It was always a big hassle, getting your stroller together, making sure I had extra diapers, milk, blankets, and your stuffed kitty. I was always exhausted. In those days I often worked late into the night, and you would wake up around 5:30 a.m. Your mom'd been waking up at that hour for the whole week, so I'd drag my bleary-eyed ass out of bed, throw on an old flannel shirt, and take you downstairs. We'd play for a few hours, and then I'd take you for a sandwich before your nap. It all felt very robotic. I was just going through the motions, just trying to get through to naptime, because then I could lie down for an hour. Sometimes I was filled with resentment about it. *When would I get a break?!*

One Saturday, I was rushing you through your lunch, trying to clean up before you were finished, checking my phone every minute for some nasty work email, getting the stroller packed, trying to get your jacket on, and you broke free from me. You crawled down from the booth and began dancing in the sandwich shop. They piped in classic rock. It was the Eagles song, "Busy Being Fabulous." I disliked the Eagles, and among Eagles songs, I especially disliked "Busy Being Fabulous." The song is about a social-climbing wife who thinks partying is more important than her family—that *appearance* is more important than reality.

You had this enormous smile on your face, and you spun around until you were so dizzy you fell down. Then you laughed at yourself. The ladies behind the counter laughed and clapped their hands.

What the hell was wrong with me? What can I possibly tell you about happiness?

Aristotle was Plato's "student," in the sense that he was mentored at Plato's academy, but he was certainly not Plato's disciple. There is none of the mysticism of Plato. Everything can be explained rationally. Everything can be defined and categorized. Aristotle creates *taxonomy*, which is the study of scientific classification. The concept of things flowing from a few general principles or categories to numerous subcategories—a very Western way of thinking about the world—begins with Aristotle.

Before we start with Aristotle, Violet, I should tell you that of all the authors in this book, Aristotle is the one I have the most trouble with. It would be an understatement to say that Aristotle was hugely significant, but he was also hugely incorrect about a great many things. He is a racist, without doubt, believing the Greeks superior to all other people. This allows him to justify things like slavery without much trouble: after all, if the Greeks are simply naturally superior, then of course slavery is a natural condition. And unlike Socrates, who believed that man was quite insignificant in the great scheme of things, Aristotle believed that man—and the planet Earth itself—were literally the center of the universe, a belief that caused 2,000 years of astronomical contortions because people just assumed that Aristotle must be correct. He was not. The heliocentric theory, which proposes that the Earth revolves around the sun, was known to later Greeks, particularly Aristarchrus and Archimedes. Yet Aristotle's ideas persisted. Both his mentor (Plato) and his most famous student (Alexander) appear to have rejected many of his teachings, and in the Roman period both Plutarch and St. Augustine took rather blunt exception to his teachings and worldview. These were pretty smart guys, too.

To me, it seems that there are two fundamental ways of approaching the world: a Platonic view, and an Aristotelian view. Plato (or at least Plato's surrogate Socrates) believed that there is some degree of mystery in the universe; that there are some things we simply may not be able to know given our limitations as human beings. He accepted the idea of divine, unknowable truths. Aristotle does not seem to go for that. To Aristotle, everything can be known, and everything can be explained. And Aristotle set out to explain everything, whether he knew what he was talking about or not. The *attempt* to define and explain the universe—whether the attempt succeeds or fails—is what's interesting to me about Aristotle. I happen to disagree with Aristotle's worldview, but I also find many of his ideas on processes, politics, and systems quite compelling.

It's okay to disagree with Aristotle or anyone else, Violet. We revere these thinkers, but they could be wrong. I have my biases, like anyone else, but I must concede that *all* of them could be wrong. Remember: be skeptical. And be aware that just because certain people lived around the same time (Socrates, Plato, Aristotle, Alexander...), you can't lump them all together and paint them with one brush. These are very different individuals with very different ideas.

As for Aristotle's dissection of happiness, well—*Nicomachean Ethics* is not something I'd keep on the toilet for giggles. But it does offer a definition of happiness that may help you, as it has helped me.

In *Ethics*, Aristotle first states that everything in life has a purpose, and the proper functioning of that purpose may be taken as that thing's "good." For the eye, the "good" is sight, for the carpenter, the "good" is the successful construction of a house, etc. But many goods are subordinate to others—the lumberjack serves the carpenter, and the carpenter serves the architect. So what is the *chief* good? What is the one good that all men seek, above all others? What is the good that all these other apparent goods (wealth, power, pleasure, wisdom) serve?

Aristotle believes that this Chief Good is *happiness.*

We all seek happiness. But what is it? Is it pleasure, wealth, power, honor, or wisdom? It seems to mean different things to different people. The artist might believe that happiness is pleasure, the politician craves power, and the businessman seeks wealth. A military man might consider honor to be happiness, and philosophers treasure wisdom. These ends—pleasure, wealth, power, honor, and wisdom—are all ends of different kinds of lives, which are lived by men with different natural aptitudes. One pursuit is not necessarily better than the others—all of these ends are "good." Contemplation is terrific, but wealth is not necessarily a bad thing, and neither is power, honor, or pleasure.

And yet, in all these different pursuits, is there some common element to the *kind* of happy life? In addition, the happiness Aristotle seeks to define is not simply a fleeting moment of joy, but a permanent state—otherwise we might call a man happy at one point in his life and unhappy in another. What creates this permanent state of happiness?

> *No function of man has so much permanence as virtuous activities (these are thought to be more durable even than knowledge of the sciences), and of these themselves the most valuable are more durable because those who are happy spend their life most readily and most continuously in these; for this seems to be the reason why we do not forget them. The attribute in question, then, will belong to the happy man, and he will be happy throughout his life; for always, or by preference to everything else, he will be engaged in virtuous action and contemplation, and he will bear the chances of life most nobly and altogether decorously, if he is "truly good," and "beyond reproach."*

Chance can make a man happy or miserable. A man may lead a charmed life and be born into prosperity and stability; or a man may lead a life laced with chaos and tragedy, but neither man can be said to be permanently happy in the sense that Aristotle is talking about. A rich businessman may be miserable, and so too may a successful artist, or a great general. So it's not really your life's pursuit that defines whether or not you are happy; what makes a man truly happy is how he bears the chance of life.

> *If activities are, as we said, what gives life its character, no happy man can become miserable; for he will never do the acts that are hateful and mean. For the man who is truly good and wise, we think, bears all the chances of life becomingly and always makes the best of circumstances, as a good general makes the best military use of the army at his command, and a good shoemaker makes the best shoes out of the hides that are given him; and so with other craftsmen.*

The truly happy man cannot be moved by either good luck or bad—he reacts to both with wisdom and prudence.

Happiness is an activity of the soul, in accordance with perfect virtue.

Well, what does that mean? What is "an activity of the soul," and what is "virtue"? Aristotle believes that moral virtue is something we learn by doing—it's a habit, just like smoking cigarettes or exercising. We have two sides to our being, a rational and an irrational side. The virtues are those qualities that lie between those states. Some have called this **the golden mean**.

For example, everyone feels pleasure and pain, and these two feelings animate many of our decisions. We want pleasure, and we want to avoid pain. But too much pleasure is not a good thing. We can't just sit around drinking and eating ice cream all day. And while we want to avoid pain, a little pain can often be instructive and helpful, as with exercise or diet. So virtue is somewhere in the middle—a *mean* that Aristotle calls **temperance**. Until very recently in Western education, virtues like these were commonly taught in school:

EXTREME (Excessive)	GOLDEN MEAN (Virtue)	EXTREME (Deficient)
Rashness	COURAGE	Cowardice
Self-indulgence, destruction	TEMPERANCE	Prudishness
Hubris	AMBITION	Laziness

We must work at cultivating the middle and avoiding the extremes. As Oscar Wilde once wrote, "Everything in moderation, including moderation." The problem is, we're hardwired for the extremes. Even our bodies have evolved to seek out as much fat and sugar as possible, because in the days when we ran around desperately looking for food, that was rare stuff. And today, in our culture, we *glorify* extremes (such as unhealthy physical beauty, excessive wealth, and even an unwillingness to compromise, which we mistakenly call "being principled"). We also promote the idea that happiness is an external thing—that it can be "purchased" or "possessed." If you just own this gizmo, you'll be happy, or if you find romantic love, you'll be happy, or if you win the lottery, then you'll be happy.

But no *thing* can make you happy, Violet. Other people can't make you happy, either. Professional accomplishments won't do it, and neither will wealth. All these things may be taken away from you. What makes you happy is not what you have, or what others think of you, but how you respond to life's ups and downs—and surprisingly, the truly happy person reacts to both success and tragedy the same way.

Happiness comes from inside you. It's *your* responsibility. Happiness is a choice, and then it is a practice.

That sounds severe, but I'm reminded of something my mother told me. Once, while I was living in Chicago, a married friend came to me and confessed that he was gay. But he didn't want to be gay. He wanted to stay married. I felt so bad for this guy, because I could tell he felt so ashamed. He didn't want to hurt his wife, or his children; he didn't want to deal with the discomfort and humiliation of coming out. What was he going to tell his priest? His mother? His friends? He was trying so hard to be someone he wasn't—not because *he* wanted to live that way, but because of the social pressures. He seemed to be asking me what to do, or to validate his decision. My mom caught wind of it, and she told me the score.

"What are you gonna do with people?" she asked. "Either they're gonna be happy or they're not. It's amazing to me how many people choose to be miserable."

Bingo.

I was choosing to be miserable, too. Of course the chemicals in your brain matter, and lots of people need help adjusting those— including me, Violet, at times in my life. But don't discount the role of behavior. A pill might fix the chemistry, but a pill can't make you happy, either, at least not in the way Aristotle means. Pill or no pill, your behavior is always going to be a factor in your happiness. For example, I suffered from a deficiency of courage. I'd always wanted to be a writer, but I didn't want to give up the comfort and security of a professional career. So I'd chosen not to do the thing that would make me happiest, because, frankly, I was afraid. I thought I had to choose between writing and "everything else." I had defined that choice. And I blamed everyone else because I "had" to make it. That was nonsense. It was understandable that I felt badly, because I was pretending to be someone I was not. That other person sought wealth and power. There was nothing wrong with those pursuits, if that's what I really wanted. But when I acquired both, and still felt miserable, I became angry. I was supposed to be happy now, right? Why wasn't I happy? The answer was simple: I was pursuing the wrong things.

I found happiness—for the first time in my life, really—by following your example.

You exuded this kind of happiness from the moment you were born. You weren't obsessed with the future or the past. You heard a song you liked, you danced to it. When I was with you—*really* with you, and not distracted by work or my own interior monologue about the things I had or didn't have—when I was dancing with you in a sandwich shop, I was happy, too. For the first time in a long time, I felt like myself.

Live the life you want to live, Violet. Don't ever be afraid to simply be who you are.

CHAPTER 6

IS THE CUSTOMER KING?

ARISTOTLE
Politics, Book I

———⟫◦◦◦⟪———

M y dad was a founding partner in a radiology practice, and
when a new hospital was going to be built in town, he and
his partners gave input to the design. While they were drawing up
the waiting room, the hospital administration told him that the
waiting room should "provide a positive customer experience." This
annoyed my father, who made a simple but important distinction:

"They're not customers," he insisted. "They're patients."

When I worked as an advocate for higher education, I heard
similar sentiments about students. Students in the educational
system were increasingly viewed as "customers," and higher education began to be viewed as a business enterprise inside administra-
tions, where the bottom line reigned supreme.

One way to improve the bottom line was to increase capacity and
reduce cost. This was called "increasing access to higher education."
Access could be increased by offering "virtual classrooms." Students
across the country could earn degrees online. They could log in at
their convenience, review a presentation or lecture, and submit their
work via an online platform. These classes could be much larger
than traditional classrooms, and they could be taught by fleets of
adjunct faculty, who could be paid flat fees per student or per course.
As part-time labor working remotely, these adjuncts would not incur
overhead expenses, like facilities costs and health care benefits.

Instead of students *earning* their degrees, they seemed now to be *purchasing* their degrees. This meant lower (or nonexistent) failure rates. You can't fail a customer. Adjuncts who complained about standards were quickly replaced. They were not there to educate students, but merely to facilitate transactions.

This consumerist mentality has even infected the way we choose to govern ourselves. Our elected officials often compare government to running a business or managing a household budget. In October 2013 the Federal Government was shut down because Congress would not agree to pay its bills. Senator Johnny Isakson of Georgia issued this statement during the debate, and it was a sentiment that was widely shared, both inside and outside Congress:

> *As a businessman and a saver, I know what the time value of money is .... But I also know what the time cost of money is: when you are borrowing money to pay off borrowed money—and that is where we are in the United States of America today .... Instead of arguing about what we can't agree upon, we ought to find common ground and run our country's household the way American families run their households. If we had to do here in Washington what every American family has to do year in and year out, this place would be a whole lot different.*

"Politics" has a dirty connotation to us today, but what Aristotle meant by the word *politics* is *Politika*, a Greek word that means "affairs of the polis." In Aristotle's time, the **polis** was a combination of a city and a state. But it was actually much more than that. To Aristotle, the polis was the natural state of mankind—it was the culmination of the family unit, and its purpose was to serve the ultimate good.

Aristotle believed that the state was composed of its constituent parts. The most basic constituent part was the family. Fundamentally, people needed each other in order to survive, so they naturally formed the family unit—the fundamental building block of all states. In families, the most natural form of government was a **monarchy**, where the father/husband was essentially a king.

When a group of related families got together, they formed a village, and according to Aristotle, the natural form of government in a village was a hereditary kingship, because this was merely a continuation of the family unit.

When a group of villages got together, they formed a polis, which we often describe as a "city-state," that is, a political entity like Athens, whose actual city boundaries may have been geographically rather small, but whose sphere of influence extended much further. In a polis, the monarchy becomes unworkable, because the kingship can no longer legitimately serve the interests of everyone in the polis, nor can the owner of hereditary right be obviously identified. Aristotle believes that the ultimate goal of the polis is the **administration of justice**, because the administration of justice is what preserves order among the various family units that constitute the political unit.

Aristotle famously writes, "Man is a political animal." What he means is that the polis is a natural body. Just as the honeybee constructs a hive, human beings are naturally disposed to form larger political bodies. Leaders of states have one main job: the administration of justice.

To understand why, we have to get into some unpleasant realities of life in antiquity.

Seeing then that the state is made up of households, before speaking of the state we must speak of the management of the household. The parts of household management correspond to the persons who compose the household, and a complete household consists of slaves and freemen. Now we should begin by examining everything in its fewest possible elements; and the first and fewest possible parts of a family are master and slave, husband and wife, father and children. We have therefore to consider what each of these three relations is and ought to be: I mean the relation of master and servant, the marriage relation (the conjunction of man and wife has no name of its own), and thirdly, the procreative relation (this also has no proper name). And there is another element of a household, the so-called art of getting wealth, which, according to some, is identical with household management, according to others, a principal part of it; the nature of this art will also have to be considered by us.

There are two elements that are going to cause us discomfort. First, Aristotle says, the natural ruler of a household is the man, and he simply asserts that men are superior to women. Doesn't even discuss it. Second, Aristotle discusses the man's relationship to his slaves as if they were vacuum cleaners.

For modern readers, both of these givens in Aristotle's argument are offensive to say the least. We see Aristotle's casual elitism laid bare—his indifference to the oppression of the majority of the world's population, and later, and even more remarkably, his specious *justification* of slavery. You can see why the Dead White Guys got a bad reputation. And from a modern perspective, there's simply no defending this stuff. But can we understand it?

First of all, even Aristotle's most famous pupil, Alexander the Great, rejected Aristotle's belief in the natural superiority of the Greeks. Alexander, after marching an army across the known world, demonstrated his belief in meritocracy regardless of other considerations. Alexander trained up foreign troops beside his own (which greatly irritated his men). He married an Eastern princess, not by force, but through consent. He came to adopt the customs and even the clothes of the people he conquered. Alexander so distanced himself from some of Aristotle's teachings that some have suggested that Aristotle may have actually had a hand in poisoning Alexander. But though Alexander rejected these particular teachings, he still revered Aristotle's ideas on government. Aristotle was wrong about a great many things—but not everything.

It's also unfair and silly for us to apply industrial, technologically advanced values to preindustrial societies. Our "enlightened" values are very new in human history. We didn't start really entertaining notions of social equality until the 19th century—about 2,200 years after Aristotle died. We practiced a brutal form of slavery in the United States until 1865, followed by a century of segregation, followed by decades of seething racial tensions that still persist. Women didn't even have the right to vote in this country until 1920. My grandmother was alive in 1920. Even today, women are still paid less than men for performing the same labor. Our commitment to diversity and gender equality did not come about because humankind suddenly produced more moral and enlightened individuals. Economic and political realities coalesced to produce them. Industrialization played a huge role in changing social values. The average

Roman citizen living in the first century didn't live all that differently than someone living 1,500 years later—actually, that Roman citizen was probably a lot better off. But for people born in the West after 1900, life was fundamentally different from how it had been for thousands of years. Urban centers exploded in size and importance, the global population began increasing at an exponential rate, and labor became increasingly specialized. Political and economic systems were completely overhauled to reflect new realities, and values changed along with them.

In preindustrial societies, the key to survival (and to the prosperity of any household or state) was to reproduce furiously, not only so you could have a bunch of farmhands and fighters, but also because the infant mortality rate was so high. Today, in our society, large families are uncommon. "Traditional" families themselves are becoming increasingly uncommon. Women bearing children today tend to have fewer children, and to have them later in life. In antiquity, a woman might begin to have children in her early teens, and then she would spend 10 or 20 years of her life either pregnant or nursing very small children. Women regularly died in childbirth, and *everyone* died much younger than they do today. Today we live into our 70s or 80s. Just 100 years ago, the average life expectancy was 45. A century prior to that, it was only 26. In antiquity, even if you survived childbirth, you weren't going to live that long. People didn't worry about cancer or heart disease, because you were more likely to die from simple infections, from starvation, or because some rival faction clawed over the walls and ran giant pikes through your skull.

So in these societies women played the most crucial and vital role—but they spent the majority of their lives simply bearing and rearing children. That was nonnegotiable for the survival of the species, let alone the society. Who had the time and energy to run states? Men. So we have to accept that gender roles were different in antiquity, and while we may not agree that it was right, there were actually some reasons besides "everyone was evil and stupid."

As for Aristotle's defense of slavery, well—it is really going to make your head explode. Basically he says that slavery is not a condition of unequal power, but of character—that some people possess "the character of a slave."

First he examines the relationship of master and slave, and he gives a natural justification for slavery. Aristotle claims that no household can be successful unless it acquires property, and that property can take all sorts of forms. The slave, according to Aristotle, is merely like a tool, or an instrument that man uses to acquire property, with no real difference in purpose to a fork or a knife, except that it is a living possession. But who would submit to being such a possession?

> *But is there any one thus intended by nature to be a slave, and for whom such a condition is expedient and right, or rather is not all slavery a violation of nature?*
>
> *There is no difficulty answering this question, on grounds both of reason and of fact. For that some should rule and others be ruled is a thing not only necessary, but expedient; from the hour of their birth, some are marked out for subjection, others for rule .... The ruler ought to have moral virtue in perfection, for his function, taken absolutely, demands a master artificer; the subjects, on the other hand, require only that measure of virtue which is proper to each of them.*

Of course we don't believe in slavery, or that people have "the character of a slave." It's nonsense of the most disturbing kind. But remember that what Aristotle is ultimately trying to do is to determine what kind of person should be in charge of the state. And would we disagree with his definition?

> *The ruler ought to have moral virtue in perfection, for his function, taken absolutely, demands a master artificer; the subjects, on the other hand, require only that measure of virtue which is proper to each of them.*

What is the function of a head of state, and how does it differ from the head of a household? The head of the household is primarily concerned with the **acquisition of wealth and property**. The head of a state also worries about acquiring wealth, but that is not his primary concern.

> *The previous remarks are quite enough to show that the rule of a master is not a constitutional rule, and that all the different kinds of rule are not, as some affirm, the same with*

each other. For there is one rule exercised over subjects who
are by nature free, another over subjects who are by nature
slaves. The rule of a household is a monarchy, for every house
is under one head: whereas constitutional rule is a govern-
ment of freemen and equals.

In Aristotle's world, as in our country prior to the 20th century, women and children had limited agency, and slaves had no agency at all. The head of the household was supreme *in his own house*. His job was to acquire wealth for his family, and his rule could basically be absolute. But in a state, the ruler must govern *other* free men, and so, the head of a state must primarily be concerned with the administration of justice, rather than simply the acquisition of wealth.

We may disagree with Aristotle on women and slavery, but still accept this concept. Yes, the state must manage its finances. But that task is subservient to the administration of justice. In fact, if we believe that governance (or politics) is the "highest end," to which all other arts are subservient, then *everything we do* should ultimately serve the state, which, in the end, should serve justice.

Commerce plays an important role in society, but the government has many other obligations besides managing the treasury. We use market metrics for everything in America—for education, for health care, for research, for social welfare programs—but it does not work that way. It *cannot* work that way, *if* you believe that the state should be just. We are not "consumers" of government—we are citizens participating in government initiatives, whatever they may be: war, social welfare programs, or tax laws.

When you are admitted into a hospital, you are not a customer. You are a patient. It doesn't matter how much money you have, or whether or not you have a "positive experience." What matters is whether or not you *leave* the hospital healthy and able to return to your life. Customers are "always right." Patients are not "always right."

Nor is education a commodity. Students may pay a fortune for a degree, but they are not entitled to credentials simply because they have paid for them. If they are unqualified, they should not be allowed to advance. That doesn't serve us *as a society*. As Robert Maynard Hutchins, editor of *The Great Books of the Western World*, once wrote:

> *The object of the educational system, taken as a whole, is not to produce hands for industry or to teach the young how to make a living. It is to produce responsible citizens.*

What a profound statement! Today our political leaders would never utter such a phrase. For them, education is seen as a dojo where one trains to compete in the global marketplace; where you are ground and filed into a cog useful to a temporary machine—and when that machine becomes obsolete, so, too, does your education. As I get older, I wonder if our leaders actually *desire* a country filled with responsible citizens—for such a population would be quite dangerous to the established order. Such a population would not abide rampant corruption or incompetence among its officials. Such a population would embrace their shared obligations to their fellow citizens, regardless of how it affected private interests. Such a population would be absolutely willing to wage a war for the common defense, but never for the wrong reasons. When it came to issues of policy, our governors would be questioned ferociously—and, because they would be possessed by civic virtue themselves, the rulers would be capable of providing good answers.

Government is not a business. Social welfare programs, infrastructure investments, and war are not undertaken because they're good business or they offer a good return on investment. We undertake them, collectively, because ultimately they are supposed to serve *justice*.

You will be pressured to believe that you are first, always, and only a customer—that you are a *consumer* of everything, including ideas, health care, education, and government programs; that you "vote with your dollars" and that "everything competes in a marketplace." In such a world, only the cheapest and most popular options survive. And that is a dangerous place to live, Violet. In the short term, it's always cheaper to let the poor starve, or to close schools, loosen environmental regulations, or let sick children die. You can save a lot of money that way, and get yourself a tax break. In the long term, it doesn't look so good on paper.

Everything is not a marketplace. The marketplace is the marketplace. It serves an important function in a larger society, but it's only one function. It exists to serve *a* greater good—it is not *the* greater good. That greater good, according to Aristotle, is *politics*:

the affairs of the polis—the administration of justice, which ensures all of our well-being. We choose to live together as free individuals under constitutional rule, with shared obligations to one another.

You're so much more than just a customer.

CHAPTER 7

WHO SHOULD BE IN CHARGE?

PLUTARCH
The Life of Lycurgus

———❦———

W hen I began my professional career at Chicago Shakespeare Theater, I had the privilege to watch the construction of an actual theater from the ground up. The company built a 40,000-square-foot space on Chicago's Navy Pier, and essentially overnight, it went from a small regional theater to an international cultural institution.

Later I went to work for a struggling association. At the time, the organization inhabited a condemned house on a wooded road in a sleepy backwater of Washington, DC. There were wooden braces holding up the second floor, and the braces themselves were buckling. One day I walked into the copy room, thinking the carpet had changed, only to discover when I stepped down that it was an enormous swarm of termites. The organization was nearly bankrupt. It had a small membership, a small conference of about 1,000 people each year, and a skeleton staff. When I left that place a decade later, we had built the largest literary conference in North America. Our budget had quintupled, and we had 40,000 members worldwide.

For more than 20 years, I've been involved with nonprofit organizations. Some have been enormously successful, and some have not. I've had the opportunity to work with great leaders and bad leaders, and I've had opportunities to be a leader myself—a capacity in which I've both succeeded and failed.

Those times when I've seen organizations humming—when they've been growing, expanding, confident, and exciting—the entire organization seemed to be animated by self-sacrifice. From top to bottom, everyone worked together, and each person focused on the greater good of the organization, regardless of themselves or their own interests. Nobody ever said, "That's not my job." These organizations were possessed by boundless creativity and constant change. They were happy places where people liked each other, where people knew each other as friends. *Everyone* was encouraged to lead, to take risks, and to innovate. Failure was perceived as a positive sign that people were trying to succeed, and never a sign of stupidity. There were expectations, but no schedules. People came and went as they pleased, but everyone always seemed to be working. Nobody had to be told what the rules were. The rules were simple and unspoken: you serve the organization, and the organization's needs are more important than any one individual's.

I've also seen (and led, I'm ashamed to say) organizations that were lost, devoid of purpose, stumbling around, in stasis, refusing to change—places where there were constant turf battles, where no one was willing to do anything an inch outside their job description, where people said things like, "But that's how we've always done it!" These were places littered with arcane procedures and labyrinthine systems. Everyone was bitter, petty, and suspicious. People couldn't wait to leave work, and they abused every privilege. In these places I've noticed that there was always an overabundance of rules and policies. The rules are codified, complex, and explained at length to new employees, who are given huge, officious handbooks on their first day, and told to study organizational charts, grievance procedures, job descriptions, and performance review criteria. Employees are taught to fill out forms, to issue reports, to attend meetings about how to conduct meetings. People quickly learn how to cover their ass. Memoranda are issued with abandon. Staff time is monitored closely for every 15-minute infraction. The staff is taught to be helpless; they are taught that when they take initiative, when they risk, and when they fail, they will be punished. Consequently everyone avoids risk, and nobody questions orders. The organization is allergic to even the slightest amount of change.

What is the difference between these two types of organizations? Why does one organization flourish, and the other fail?

⚊ ⚊

Lycurgus became the King of Sparta by accident. When his brother died, Lycurgus was handed power. He immediately discovered that the queen (his dead brother's wife) was pregnant with the former king's child. Lycurgus decreed that the unborn child was the true heir to the throne. The queen, who was in love with Lycurgus, tried to make a deal with him. She said, "I'll tell you what, Lycurgus. I'll go ahead and have an abortion, and that way, you can be king forever." This would've been a pretty sweet deal for Lycurgus, but instead, he begged the queen not to try to have the abortion, on the pretense that she might injure herself in the process. He promised her that once the baby was born, he would have it killed.

Except he didn't do that.

As soon as the boy was born, Lycurgus took him away from his mother, and he brought him before the men of Sparta. He held the boy up and proclaimed, "Men of Sparta, here is a king born unto us." And then he laid down the baby and named him Charliaus, which means "the joy of the people."

It wasn't easy being King of Sparta. Various plots were laid against Lycurgus and his little adopted child, so Lycurgus decided to go into voluntary exile from the city. He traveled around the world studying other governments. The first place he went was Crete, where he was impressed by the disciplined and sober way of life. After Crete, he went to Asia, where he lived among the Ionian people. The Ionians were very rich, and they lived luxurious lives that Lycurgus found distasteful. But they did have one thing that Lycurgus liked: the poetry of Homer. According to Plutarch, it was Lycurgus who first transcribed Homer's works and brought them to the Greeks. After Asia, Lycurgus went to Egypt, where he was impressed by the separation of the military from the rest of society.

Upon returning to Sparta, he began to reform the government, and in fairly radical ways.

He applied himself, without loss of time, to a thorough reformation, and resolved to change the whole face of the commonwealth; for what good would a few particular laws and a partial alteration avail? He must act as wise physicians do, in the case of one who labours under a complication of diseases, by force of medicines reduce and exhaust him, change his whole temperament, and then set him upon a totally new regimen of diet.

The initial sacrifice was his own: he gave up his own power. He established a senate, which had power equal to the king's. The senate was made up of 28 men over the age of 60, who were widely considered the best citizens in the country. Not only that, but he decided there should be *two* kings, not one, so that each may serve as a check upon the other.

Lycurgus created the **mixed regime**. The mixed regime is a form of government that takes the best elements from more primitive forms of government: monarchy, aristocracy, and democracy. In the 9th century BCE, this was a radical vision of government—and it's not too different from the form of government you live under today. When our founding fathers looked to antiquity for the model form of government, they did not look to Athens, which was a pure democracy, but to the Spartan Republic created by Lycurgus. (When a visitor once asked why Sparta did not set up a democracy, a Spartan remarked, "Begin friend, and set one up in your family.")

The next reform Lycurgus undertook was to address the inequality in Sparta.

For there was extreme inequality amongst them, and their state was overloaded with a multitude of indigent and necessitous persons, while its whole wealth had centered upon a very few. To the end, therefore, that he might expel from the state arrogance and envy, luxury and crime, and those yet more inveterate diseases of want and superfluity, he obtained of them to renounce their properties, and to consent to a new division of the land, and that they should all live together on an equal footing; merit to be their only road to eminence, and the disgrace of evil, and credit of worthy acts, their one measure of difference between man and man.

A small part of land was set aside for the center of the city, and then everybody got a plot of land that was roughly the same size.

If all this wasn't radical enough, Lycurgus rid the city of gold and silver. Realizing that the people would still need a method of exchange, he made iron the currency of the people. Iron is heavy, and others considered it worthless. As a result, nobody bothered stealing it. He even *ruined* the iron for weapon making, pouring vinegar over it so it couldn't be used to make swords and shields.

Once Sparta began using iron as currency, nobody sent merchants to Sparta anymore. Rhetoric masters, fortune-tellers, pimps, swindlers, and lawyers didn't go to Sparta. Why would they go to Sparta? There was no money to be made there.

You might think a state like this would be dreary and gray, but Sparta blossomed into the most beautiful state in Greece. Because they had no unnecessary luxuries, the Spartans became excellent craftsmen of all the necessary things in life—chairs, tables, and especially cups. They made awesome cups in Sparta. Before you think that's small comfort, Violet, remember that these were people who didn't have bottled water, so clean, delicious water was hard to come by. The Spartans invented a cup that filtered out mud and grit, so that when you drank, you only got clean, pure water. People all over the world loved Spartan cups. They became prized luxuries in other states.

Lycurgus insisted that all the people would eat the same foods, and that they would eat together in clubs at huge tables. The only exception to this was if you went hunting, and bagged yourself a deer. Then you could eat at home. But you still had to send some meat to the common table.

The Spartans were an unusually sober and temperate society. To a Spartan, there was nothing so distasteful as a drunk. They'd eat together, with a little bit of watered-down wine, and then they would walk home together in the dark.

Contrary to their depiction in popular culture, the Spartans avoided war, and never waged war too long with the same enemy, lest they reveal their military secrets to them.

The Spartans did not believe that children belonged to the family, but to the city as a whole. And they practiced selective breeding. If a man wanted to have a baby with another man's wife, all that was needed was everybody's consent. So adultery wasn't really a problem.

Once the children reached a certain age—about seven—they were taken from their families and put into camps together. No distinction was made between boys and girls. All the children would exercise together, completely naked. Women were equal to men in Spartan society, and here, Plutarch takes some rather blunt issue with Aristotle.

For Aristotle is wrong in saying that after he had tried all other ways to reduce women to more modesty and sobriety, he was at last forced to leave them as they were, because that in the absence of their husbands, who spent the best part of their lives at war, their wives ... took great liberties and assumed the superiority; and they were treated with overmuch respect and called by the title of lady or queen. The truth is, he took in their case, also, all the care that was possible; he ordered the maidens to exercise themselves with wrestling, running, throwing the quoit, and casting the dart, to the end that the fruit they conceived might, in strong and healthy bodies, take firmer root and find better growth, and withal that they, with this greater vigor, might be the more able to undergo the pains of child-bearing .... Hence it was natural for them to speak as Gorgo, for example, the wife of Leonidas, when some foreign lady ... told her that the women of [Sparta] were the only women in the world who could rule men; "With good reason," she said, "for we are the only women who bring forth men."

Badass!

Spartan boys had tough upbringings. They were not given warm blankets or beds, so their bodies became hard and conditioned to withstand the elements. The boys grew up under the watch of the elders, and they were informed about politics and matters of governance. They were never given enough to eat, so they would learn to be crafty and steal food. But if they were caught stealing, they would be beaten mercilessly.

Because of the nature of how they lived, perhaps, they became exceedingly good with short sayings and aphorisms:

When asked about the city's fortifications:
"The city is well fortified which has a wall of men instead of brick."
When asked how Sparta could continuously beat back invasion:
"By continuing poor, and not coveting each man to be greater than his fellow."
When asked why Spartans were so quiet:
"He who knows how to speak knows also when."
When an Athenian insulted a Spartan by saying they had no formal learning:
"You say true, sir, we alone of all Greeks have learned none of your bad qualities."
When asked how many Spartans there were:
"Enough to keep out the wicked men."

When they had to fight, they were unlike any other fighting force in the world. They did not run or march to battle. They *danced*.

It was at once a terrible sight to see them march on to the tune of their flutes, without any disorder in their ranks, any discomposure in their minds, or change in their countenances, calmly and cheerfully moving with the music to the deadly fight.

Unlike other Greek societies, they married for love. Since there was no poverty or wealth among them, they had no lawsuits. And perhaps most strangely, they never wrote any of their laws down, believing, as Lycurgus said, "the law of the people was best written on their hearts." And while they were terrifying in battle, they neither pursued their enemies nor imposed harsh penalties on those they conquered, believing that people would understand: the best way to fight a war with the Spartans was to turn around and run the other way.

At the end of his life, having established his government and laws, Lycurgus went to the senate and the two kings, and he told them that he was going on a journey. He asked them to observe the laws until he returned, and the people agreed. Then he went to Delphi and asked the Oracle if he had made good laws, and the Oracle said that he had.

Upon hearing this, Lycurgus went out into the wilderness and starved himself to death. He was an old man now, and he'd felt he'd been of use. He didn't want to use any resources that could be better spent on the young.

The Spartans kept their word. For 500 years, Sparta was the leading city of Greece. Centuries after Lycurgus lived, many people criticized his laws. One King Theopompus was said to have remarked that Spartan kings were only able to rule for such a long time "because their people know so well how to obey."

But Plutarch disagrees.

> *For people do not obey, unless rulers know how to command; obedience is a lesson taught by commanders. A true leader himself creates the obedience of his own followers; as it is the last attainment of the art of riding to make a horse gentle and tractable, so it is the science of government, to inspire men with a willingness to obey .... All those who have written well of politics, as Plato, Diogenes, and Zeno, have taken Lycurgus as their model, leaving behind them, however, mere projects and words; whereas Lycurgus was the author not in words, but in reality, of a government which none else could so much as copy.*

Lycurgus became king of a troubled, corrupt, and dysfunctional kingdom. His bold and radical reforms were not accepted because they were excellent, reasonable policies. Surely there were smarter and stronger men who'd come before Lycurgus. But people aren't convinced to change by reason or force.

Lycurgus led by example, and he was the first to sacrifice for the sake of his state. How could anyone doubt that he had their best interests at heart, when he himself was the first to surrender power to others? They continued to be inspired by his courage, his discipline, his curiosity, and his open mind. Their state became a reflection of those traits. Lycurgus held himself to the highest personal standards. He knew that the only way to change his city was through personal sacrifice.

When I was young, I thought that people followed money, charisma, or power. But I guess what I've learned after all these years working is this: character matters the most, Violet. Whether it's a tiny nonprofit, a multinational corporation, or even a state, organizations tend to resemble the character of the people in charge. When I've seen organizations excel, the leaders have been virtuous, self-sacrificing, and animated by a greater goal. They view leadership as a sacrifice and a responsibility. They are the first to sacrifice, and they seek neither glory nor credit. In these instances, their organizations grow and expand almost effortlessly—the success is like a byproduct, or a symptom, of the character of its leader.

When I've seen organizations fail, the leaders have been petty, myopic, and selfish. The leader craves power only for the benefits that power might bestow upon him or herself. These individuals believe leadership to be an entitlement or possession—something they "deserve" or "are owed." Others will do the sacrificing simply by being commanded to do so. If necessary, force can be applied to compel obedience. The organization exists to serve the people in charge, not the other way around.

So, as you begin your career, try to associate yourself with bosses of good character, because those are the individuals who will take you places. When you interview for a job, remember that you are interviewing them as well. Observe the way your interviewer interacts with people, especially those in subordinate positions. You should do your homework and ask questions about the particular organization you're looking to join, but you should also take care to observe the people in the office. Do they look busy and happy? Are they talking with one another, do they seem happy to be in one another's company? Or do they look lonely, timid, or frightened? How are you greeted when you walk in the door? How does it *feel* in the place? This will tell you a lot about the person in charge—and whether or not you want to work for that person. *Even if you don't meet that person,* you will be able to tell. You should be greeted warmly, like a guest, and it should seem exciting, vibrant, and friendly. You should *want* to join them. I've been in interviews before where people said all the right things, but something felt off. When I've listened to that feeling, I did well in my choices. When I ignored it, or thought I could change it, I've made huge mistakes.

One good leader can have a profound and enduring impact; they can shape the culture of an organization or state. According to Plutarch, 400 years after Lycurgus died, Philip of Macedonia sent a long, threatening letter to Sparta, promising that if he invaded Sparta, he would destroy the city and kill everyone in it. If he invaded, he would burn down their homes and enslave women and children.

Philip had second thoughts when he received the uniquely Spartan reply:

"If."

CHAPTER 8

THE STATE AS CHURCH

PLUTARCH
The Life of Numa Pompilius

━━━━◦◦◦◦◦━━━━

Your second birthday fell on Easter Sunday, so your mom and I invited all your little friends over for an Easter egg hunt on the day we understood as "Holy Saturday." When your mom and I were growing up, Holy Saturday was officially the saddest day of the year. Jesus Christ had been crucified on Good Friday. Schools and businesses were closed on Good Friday. On Holy Saturday, Jesus was neither on earth nor in heaven, so on this day God was absent from the universe. When I was seven years old, Sister Mary Veronica informed me that Holy Saturday was the day that "Jesus rested in his tomb." The saddest day of the year.

The Good Fridays of my youth were spent at St. Peter's church in Geneva, Illinois, wandering around the Stations of the Cross. It was a day of confession, where I would sit in the vestibule and confess my childhood crimes to Father Jim. St. Peter's wasn't much to look at—it was basically a pole building in the middle of a cornfield. And yet it was still a place of mysticism and mystery, filled with strange ancient rituals, reeking of incense and secrecy. As a boy, I learned that every altar of every church concealed the physical remains of a martyr, and that mine hid a finger bone of some unknown saint who'd been set on fire a thousand years ago. This was exactly the sort of thing the Catholics would do: dismember the bones of the devoted and distribute them to parishes according to rank or merit, collecting them like ghoulish baseball cards.

On the Good Friday prior to your second birthday, your mom and I stuffed plastic eggs full of Sesame Street stickers, M&Ms, and your mom's favorite Easter candy: purple marshmallow Peeps. This is what Easter had become for most Americans. It was all about the Easter egg hunt. Even the president had one, right on the White House lawn. So we were busy making little baskets, filling them with grass, and hiding plastic eggs in the yard. I saw our neighbors doing the same thing, and we laughed at the absurdity of what we were doing.

Why *were* we doing it?

—~—

Jesus Christ was born during the first century of the Roman Empire, and he was executed under Roman law. Rome had been founded eight centuries prior by another "god," a man named Romulus (hence the name, Rome). In the legend, Romulus was raised by wolves. He died under very mysterious circumstances, especially for a deity.

> *It was the thirty-seventh year, counted from the foundation of Rome, when Romulus, then reigning ... did offer a public sacrifice at the Goat's marsh, in presence of the senate and the people of Rome. Suddenly the sky was darkened, a thick cloud of storm and rain settled on the earth, the common people fled in afright, and were dispersed, and in this whirlwind Romulus disappeared, his body never being found either living or dead. A foul suspicion presently attached to the patricians, and rumors were current among the people as if that they, weary of kingly government, and exasperated of late by the imperious deportment of Romulus toward them, had plotted against his life, and made him away, so that they might assume the authority and government into their own hands.*

So it came time for the Romans to decide upon a new king, but nobody in Rome could agree. Eventually, the Romans selected Numa Pompilius. He didn't want the job. He was happy living a life of contemplation.

*In private, he devoted himself not to amusement or [money],
but to the worship of the immortal gods, and rational contemplation of their divine power and nature.*

When Numa was offered the job of king, he responded with indifference:

*Every alteration of a man's life is dangerous to him; but
madness only could induce one who needs nothing, and is
satisfied with everything, to quit a life he is accustomed to;
which, whatever else it is deficient in, at any rate has the advantage of certainty over one wholly doubtful or unknown.*

Numa was also wary because of what happened to his "divine"
predecessor Romulus, which nobody believed to be a miracle. He
reminded the Romans that the last person to be king was probably
murdered by the senate. So it didn't sound like a great career opportunity. And besides, Numa said, Romulus was supposedly descended
from the gods, whereas he (Numa) was a mere mortal.

*The very points of my character that are most commended
mark me as unfit to reign—love of retirement and of studies
inconsistent with business, a passion that has become inveterate in me for peace, for unwarlike occupations, and for
the society of men whose meetings are but those of worship
and kindly intercourse, whose lives in general are spent upon
their farms and their pastures. I should but be, methinks,
a laughing-stock, while I should go about to inculcate the
worship of the gods, and give lessons in the love of justice and
the abhorrence of violence and war, to a city whose needs are
rather for a captain than for a king.*

The more Numa tried to reject the job, the more the Romans wanted
him to be their king. Eventually, Numa's father convinced him
to accept, telling Numa that by doing so, he would be in the best
possible position to serve the gods. And that is what Numa did to the
Roman state: he introduced the gods into it.

Here Plutarch reminds us again of Plato's *Republic*:

Plato's expression of a city in high fever was never more applicable than to Rome at that time; in its origin formed by daring and warlike spirits, whom bold and desperate adventure brought thither from every quarter, it had found in perpetual wars and incursions on its neighbors its ... sustenance and means of growth.

As King of the Romans, Numa wove religion and worship into the daily (and civic) lives of the Romans. He was quite successful. He sacrificed often, and he tried to temper the warlike spirit of Rome. He also filled the Romans with religious fear.

At times, also, he filled their imaginations with religious terrors, professing that strange apparitions had been seen, and dreadful voices heard; thus subduing and humbling their minds by a sense of supernatural fears.

Numa also formed a priestly order in Rome, and this system would later be co-opted by the Catholic Church. He became the first *pontifices*, which derives from the word *potens*, which means "power." The Roman Catholic pope—who is the leader of the Roman Catholic faith, and who resides in the Vatican in Rome—is often referred to as "the Pontiff."

The office of Pontifex Maximus, or chief priest, was to declare and interpret the divine law, or rather, to preside over sacred rites.

Numa also made many secular reforms. In order to stop Rome from getting into wars, he instituted a diplomatic corps filled with ambassadors. And whenever Rome was slighted by some other country in some way, these ambassadors would be dispatched to try to resolve the problem amicably. If they could not, Rome went to war.

He took all the land that Romulus had won through war and divided it among the people into segments called *parishes*. Numa believed that in order for Rome to become a peaceful people, they would have to be more personally involved with agriculture.

> *For there is no employment that gives so keen and quick a relish for peace as husbandry and a country life, which leave in men all that kind of courage that makes them ready to fight in defense of their own, while it destroys the license that breaks out into acts of injustice and rapacity.*

The most important secular reform Numa made was to separate people not by their ethnicity, but by their trade. Numa instituted the Guild system at Rome.

> *So, distinguishing the whole people by the several arts and trades, he formed the companies of musicians, goldsmiths, carpenters, dyers, shoemakers, skinners, braziers, and potters; and all other handicraftsmen he composed and reduced into a single company, appointing every one their proper courts, councils, and religious observances .... In this manner all factious distinctions began, for the first time, to pass out of use, no person any longer being either thought of as of a Sabine or a Roman ... and the new division became a source of general harmony and intermixture.*

He also reformed Rome's calendar in ways that are still in use today.

> *He also altered the order of the months; for March, which was reckoned the first, he put into the third place; and January, which was the eleventh, he made the first, and February, which was the twelfth and last, the second. Many will have it, that it was Numa, also, who added the two months of January and February.*

Most of our months have Roman names. December is called December because to the Romans, it was once considered the tenth month (*deca* being the word for "ten" in Latin). January is named for the two-faced Roman god Janus. March is named after Mars, the god of War. July and August are named after Julius Caesar and his successor, Augustus Caesar. And April, which is the month when you were born?

*[Some say] April is named from Aphrodite ... but others ...
say it is called April from aperio, Latin for "to open," because
that this month is high spring, and opens and discloses the
buds and flowers.*

Like violets!

All of these religious and secular reforms served their purpose. It
was said that Numa presided over 43 years of peace at Rome.

*For not only had the people of Rome itself been softened and
charmed into a peaceful temper by the just and mild rule of
a pacific prince, but even the neighboring cities, as if some
salubrious and gentle air had blown from Rome upon them,
began to experience a change of feeling, and partook in the
general longing for the sweets of peace and order, and for life
employed in the quiet tillage of soil, bringing up of children,
and worship of the gods.*

On top of ordering the calendar, creating the offices and infrastructure that would eventually become the infrastructure of the Roman
Catholic Church, and inventing the first "state department," Numa's
most consequential innovation was weaving religion into the fabric
of civic life. It's no accident that post-Roman states, including our
own, have so much religion intermixed with our civic rituals. Numa
Pompilius is the reason the President of the United States hosts an
Easter egg hunt on the White House lawn. And he's also the reason
why the president tends to invoke the almighty on a regular basis.
People don't just need a state to give laws—they also need the state
to sponsor certain virtues.

Numa understood that the law was not so important as the
culture. Laws change, cultures endure. The American republic,
despite its pretense to secularism, is very much united by religious
rituals and ideals. Like it or not, the United States is a Christian
nation. Legally, we're not. Culturally, we are.

For example, legally, the American Constitution prohibits any
"religious test" for our elected officers like the president. That's
the law. But in practice, a great deal of time is spent parsing every

candidate's religious faith and practices. Many of our presidents even claim, as Numa did, that they converse personally with the Almighty.

On your second birthday, as you and your little friends hunted Easter eggs in our backyard in Alexandria, Virginia, you were actually stuffing your basket with symbols of the grave of Jesus Christ. Early Christians used to paint eggs red, believing that the egg symbolized the empty tomb of Jesus Christ, and the red paint symbolized his blood. A bird would hatch from the egg, symbolizing Christ's ascension into heaven.

These early Christians understood the power of custom and ritual, because they were following the Roman example. Religion is now so intertwined into our everyday life that we don't even realize it. Once a year, we stuff plastic eggs full of marshmallow birds. We don't know why. We just do it. We're still doing things the Romans did.

The power of history is not in understanding obscure dates and strange names like "Numa Pompilius." The power comes from understanding *why* things are as they are. Why are the months ordered and named as they are? Why am I sitting on my porch in Alexandria stuffing marshmallow birds into plastic eggs? Why are we at war in the Middle East? Why has our economy collapsed? Why have the terrorists attacked us? These events do not occur in temporal vacuums, and they are not simply the result of events that have transpired in the last five minutes, five months, or five years. Often the true cause (or causes) of our problems extend decades or even centuries into the past.

Whether you believe in Jesus or not, your view of the world is focused through a Christian lens, with its notions of justice, peaceful protest, individual rights, and the afterlife—all of which owe a debt to the Romans, the Jews, and the Greeks before them. Many of the teachings of Jesus Christ are similar to those of Socrates, with his ideas about an absolute and just God, the immortal soul, and acceptance of unjust persecution. That's not a coincidence, Violet.

There is a secret history to everything you believe. You did not arrive on this Earth with the compulsion to paint hard-boiled eggs, any more than you arrived filled with a love of "democracy," "capitalism," or "freedom." I don't mean to suggest these notions are right or wrong—but they are certainly not natural givens. I imagine you as balancing atop a very thin, needlelike spire that extends far above the clouds. From your vantage point you can see the expansive sky, the sun and stars, and all the birds in the air. But far beneath your feet, obscured by the cloud cover, is the enormous foundation that supports your weight, and it gets wider and wider the farther down you go. If you truly want to understand yourself, climb down from the present, and learn about the past.

CHAPTER 9

PUNCH THE BULLY IN THE FACE

PLUTARCH
The Life of Alexander

———

W hen I was 20 years old, I was in Murphy's Pub in Champaign, Illinois, getting drunk with my friend Sean Lee. As I was walking out a frat guy at a table put his hand on my chest.

"What'd you say about my girlfriend?" he asked.

I hadn't said anything about his girlfriend. I didn't know this guy or his girlfriend. I had my coat on. I was leaving. But I knew what was really going on. This guy was drunk, and he saw me, all five foot, seven inches of me, and he thought he'd kick my ass a little bit. And he proceeded to do that—quite capably, I might add.

I'd been here before. I've always been small, and I was bullied as a kid. I thought the best thing to do was to get away as fast as possible. Leave the situation. *Run.* If I stayed I was going to take a beating. But the bar was crowded, this guy was in my way, and now all his buddies were standing behind him egging him on.

"I'm sorry?" I said.

Then he broke a beer bottle over my head. You see that in movies like it's no big deal. It's a big deal. It hurt. It knocked me down. My head was bleeding. I lay on the sticky floor in my arty black trench coat. I assumed the fetal position as the guy began to kick me in the ribs while his buddies hollered. I could see the bouncers in the background. Nobody was doing anything, and nobody was gonna do anything.

Then I saw one of the most amazing things I have ever seen in my life. Sean Lee grabbed my attacker by the shirt, and like a superhero, he whipped the guy around in the air, knocking a couple people off their barstools in the process.

A small gladiatorial pit emerged, like somebody dropping a boulder in a pond. I was in the middle of the pit, and so was Sean Lee. So was the guy who'd hit me. When I stumbled to my feet, I saw Sean Lee kneeling on top of that guy, and he was gouging my attacker's eyes out with his index and pinkie fingers. Both he and Sean were screaming, but only one was screaming in pain. Sean was screaming a savage battle cry.

It didn't last long. Maybe a minute or less. It felt like forever. The guy's friends grabbed Sean by the arms and hauled him off their friend, who ran past me with his hands over his eyes. I could see blood running down from under his palms. Sean struggled and kicked and fought, but he was brought down and beaten very badly.

I stood there watching. I did nothing. I was terrified.

Hours later at the emergency room, Sean sat on an examination table. His face was swollen, his lip was fat and bleeding, his nose looked broken, and both his eyes were black and blue. I had a relatively minor cut on the side of my head.

He lit a cigarette in the emergency room. Man, that guy was cool! Before the doctor came and told him to put it out, he exhaled a long train of smoke and looked up at me.

"Why didn't you *do* anything?" he asked.

For centuries the Persian Empire had been harassing the Greeks. The Persians invaded Greece, they occupied Greek cities, they demanded enormous tributes, and they meddled in the Greeks' domestic affairs and civil disputes.

That ended with Alexander the Great.

By the time Alexander was 20, he was the king of Macedonia. By all accounts, he was a man of small stature. When he captured the Persian queen, she is said to have prostrated herself before Alexander's taller friend Hephaestion. Learning of her mistake, the captured queen quivered in panic.

"Worry not, mother," Alexander assured her. "For he too is Alexander."

That could've been said of anyone who served under Alexander the Great, because he inspired complete devotion in his men. They gladly died for him. Many of them believed he was a god—not "godlike," but an actual deity sent down to Earth to achieve the impossible, to do what no man before or since has ever done: to conquer and unite the entire world. His example inspired men like Hannibal, Julius Caesar, Augustus, and Napoleon—none of whom came close to matching his accomplishments.

You live in Alexander's shadow, Violet. You're *Western* because of Alexander. He is responsible, perhaps more than any other individual in history, for preserving and expanding the Western intellectual tradition. Socrates instructed Plato, who then mentored Aristotle, who then tutored Alexander. Alexander was the Philosopher King imagined in Plato's *Republic,* made real and come down to earth.

He did not disappoint.

Alexander's very conception and birth were shrouded in superstition. The night before his conception, both of his parents had strange dreams. His mother dreamed that she was struck by lightning, and his father dreamed that he sealed up his wife's body with the symbol of a lion. And on the day he was born, the great temple of Diana at Ephesus was burned to the ground. The ancients claimed that the temple's patron goddess (Diana) was away from the temple, assisting with Alexander's birth. All the fortune-tellers watched the temple burn and cried and beat their faces. They swore that something had been brought forth that would destroy all of Asia.

Alexander's father, Philip, was the King of Macedonia, and he himself was a military genius. Philip had already conquered most of Greece by the time Alexander was born, so Alexander grew up surrounded by luxury, wealth, and power. But from a very young age, Alexander was always upset when he heard news of his father's successes.

Whenever he heard Philip had taken any town of importance, or won any signal victory, instead of rejoicing at it altogether, he would tell his companions that his father would anticipate everything, and leave him and them no opportunities of performing great and illustrious actions.

From the time he was a just a little boy, Alexander had dreams of glory, and he showed a remarkable amount of potential.

> *While he was yet very young, he entertained the ambassadors from the King of Persia, in the absence of his father, and entering much into conversation with them, gained so much upon them by his affability, and the questions he asked them, which were far from being childish or trifling (for he inquired of them the length of the ways, the nature of the road into inner Asia, the character of their king, how he carried himself to his enemies, and what forces he was able to bring into the field).*

The Persian ambassadors smiled at this precocious little boy, unaware that even at such a tender age, Alexander was plotting to attack Persia, and he was using every opportunity to gain a tactical advantage. They told him everything he wanted to know. What could be the harm?

One of the most famous stories about Alexander involves his beloved horse, Bucephalus. Bucephalus went with Alexander on all his campaigns, and there was even a city named in his honor. Plutarch describes how Alexander tamed the horse:

> *Philonicus the Thessalian brought the horse Bucephalus to Philip, offering to sell him for thirteen talents; but when they went to the field to try him, they found him so very vicious and unmanageable, that he reared up whenever they attempted to mount him, and he would not so much as endure the voice of any of Philip's attendants. Upon which, as they were leading him away as wholly useless and intractable, Alexander ... said, "What an excellent horse do they lose for want of address and boldness to manage him." Philip at first took no notice of what the boy had said, but when he heard him repeat the same thing several times, and saw he was much vexed to see the horse sent away, "Do you reproach," said Philip, "those who are older than yourself, as if you knew more, and were better able to manage him than they?" "I could manage this horse," replied Alexander, "better than the others do." "And if you do not?" asked Philip, "what will*

you forfeit for your rashness?" "I will pay," answered Alexander, "the whole price of the horse."

After he had said this to his father, all his father's men laughed at him. Thirteen talents was a *lot* of money—the equivalent of hundreds of thousands of dollars to us. So Philip told his son to go ahead and try it.

Alexander took the horse's bridle, and led the animal away from the sun, seeing that the horse was aggravated by its shadow. He stroked the horse gently, and spoke to it softly, and then, in one quick motion, he leaped into the saddle and rode the horse as if the two had known each other their whole lives. His father was so impressed by this act that he said to his son,

O my son, look thee out a kingdom equal and worthy of thyself, for Macedonia is too little for thee.

His father recognized Alexander's intellect immediately, and so, for his tutor, Philip selected the most famous philosopher of his time: Aristotle. Alexander proved to be a promising student. He was a voracious reader, and he loved Homer most of all. He kept two things under his pillow while on campaign: a dagger and a copy of the *Iliad,* edited by Aristotle himself. He didn't just read literature. He was a trained physician, and when his men were sick, he prescribed them medicines and diets to cure them. He read treatises on science, metaphysics, and religion.

Philip was assassinated when Alexander was only 20 years old, and the kingdom fell to Alexander. Upon assuming the throne of Macedonia, Alexander found himself beset by dangers on all sides. Philip had built an empire, but the barbarian tribes and Greek cities he had conquered sensed an opportunity to rebel once Alexander came to the throne. He was just a boy, after all, only 20 years old.

Alexander moved swiftly to quell the barbarians, and then he turned his attention to Thebes, which was in open revolt. Alexander's conquest of Thebes was his first great military test, and he understood that he wasn't just dealing with Thebes—he was dealing with all the Greek cities, especially Athens. He had to send a message to the Greeks that rebellion was unwise.

Alexander tried to reason with the Thebans. He offered clemency to Thebes if they would hand over the leaders of the rebellion. The Thebans not only refused, they insulted Alexander. So Alexander made a very severe example of Thebes. After he put down the revolt, he killed six thousand men, and he sold 30,000 Thebans into slavery. He essentially depopulated one of the most ancient and famous cities of Greece.

Now it is fashionable to look upon an act like this and judge Alexander harshly. He was overly cruel, or he was ruthless, so this atrocity colors all of the man's accomplishments. Alexander himself knew it was harsh, and Plutarch reports that he regretted the brutality of it for the rest of his life. On the other hand, Alexander was a man who had a comprehensive vision of the future—not just his own immediate future, or the future for the next 50 or 100 years, but the future of all mankind. He dreamed of uniting the entire world into one world-nation. That wasn't going to happen without conflict.

Alexander did terrible things, Violet. He killed a great many people personally, including many of his friends. Later on in his life (when he was still a very young man, actually), Alexander may have become a drunk. As his military conquests became more and more incredible, he also began to believe his own press, and he became increasingly unwilling to listen to criticism or dissent. The punishments he meted out for disloyalty or sedition were swift and brutal. Believing he was in fact a god, his men believed that he arrogantly took on divine airs, and acted above them. He became increasingly consumed by a fascination with superstition and omens, and he put his armies through a tremendous amount of anguish and hardship.

But at the same time, the scale of his accomplishment staggers the imagination, especially when you consider that he died at 32. Besides marching a small army across the known world and never losing a battle, Alexander was a man of enormous intellectual curiosity. He founded the great city of Alexandria in Egypt. This city became the intellectual capital of the entire world, and scholars from all the reaches of Alexander's vast empire came and shared their knowledge at the great Library of Alexandria, which Julius Caesar later tried to burn to the ground. Far more than Plato's Academy or Aristotle's Lyceum, the Library of Alexandria would serve as the template for our modern universities: a place where great minds could come together and debate, rather than a didactic school led by a single mind. It was here that scientists and philosophers from around the world convened, where experiments in mathematics, biology, and every branch of science flourished for centuries. These discoveries led to practical innovations that would change mankind. Alexander placed wisdom above riches and power, and his values may best be exemplified in this story from his campaign in Persia:

While on campaign, his soldiers brought him an amazingly ornate Persian casket, adorned with gold and jewels. All of Alexander's men took turns wondering what could possibly be so precious as to deserve to be laid inside such a valuable casket. Alexander took his weathered, beat-up copy of the *Iliad* and laid it inside.

He dreamed so big it inspired the world. When Alexander announced his plan to conquer Persia, it was perceived as an insane and suicidal ambition. At the time of Alexander's invasion, Persia was *enormous*. It stretched across Asia and the Middle East. In modern terms, the territory Alexander set out to conquer included Turkey, Syria, Egypt, Iraq, Iran, Afghanistan, and Pakistan. No other Western power in history has been able to do what Alexander did—not even the United States of America.

How did he do it? It wasn't with horses and spears. It was with Alexander's signal gifts: courage and generosity.

First, Alexander never asked his men to do anything he would not. At every battle, in every circumstance, he plunged himself headlong into danger. He was not the type of commander who stood in the back and sent his armies to die. He was right there in the front leading the charge. This was in stark contrast to his Persian counterpart, King Darius. At the battle of Gaugemela—at which Alexander's army was said to be outnumbered by as much as 20 to one—Alexander led the charge of his Macedonians while King Darius sat in an imperial chariot at the rear of his forces. Rather than deal with the danger in front of him, Alexander plunged straight for Darius, racing through the Persian ranks to confront Darius personally. When Darius saw Alexander approaching, he leaped off of his chariot, mounted a horse, and ran away. He deserted his men. This retreat not only demoralized the Persian troops, it made them admire Alexander.

Through his bravery and personal example, Alexander inspired friendships across enemy lines. Other armies stood in awe before him. He even put himself at more risk by making sure everyone could identify him. He wore special armor and a very distinct helmet, so that he could not be mistaken for any other soldier. He basically made himself a giant target. And then he personally raced through hordes of enemy forces, escaping death as if protected by the gods themselves.

But Alexander's courage was accompanied by an amazing generosity. While he was sailing to invade Persia, he gave away all of his lands and estates to his men, leaving nothing for himself. When one of his soldiers asked what would be left for Alexander, Alexander replied, "My hopes." This so touched the soldier that he refused to take Alexander's gift, imploring Alexander to let him share instead in the hopes.

> *Alexander was naturally most munificent, and grew more so as his fortune increased, accompanying what he gave with that courtesy and freedom which, to speak truth, it is necessary to make a benefit really obliging.*

It is easy to be generous to your friends, Violet. It is far more difficult is to be generous to your enemies, and here was the essence of Alexander's military genius.

When Alexander seized Thebes, he was really trying to send a message to Athens. Once he had made his point, though, Alexander did not press it with further brutality—in fact, he forgave the Athenians, and then he paid them the highest compliment he could.

> *He not only forgave them all past offenses, but bade them look to their affairs with vigilance, remembering that if he should miscarry, they were likely to be the arbiters of Greece.*

The once rebellious Athenians were suddenly filled with pride, and with affection for Alexander.

After he won his first amazing battle in Persia, he captured the wife and daughters of the Persian King Darius, along with all their riches. A shortsighted man would've plundered their treasure and sold them into slavery. But Alexander insisted that they be treated with the highest respect, and that nothing of theirs should be touched. He promised to restore them to liberty as soon as it was safe. In fact, he ordered that they be paid *larger* pensions than they had been paid before.

He treated these illustrious prisoners according to their
virtue and character, not suffering them to hear or receive, or
so much as to apprehend anything that was unbecoming. So
that they seemed rather lodged in some temple, or some holy
virgin chambers, where they enjoyed their privacy sacred and
uninterrupted, than in the camp of an enemy.

More than any battle, this single act of generosity won him the love and respect of the Persians he was conquering. When Darius's wife died, Alexander held a state funeral for her, sparing no expense, and even weeping himself. When word of his wife's death reached Darius, he cursed Alexander, believing his wife had been rudely treated. But a slave who had been with the queen challenged his own king in Alexander's defense:

"Oh King," replied the Eunuch, "as to her funeral rites, or
any respect or honor that should have been shown in them,
you have not the least reason to accuse the ill fortune of your
country; for to my knowledge neither your queen, nor your
mother, nor your children, wanted anything of their former
happy condition ... and after her decease, I assure you, she
had not only all due funeral ornaments, but was honored
also with the tears of your very enemies; for Alexander is as
gentle after victory as he is terrible in the field."

After that, even *Darius* admired Alexander. And Alexander was trying to kill him!

After Alexander won his great battle against the Indian warlord Porus, he took the defeated king into his tent and asked him what he could do for him. "Treat me as a king," replied Porus. Recognizing Porus's courage and ability, Alexander let Porus keep his throne, and then he gave him *more* land and people to govern.

Alexander also thought that the people he conquered were every bit as capable as his own Macedonians. This was in stark contrast to the views of Aristotle, who viewed the Macedonians and Greeks as naturally superior to other races. In India, much to the chagrin of his Macedonians, Alexander had 30,000 boys trained up to fight alongside his men. He didn't conquer people. He embraced them.

He even adopted foreign customs. Before taking a Greek wife,

Alexander asked for the hand of the Persian princess Roxana. He had already conquered Roxana's kingdom, but instead of simply taking her by force, which he could've easily done, he asked her father for his consent.

Alexander was a military genius, Violet. We use that word a lot to describe great generals, but most of the time it's undeserved. Alexander marched an outnumbered, undersupplied army across three continents and he *never lost a battle*. His military innovations were studied and employed by military minds up to our current age. Alexander was a genius at waging war the way Einstein was a genius at physics. He used his opponents' strengths against them, and he understood his enemies almost to a supernatural extent. He selected his battlefields for the strategic advantage they provided. He had complete faith in his men, and he led them by personal example of discipline, temperance, courage, and generosity.

Alexander's military tactics are applicable in every area of your life, and they can teach you about the importance of patience, timing, strategy, and thinking "outside the box." One of my favorite stories about Alexander is when he cut the knot of Gordium:

> *Then he subdued the Pisidians who made head against him, and conquered the Phyrigians, at whose chief city, Gordium, which is said to be the seat of Ancient Midas, he saw the famous chariot fastened with cords made out of the rind of the cornel tree, which whosoever should untie, the inhabitants had a tradition, that for him was reserved the empire of the world. Most authors tell the story that Alexander finding himself unable to untie the knot, the ends of which were secretly twisted round and folded up within it, cut it asunder with his sword. But Aristobulus tells us it was easy for him to undo it, by only pulling the pin out of the pole, to which the yoke was tied, and afterward drawing off the yoke itself from below.*

But the two most important lessons Alexander can teach you are these: have courage, and be a gracious winner.

Have courage, Violet! Stand up for yourself. There is nothing more unseemly in my character than my cowardice. Conflict and violence are natural parts of life, even when they don't manifest physically. Standing up for an unpopular belief is an act of courage.

It's not true that "Violence never solved a thing." Ultimately, violence solves an awful lot of big problems. The Revolutionary War, the Civil War, and World War II were fairly violent affairs. They also answered huge moral questions.

But the application of force will certainly *not* solve anything without the magnanimity of the winner. And those rulers who followed this example of Alexander have had the most profound successes. After the Civil War, for example, Abraham Lincoln was incredibly generous to the South, even advising U.S. Grant to "let them up easy." And after World War II, Harry S. Truman agreed to the Marshall Plan, which was an amazingly generous plan to rebuild enemy states like Germany. In the short term, both Lincoln's clemency and Truman's generosity were seen as weak and stupid, even crazy—but in the long term, these proved to be remarkably wise and fruitful judgments.

After World War I, the winners acted far differently. They imposed brutal penalties on Germany. They demoralized the "losers," they bankrupted them, they stole their land, and they treated them with abject cruelty. They *humiliated* their opponent, instead of offering a true hand of peace and friendship. And what happened? Anger, resentment, and hostility bubbled up for decades, until the people of Germany embraced the extreme nationalism preached by Adolf Hitler. They wanted their pride back.

That night when Sean Lee looked up at me, and asked me why I hadn't done anything to help him, I felt *disgrace,* Violet, and I continued to feel it for a long time. This man had put himself at great risk by taking up my part, and because I was terrified of a little pain, I allowed that night to haunt me for years. I still think about it whenever I have to do something difficult.

I don't want you getting into bar fights, Violet. But I don't want you to be a coward, either. Sometimes there's going to be a fight whether you want one or not, and when that happens, the odds might be stacked against you. It's okay to be scared, but stand your ground, and punch the bully in the face.

Then do what Alexander would do—extend your hand in genuine friendship.

CHAPTER 10

HUBRIS

PLUTARCH
The Life of Julius Caesar

———◦◦◦———

*H*ubris is a Greek word that means an excessive pride or arrogance that leads a person to their downfall. Greek literature is filled with examples of hubris, and many of Shakespeare's plays deal with the concept as well—including his play *Julius Caesar,* which was based largely on the account of Plutarch.

Julius Caesar was—for better or worse—one of the most conse quential figures in Western history. Caesar upended the Roman Republic, and he laid the foundation for the Roman Empire. "Europe" as we understand it did not exist before Caesar, as his conquest brought much of modern Europe under Roman dominion.

We can still hear the voice of Julius Caesar. Great figures of antiquity like Pericles, Alexander, and Augustus left little or nothing by way of personal biography, but Caesar left us plenty. In his own literary works (*The Civil War* and *The Conquest of Gaul*) Julius Caesar's charisma still survives, all these centuries later. He writes about himself in the third person: *"Then Caesar kicked some ass,"* and *"Then Caesar outsmarted them all."* Not direct quotes, of course—but not too far off the mark, either.

Plutarch gives us a more complex picture. As a young man, Caesar was captured by pirates, and instead of being terrified, he befriended all of them.

When these men at first demanded of him twenty talents for his ransom, he laughed at them for not understanding the value of their prisoner, and voluntarily engaged to give them fifty .... For thirty-eight days, with all the freedom in the world, he amused himself with joining in the pirates' exercises and games, as if they had not been his keepers, but his guards. He wrote verses and speeches, and made them his auditors, and those who did not admire him, he called to their faces illiterate and barbarous, and would often, in raillery, threaten to hang them. They were greatly taken with this, and attributed his free talking to a kind of simplicity and boyish playfulness.

That Caesar was such a scamp! Except that when his ransom had been paid, Caesar did indeed capture the pirates, and he had every last one of them crucified.

From the start, Caesar was a talented speaker, and he was exceedingly liberal with his money. He gained political office in Rome, where he began to tamper with the constitution. Some elder statesmen like Cicero detected Caesar's real ambitions. He saw Caesar's generosity, affability, and good humor as a pretense, behind which lurked a lust for power. Cicero said sarcastically:

But when I see his hair so carefully arranged, and observe him adjusting it with one finger, I cannot imagine it should enter into such a man's thoughts to subvert the Roman state.

Caesar craved absolute power from the start. And indeed, just as Socrates described the tyrant's path to power, Caesar cast himself as a man of the people, and he made generous gifts to them. So much so that he found himself in great debt, so he made an alliance with Crassus, a very wealthy man in Rome. After Crassus paid off Caesar's debts, Caesar was traveling near the Alps when he came upon a wretched barbarian village. Caesar's men made fun of the villagers, and Caesar is said to have remarked:

For my part, I had rather be the first man among these fellows than the second man in Rome.

And another time, after he had read the history of Alexander the Great, Caesar is said to have been moved to tears, exclaiming to his men that he had just cause to weep, since "Alexander at my age had conquered so many nations, and I have all this time done nothing that is memorable."

Caesar knew that he could only attain that glory through military success. Caesar's greatest rival, Pompey, was revered as a military commander of the highest order, but Caesar had no accomplishments to his credit. The problem was, Caesar was relatively old when he took command, and he was also sick. He suffered from epilepsy, which he controlled through a very strict diet and exercise regimen.

Eventually, Caesar was given an army and sent to Gaul (France), which at the time was inhabited by numerous barbarian tribes hostile to Rome. Caesar's political enemies thought this was an ideal place to send Caesar. What could Caesar possibly accomplish in Gaul? He didn't know how to fight wars, and Gaul was a huge, dangerous place. They thought he'd get himself killed within six months.

But over the next decade, Caesar proved himself a remarkably capable and ingenious military commander. He subdued all of Gaul and parts of Germany, and became the first Roman to lead an expeditionary force against Great Britain. Caesar dramatically enlarged the Roman state, easily doubling its size and greatly increasing its wealth. He became a military match for great Pompey. He instilled enormous loyalty in his men, who became battle-hardened veterans under his command. He eliminated almost every potential external threat to Rome, transforming most of Western Europe into one giant Roman colony.

> For he had not pursued the wars in Gaul full ten years when he had taken by storm above eight hundred towns, subdued three hundred states, and of the three millions of men, who made up the gross sum of those with whom at several times he engaged, he had killed one million and taken captive a second.
>
> He was so much master of the good will and hearty service of his soldiers that those who in other expeditions were but ordinary men displayed a courage past defeating or withstanding when they went upon any danger where Caesar's glory was concerned.

Caesar was not only ambitious, but he had the ability to inspire and
lead people, just like Alexander. He had great personal courage and
he was a brilliant tactician.

> *There was no danger to which he did not willingly expose*
> *himself, no labor from which he pleaded an exemption.*

As Caesar's power grew, Pompey became nervous back in Rome.
Eventually both men knew they had to destroy the other if they
wanted a shot at the title: most powerful man in Rome. This rivalry
threw the government at Rome into chaos.

> *So that after having many times stained the place of election*
> *with blood of men killed upon the spot, the people left the*
> *city at last without a government at all, to be carried about*
> *like a ship without a pilot to steer her; while all who had any*
> *wisdom could only be thankful if a course of such wild and*
> *stormy disorder might end no worse than in a monarchy.*

At this point, Pompey demanded that Caesar lay down his arms, and
warned him not to bring his army across the Rubicon, a river that
divided Italy from Gaul. Caesar replied that he would do so if Pompey
also laid down his arms. Pompey refused. Caesar approached the
Rubicon with his army.

> *When he came to the river Rubicon, which parts Gaul within*
> *the Alps from the rest of Italy, his thoughts began to work,*
> *now he was just entering upon the danger, and he wavered*
> *much in his mind when he considered the greatness of the*
> *enterprise into which he was throwing himself. He checked his*
> *course and ordered a halt, while he revolved with himself, and*
> *often changed his opinion one way or the other ... computing*
> *how many calamities his passing that river would bring upon*
> *mankind .... At last, in a sort of passion, casting aside calcu-*
> *lation, and abandoning himself to what might come true, and*
> *using the proverb "The die is cast," he crossed the river.*

It's possible that Caesar may have actually said, "Toss the dice
high," which gives a very different sense of the man's character. But

this is where we get the phrase "crossing the Rubicon," which means making a fateful decision from which there is no turning back.

Pompey ran. Within 60 days, Caesar was in complete control of Rome. At this point, he ordered the public treasury to be opened, so that he could fund his army. A tribune named Metellus stood before the treasury door and pleaded with Caesar not to do this. Charming Caesar finally revealed his true character:

> Caesar replied that arms and laws each had their own time; "If what I do displeases you, leave the place; war allows no free talking. When I have laid down my arms, and made peace, come back and make what speeches you please. And this I will tell you in diminution of my own just right, as indeed you and all others who have appeared against me and are now in my power may be treated as I please."

Caesar showed clemency to many Romans who had stood against him—but he always offered that clemency when it was politically expedient. He quickly installed a puppet senate, which named him Dictator.

Caesar faced a real challenge in Pompey, and at one point, he nearly lost the war. But eventually, he defeated Pompey's troops at Pharsalus. Pompey had a much larger army than Caesar, and he was a capable general, but Caesar's men had been fighting wars for more than a decade, and they were much more accomplished soldiers. Caesar ordered that during the fight, his men were to throw their javelins at the opposing army's faces instead of their horses.

> In hopes that young gentlemen, who had not known much of battles and wounds, but came wearing their hair long, in the flower of their age and the height of their beauty, would be more apprehensive of such blows, and not care for hazarding a danger at present and a blemish for the future.

Caesar was right. Pompey's forces ran, and Caesar's forces routed them. Pompey fled to Egypt, believing the Egyptians would welcome him, as he'd been a friend to them. The Egyptians, understanding that Caesar was now the true master of Rome, welcomed Pompey with open arms—and then they killed him.

When he returned to Rome, Caesar was not as popular with the people as he used to be. For one thing, he ordered an unseemly triumph to celebrate his victory over Pompey. Since Pompey was a Roman citizen, and not some foreign enemy, the people thought this was distasteful. Caesar also openly insulted men of consequence, and he installed incompetent, wasteful, drunken lieutenants in positions of power.

> *He was also reflected on for Dolabella's extravagance, Amantius's covetousness, Antony's debauchery, and Corfinius's profuseness …. But Caesar, for the prosecution of his own scheme of government, though he knew their characters and disapproved of them, was forced to make use of those who would serve him.*

He still had enemies. The great Cato and Scipio had fled to Africa, where they raised an army to resist him. Caesar ultimately defeated this army as well. But he faced a public relations disaster when Cato, who was a highly respected man in Rome, disemboweled himself rather than submit to Caesar.

Caesar became more and more haughty, and not only had himself named "dictator for life," but also had piles of titles heaped upon him. This alienated many of the moderate people in Rome, who found the whole business distasteful and extravagant.

People were getting tired of Julius Caesar's desire to be king. It wasn't enough that he basically *was* king, he wanted to be *called* king. And slowly but surely, a conspiracy began to evolve in the puppet senate, led by Brutus. Finally, one day in March, Caesar went down to the senate, because Brutus told him that his puppet government was going to finally name him king. Caesar went down expecting his puppets to put a crown on his head. Twenty-three senators took turns stabbing him to death.

Julius Caesar changed Western history. He doubled the size of Rome through his conquest of Gaul. He overthrew its republic and laid the foundation for empire. The Roman Empire that followed him would leave an unparalleled cultural and intellectual legacy. The states of Western Europe would be forever informed by their Roman experience. Christianity would emerge, flourish, and spread under the Roman Empire. Greek ideas would be preserved and transmitted down over centuries. Our own notions of statehood, laws, culture, religion—even the way we measure time—all have their roots in the acts of Julius Caesar.

As a historical figure, he is indeed impressive. But as a man, he was an utter tragedy. He was raised by his ambition and brought low by it. He sought too much power, and he paid the price for his arrogance.

Was Caesar powerful? For a time. But as Solon said, "Count no man happy until the end is known." Would you call Caesar a happy man? He died horribly, short of his ambition, bleeding like a stuck pig on a cold marble floor. In the end, he followed the path of all tyrants that Socrates warned of in *Republic*. He became a prisoner of his own power, unable to trust anyone.

Perhaps it would've been wise to show a little humility.

CHAPTER 11

WHAT WOULD JESUS DO?

ST. MATTHEW
The Gospel of Jesus Christ

———◦◦◦———

When you were born, and for as long as I can remember before that, our politicians l-o-o-o-o-ved to talk about how much they admired Mr. Jesus Christ. But they seemed to have some rather curious ideas about what Jesus actually said, and also how he lived and died.

We do know what the man said, Violet. According to Matthew, who was actually present when Jesus was alive, these are the actual words of Jesus Christ.

> *Blessed are the poor in spirit, for theirs is the kingdom of heaven.*
> *Blessed are those who mourn, for they shall be com-forted.*
> *Blessed are the meek, for they shall inherit the earth.*
> *Blessed are those who hunger and thirst for righteousness, for they shall be satisfied.*
> *Blessed are the merciful, for they shall obtain mercy.*
> *Blessed are the pure in heart, for they shall see God.*
> *Blessed are the peacemakers, for they shall be called sons of God.*
> *Blessed are those who are persecuted for righteousness' sake, for theirs is the kingdom of heaven.*
> *Blessed are you when men revile you and persecute you*

and utter all kinds of evil against you falsely on my account. Rejoice and be glad, for your reward is great in Heaven, for so men persecuted the prophets who were before you.

Here's what Jesus said about being persecuted:

Do not resist one who is evil. But if any one strikes you on the right cheek, turn to him the other also; and if any one would sue you and take your coat, let him have your cloak as well; and if any one forces you to go one mile, go with him two miles.

You have heard that it was said, "You shall love your neighbor and hate your enemy." But I say to you, Love your enemies and pray for those who persecute you.

Here's what Jesus said about how one should worship God:

And when you pray, you must not be like the hypocrites; for they love to stand and pray in the synagogues and at the street corners, that they may be seen by men. Truly, I say to you, they have received their reward. But when you pray, go into your room and shut the door and pray to your Father who is in secret; and your Father who sees in secret will reward you.

Here's what Jesus said about judging people:

Judge not, that you not be judged. For with the judgment you pronounce you will be judged, and the measure you give will be the measure you get. Why do you see the speck that is in your brother's eye, but do not notice the log that is in your own eye?

Here's what Jesus said about getting into heaven:

You shall not kill, You shall not commit adultery, You shall not steal, You shall not bear false witness, Honor your father and mother, and You shall love your neighbor as yourself .... If you would be perfect, go, sell what you possess and give to the poor.

Here's what Jesus said about the religious people of his day:

They preach, but do not practice.

When Jesus was seized by the authorities, to be taken off to be cruci-fied, one of his disciples drew his sword to defend him. Jesus told him to put it back.

Put your sword back in its place; for all who take the sword will perish by the sword.

Before he died, Jesus summarized the whole of his teaching:

So in everything, do to others what you would have them do to you, for this sums up the Law and the Prophets.

That's what the man said, Violet. It's probably what he meant, too.

CHAPTER 12

CAN PEOPLE CHANGE?

ST. LUKE

The Acts of the Apostles

———◦◦◦———

I used to make fun of homosexuals. Everybody used to make fun of homosexuals (or "homos" as we called them). Homos were weird and funny! The movies of my childhood were filled with homosexual stereotypes. Usually there was a tan blond guy with a lisp and a pink sweater tied around his neck. Society didn't accept homosexuals. If you were gay, it was definitely something to hide. To a man, "gay" was an insult that meant you liked other men, but it also meant "stupid." I'd use it casually in conversation. I'd say, "Don't be gay," or "That game is gay."

When I was 12 years old, one of my favorite comedians was Sam Kinison. He made jokes about gay people getting AIDS. AIDS was funny, too, because gay people got it! When I was a boy, nobody had sympathy for people with AIDS. Even the president didn't care. AIDS was "God's punishment" for their homosexuality.

Gay people were bullied all the time. Sometimes they were tortured and murdered. There was the case of Matthew Shepard, who, at 22 years old, was kidnapped by three guys who drove him to the middle of nowhere, tied him to a fence, and beat him with a pistol until his brain stem broke. That was in 1998.

But when I graduated college, I went to work at Chicago Shakespeare Theater, where I worked for a gay man who fit none of the stereotypes. He didn't wear pink sweaters and he didn't have a lisp.

He wore a suit like Don Draper and he meant business. He was brilliant, and not in an artistic way. He was a businessman, a producer. One of his favorite sayings was "They call it show *business*, not show *art*." This man so impressed the city's elite that they gave him the most expensive acre of lakefront property in Chicago for one dollar. Then they gave him about $40 million to help build his Shakespeare Theater, which was constructed in nine months. When the theater was finished, some of the most famous Shakespeareans in the world—including knights of the British Empire—remarked that it was the finest performance space *in the world*.

He accomplished all that in 10 years—such a little bit of time!

I learned more from that man in six months than I had in four years of college. Although I only knew him for a brief time, he had a huge influence on my life. Everything I learned about nonprofit organizations I learned from him. Systems, marketing, politics, fundraising—that guy could do it all. He was one of the few actual geniuses I've met in my life. He was a man of vision, integrity, courage, and he was one of the toughest dudes I ever met.

Once he asked me to analyze our subscription sales, because he'd set an insane target of doubling subscriptions in nine months. I told him that was impossible. He told me to make a plan. I made a little chart for him, showing how sales peaked in a certain month, and I suggested that we concentrate our marketing efforts in those months. My chart proved it! He looked at the chart, shook it in my face, and said, "I would hope that sales peaked that month, because that's when we spent all our advertising money!" and then he sighed, remembering I was just a stupid kid, and he gave me one of the most important lessons of my life:

"Matt," he said. "The shape doesn't shape you. You shape the shape."

You shape the shape, Violet! This is advice from a great man, and I can imagine Alexander the Great saying exactly the same thing. Don't let circumstances dictate your behavior. Great people do not believe that they are victims of circumstance. They believe in creating their own circumstances. They are in charge of their own destinies, and they are willing to fail to achieve their objectives. They don't make excuses. They don't let obstacles defeat them. They set audacious goals and they put their ass on the line. They take huge risks. They don't let process stand in the way of outcomes. They work harder than other people, and they are brutally honest, both with others and with themselves.

This man taught me that I was looking at the *world* the wrong way. Before I met this man, I believed that I was constrained by all manner of limits. Personal limits, financial limits, you name it. So I made excuses. I-didn't-have-enough-money, or there-wasn't-enough-time, or this-is-how-we've-always-done-it, or the-system-can't-handle-it. Excuses are bullshit, Violet. There's never enough money, it's always a bad time, and what happened yesterday is irrelevant. Oh, you screwed up and made a fool of yourself? Doesn't matter. Produced a flop and lost all your money? Doesn't matter. All that matters is what you do *right now*. Identify your goal and work backward from it. Don't ask others for permission. Don't be ashamed to ask for help, but don't ask anyone to hold your hand, either. You can't succeed before failing first. Quit crying about how tough it is. Do it. Start right now, where you are. Need more money? Go get more money. Need more time? Looks like you'll be staying late! The system can't handle it? Build a new system. And after all this, if you find that what you're doing isn't working, it can still be done. *Anything* can be done. We can build a $40 million Shakespeare theater on a goddamned pier in nine months.

He wasn't asking me to duplicate the past. He asked me to create a new future. He knew it would cost more money. He knew it would mean completely changing how we did things. Those were details, and details were irrelevant. He also knew I had no idea what I was doing. He would mentor me, but he also expected me to be entrepreneurial, and find answers myself. And, despite his insistence that I meet this goal, he wouldn't punish me if I failed—he'd punish me if I didn't try.

He had a goal, too. It wasn't to double subscriptions, or even to build another regional Shakespeare theater. He wanted to create an international center of culture in Chicago, because according to him, Chicago deserved it. My role in his vision was very minor, but to this day, I am so proud, and so grateful, to have been a part of that experience, and to have shared in his vision.

This man took a chance on me and basically gave me my career. I was working in a warehouse for $8 an hour when he hired me. I learned so much from him, but the most important lesson was that I was a bigot and a fool. I needed to change not only what I said, but also what I thought, and how I behaved. I had to confront my prejudice honestly, be ashamed of my behavior, and change.

The scales had been lifted from my eyes.

———————

Paul did not start out as Paul. He started out as a man named Saul. He hated Christians. He *enjoyed* finding Christians and prosecuting them and putting them to death.

> *But Saul was ravaging the church, and entering house after house, he dragged off men and women and committed them to prison ....*
>
> *But Saul, still breathing threats and murder against the disciples of the Lord, went to the high priest and asked him for letters to the synagogues at Damascus, so that if he found any belonging to the Way, or women, he might bring them bound to Jerusalem.*

But then something remarkable happened to Saul:

> *Now as he journeyed he approached Damascus, and suddenly a light from heaven flashed about him. And he fell to the ground and heard a voice saying to him, "Saul, Saul, why do you persecute me?" And he said, "Who are you, Lord?" And he said, "I am Jesus, whom you are persecuting, but rise and enter the city, and you will be told what you are to do." The men who were traveling with him stood speechless, hearing the voice but seeing no one. Saul arose from the ground; and when his eyes were opened, he could see nothing, so they led him by the hand and brought him into Damascus. And for three days he was without sight, and neither ate nor drank.*

Saul is tended to by a man named Anani'as. The Lord commands Anani'as to go to Saul and heal his sight. But Anani'as has heard all about Saul and his persecution of the Christians, and about all the evil he has done. And the Lord says to him:

Go, for he is a chosen instrument of mine to carry my name before the Gentiles and kings and sons of Israel.

Anani'as goes to Saul and lays his hands upon Saul's eyes.

And immediately something like scales fell from his eyes and he regained his sight.

Saul is converted, and he changes his name to Paul. He becomes the most fervent missionary for Jesus Christ, and he travels all around the Roman world spreading the story of Jesus.

Such journeys were common in the Ancient world. Roman infrastructure made it relatively easy to travel, the common Greek language made it easy to communicate, and Paul's Roman citizenship saved his life on a number of occasions. As a Roman citizen, Paul could not simply be imprisoned, beaten, or executed, as many early Christians were. He could not be brought up on trumped-up charges, like Jesus. As a Roman citizen, Paul had rights, and his accusers had to eventually present a legal case against him. The Romans eventually set Paul free, after he made his case to them. During his defense, Paul admitted his sins:

I myself was convinced that I ought to do many things in opposing the name of Jesus of Nazareth. And I did so in Jerusalem; I not only shut up many of the saints in prison, by authority from the chief priests, but when they were put to death I cast my vote against them. And I punished them often in the synagogues and tried to make them blaspheme; and in raging fury against them, I persecuted them even to foreign cities.

Whether or not you believe in the divinity of Jesus Christ, Violet, you will experience this moment in your life. You will be absolutely convinced that you are right about something. In fact, you will be *so* convinced that you won't even think about it.

But then later, you will be given very good reasons to reassess your position, and you will have the opportunity to reflect on something you've done. Something evil. And you will find yourself on your own Road to Damascus. People can change, Violet. *You* can change, and you can do so whenever you like.

The shape doesn't shape you. You shape the shape.

CHAPTER 13

HOW CAN GOD LET BAD THINGS HAPPEN?

ST. AUGUSTINE
The Confessions

The summer after I turned 11, I watched a bunch of my friends kill frogs. One of the neighborhood kids had a pond in the back of his house, and everyone walked down to the edge and just scooped them up. They put the frogs into shoeboxes, and then they lit firecrackers and dropped them in the boxes. I watched them do this over and over again, though I never did it myself. They were laughing about it, so *I* laughed about it. I wanted the other boys to like me.

I distinctly remember opening an orange Nike box, which was burnt black on one side from the firecracker explosion. Once the smoke cleared, I saw a little frog inside, and he was still alive. Its face was bloody, but it was sitting there, its little chin pulsing, terrified, in pain. It wasn't dead. They wanted to drop another firecracker in to finish it off.

I made some excuse to leave. I didn't want any more of it, but I could hear them laughing, lighting off more firecrackers as I pedaled away on my ten-speed. As I was pedaling down Forest Avenue, I started to cry thinking about all those poor frogs. They hadn't done anything to deserve such a fate.

Why hadn't I stopped my friends? Why had I even *laughed* about it, when inside it felt sick and wrong? How could I participate in something like that?

St. Augustine was a Roman citizen who lived about 400 years after Jesus was born. Augustine held important jobs in the latter days of the Roman Empire, including Court Rhetorician. Augustine wasn't just another bureaucrat in the empire. He was a big deal outside the church. People paid him a lot of money, and they sought his counsel on important affairs.

Rhetoric in the classical sense does not really have the same meaning as it does for us today. In classical times, rhetoric was a very highly prized technical skill. It might be equivalent to being an excellent lawyer today. Rhetoric was a process by which one used reason and linguistic skill to make and assess arguments. It was used in business, in law, in government, in philosophy, science, and even in the church. Rhetoric masters were generously compensated, and wealthy citizens would send their children to be taught by rhetoricians the way we send children to college. In Greek times, teachers of rhetoric were called *sophists,* and over time, the words *rhetoric* and *sophistry* have each acquired negative connotations. Today we are suspicious if someone is "using rhetoric," and we presume that someone who is guilty of "sophistry" is making a spurious argument.

But this was not the definition in Augustine's time. *The Confessions* is largely a work of a great rhetorician. Augustine methodically builds a compelling and *logical* argument for Christianity, while he carefully addresses, defends, and explains the inherent problems or contradictions of his cause. Augustine himself did not accept Christianity until late in life, and he did so only after decades of rigorous and logical examination.

In Book II of *The Confessions,* Augustine describes an incident from his childhood in which he and his friends stole some pears. They didn't need the pears, and they quickly put them to waste. Augustine wonders what it was about the act of robbery that compelled him to commit the sin.

I was driven by no deprivation—unless by a deprivation of what is right, a revulsion at it, while I was bloated out with evil. I stole things I had much more of, and much better. I wanted the stealing, not the thing stolen. I wanted the sin.

He doesn't understand his own motives for stealing the pears. It wasn't for money, because the pears weren't worth anything. He examines other sins to see if he can ascertain his motive. Most sins have logical motives—even murder is logical. In general, people at least have some *reason* to murder. They might do it out of anger, for some wrong that's been done to them. They might do it for sexual reasons, or for personal gain, or to prevent something from becoming known.

As Augustine considers the wide range of sins, he concludes that most sins can be explained rationally. Pride is meant to feign loftiness, aggression is meant to instill awe, cowardice is for self-preservation, and so on.

But the Great Pear Robbery is different, because there is no reason behind it. Augustine did not need the pears; he didn't even *desire* the pears. He wasn't hungry, and he didn't eat them. What he desired was the *act of stealing them*. He likens his crime to Adam feasting from the Tree of Knowledge.

> *What rottenness is here, what living enormity, what a downward plunge into death—to be allured by what was not allowed, just because it was not allowed.*

He knows that he would not have committed this stupid crime had he been alone. It was the act of committing the crime with his friends that compelled him to sin.

> *There is no way I would have done it alone. So I must have loved a partnership with my fellows in the theft …. For what else could that [partnership] be called in reality? …. How infectious, then, is this affection, the mind's inexplicable swerve, the way laughter and pranks become a readiness to harm, a willingness to inflict loss, without any compensating gain, no sense of a wrong being requited. Someone has but to say Let's do it!*

For most of his life, the very existence of evil troubles Augustine, because it does not make logical sense. He can't reconcile the existence of a just and merciful god with the existence of evil. If you believe in God, and believe that God created everything, and everything God created is good, then how can you also believe that God created evil? Because if God created evil, then evil would, by definition, be good. How can evil be good? Philosophers call this **the problem of evil.**

Augustine spends much of his life applying reason to solve this problem. Early in his life he conceives God as a material being, even wondering about the composition of God's fingernails. Then he allows that God may be, in fact, all good, but that there must be some "anti-God" out there, an evil force that is constantly warring with God. This would explain evil. He seeks his answers in astrology and astronomy. But the sciences can only go so far.

One could understand everything about astronomy without understanding wisdom.

Augustine is a reasonable man, and he believes in logic. But his spiritual quest is frustrated because the spiritual world cannot be understood in material terms. It is not until Augustine discovers Plato that he begins to believe that there is a world beyond the material one.

At the time Augustine lived, Aristotle was the most revered philosopher. Even though Augustine seems ancient to us, he was born nearly 700 years after Aristotle died. For a thousand years between the fall of the Roman Empire and the advent of the Renaissance, thinkers simply referred to Aristotle as "the Philosopher." So most philosophers, like Augustine, kept trying to make everything fit into an Aristotelian worldview—one where everything was empirical and measurable.

At one point, Augustine reads a book by Aristotle called *The Categories.* In the book, Aristotle contends that there are 10 categories of things, and Augustine laughs at himself for trying to make everything fit into neat little categories like Aristotle.

It made me treat the ten categories as applicable to everything, even to your wondrously simple and unique nature, as if greatness and beauty could be predicated of you as they are of a corporeal body, whereas your greatness and beauty are yourself.

Aristotle was an empiricist. He's someone who tries to define the world, and this leads him to this scientific obsession with categories, lists, and rules. That works remarkably well in the material world, but eventually, it reaches a limit.

Plato admitted to some degree of *faith*. That doesn't mean Plato did not believe in science or scientific principles—quite the opposite. In *Republic,* it was Plato's Socrates who first suggested that our senses were imperfect, and that there was a world beyond what we could comprehend through crude mediums like sight and sound. In a sense, we were all prisoners in the cave. The "real" world beyond the cave could never be seen by man, and it could really only be understood in the abstract. Socrates even suggested that the true universe could only be understood mathematically. This is very similar to our modern scientific conception of the universe. We know that there are alternate visual and auditory spectrums that we don't have access to. Scientists even believe there may be an infinite number of parallel dimensions. There may be some mathematical law that governs the universe, but we just don't know what it is yet.

Plato's Socrates *also* believed that somewhere deep in this unseen world, abstract concepts like justice existed in some kind of ideal form. These ideas are themselves shadows of an ultimate truth, which we know as **the idea of the good.** The idea of the good is a supernatural, unknowable, invisible thing that man can never comprehend. This force animates everything in the universe, but it's like the sun: you can't look right at it. You can only see its effects in the world, and the shadows its light creates. Our world is incredibly primitive compared to this ultimate world. The universe is separated into segments along a line, into "spectrums," and we exist in the most primitive segment, incapable of observing the higher realities above us.

Plato's idea of the good is very much like the conception of God that Augustine will eventually embrace. And as Augustine has increasing difficulty trying to bend and contort God to fit inside narrow material laws, he will turn further away from Aristotle, and move closer and closer to Plato.

The books of the Platonists that I had read prompted me to seek an immaterial truth.

Throughout his life, Augustine has treated scripture literally, but as he begins to understand that there may be an immaterial truth, he comes to understand scripture *symbolically*. He stops attempting to cram everything into categories. And he finds an elegant solution to the problem of evil.

God doesn't make bad things happen. *We* do. God gave us choice. God gave us *free will*. How we use that free will is up to us.

Consider gold. In Augustine's time, gold was not really all that useful. You couldn't use it to make weapons, because it was too soft. Other metals, like iron, were much more useful, and yet much less valuable. Why had wars been waged over this relatively useless thing? Was gold "evil"? Gold itself is nothing. It's just a rock. The choice to pursue it was what was evil.

> *I had looked for evil and found that it was not a reality in itself but the twisting motion of a man who turns away from the highest reality—that is, from you—by "emptying himself inwardly" and bloating himself outwardly.*

It's not logical to blame God (or anyone else) for the decisions we make. We have moral responsibility. We are responsible for our own choices in life. *You* are responsible for the choices you make, Violet. You can't blame anybody else. You can't blame God, your parents, your friends, or the state. Yes, there will be times when making the right choice is extremely difficult; when it means alienating yourself from established views, or even from your friends and family. Don't be afraid to make the right choice. Trust your soul. Listen to what it's telling you to do.

When I think about those frogs now, I don't excuse myself from the crime just because I did not personally kill them. My inaction was the sin. We can tolerate all sorts of evil when others also remain silent. I'm absolutely certain that the other boys who were there that day—maybe all of them—felt the same shame and regret for killing those frogs. But nobody said anything. We laughed to conceal our shame. That was our choice. That was *my* choice. Nobody made me do it. It's my fault.

Throughout *The Confessions*, Augustine often compares adults to children, and you will find that the games of childhood are really not so different from the "games" of adulthood, in which we compete with one another to acquire property and status. Augustine recalls being caught cheating as a child, and reflects that cheating as a child is no different from cheating as an adult.

I had no excuse from lack of memory or talent, which you made sufficient for my age; I simply loved games more, and I was disciplined by those who had their own games (since gain is the game of adults).

I can now see my own childhood sin reflected in the corporate and political scandals of my time. There may have been a few people committing the actual crimes that led to the collapse of companies like Enron or Lehman Brothers, or the unraveling of the Madoff Ponzi scheme, or the torture scandal of Abu Ghraib. But there were others who knew what was happening and chose to do nothing, and to say nothing. That doesn't make them innocent.

You always have a choice. As Marcus Aurelius wrote, "And you can also commit injustice by doing nothing."

CHAPTER 14

DO THE ENDS JUSTIFY THE MEANS?

MACHIAVELLI
The Prince

I n my 20s, I lived in a state of complete chaos. When I was 23 I was
a drunken, fat mess. I was living with two heroin addicts—one of
whom was a 17-year-old girl—in an apartment I couldn't afford, in
a city I despised, in a job I couldn't stand anymore. Every morning I
would wake up and look at myself in the mirror, hungover, my eyes
bloodshot, huge bags under my eyes, and I would swear that I would
change. *Today was the day I was gonna get my shit together!*

By midnight I'd be drunk again. Or stoned. Or worse. The whole
room would be filled with smoke, and next to the bed would be an
ashtray full of cigarette butts. By midnight I was ready and resigned
to do exactly the same thing again the next day. I abused all sorts of
drugs, and now I think I was just lucky to stay clear of heroin. And
I did most of this in complete secrecy.

This went on for about two years.

Years later I was on the other side of the country, standing in front of
an Olympic-size swimming pool. My gut hung over my swimsuit. I
dove in the water, and it was freezing, and I began swimming. After
four laps, I got out, went to the locker room, and threw up.

Six months later I was swimming a mile every morning, and I had a very strict regimen. In the morning, coffee, fruit, and yogurt, then work, then several hours of writing, and then school at night. No more hard liquor, no drugs, and seldom more than two light beers. I wasn't ready for a relationship, and I knew it. I don't want to paint it as a complete turnaround—I eventually quit smoking, and I gave up hard liquor and drugs, but I still drank beer. I guess the difference was I didn't drink 12 of them on any given Tuesday. Mostly I wrote, sometimes up to 10,000 words a day. I understood that almost all of it was crap. It didn't matter to me. At the time, I needed disciplined, rigid structure in my life—and as you yourself know, I am still rather obsessive about my routine.

One day I met a girl at a bookstore named Kristin. Kristin was beautiful, funny, and interesting. Kristin listened to all the bands I liked. Kristin was trying to get her shit together, too. She was a recovering alcoholic, but she still liked to get high. I liked to get high, too, but I'd given that up. Pretty soon Kristin was coming over uninvited. She was calling me at three in the morning, about to pass out in her car, and I'd go pick her up and bring her home. One night Kristin came over, broke into my house, stole my roommate's booze, and when he came home, she made a pass at him.

I broke it off with Kristin. And when I did I was extremely cruel. I called her a worthless drunk. I grabbed her by the arm, dragged her to her beat-up old brown Chevy, threw her inside, and told her to get lost, or I'd call the cops. She cried. She told me she was trying to get it together. She begged me to give her one more chance. I told her I never wanted to see her again.

A few weeks later, Kristin called me in the middle of the night, drunk and literally lost, begging for me to help her. I hung up on her.

Eight years later I was married, I owned a home, and I had a great career. One morning I was surprised to read about Kristin in the newspaper. She was dead of a drug overdose. Her picture was right there in the paper, a beautiful girl from some other time before all this, smiling, with her family, happy. She looked young, beautiful, and full of promise. She looked truly happy.

She died at 32, awaiting trial for armed robbery. She and two guys tried to knock over a drugstore. Kristin was the getaway driver. The car was described in the report. When she was arrested, Kristin was still driving the same car I'd thrown her in.

About this woman I'd known so briefly at such a strange time in my life, and whom I'd treated with great cruelty, I didn't feel guilt, or surprise, or even remorse. Honestly, I felt relief: relief that I'd thrown her in that car, relief that I wasn't kind to her, relief that I'd somehow managed to get control of myself before my own life went completely off the rails.

~

Machiavelli doesn't care about how things ought to be. He's not trying to create a utopia. He takes a cold look at the facts and human nature, and he says, basically, "All right, this is how people *really* are. This is how they *actually* behave. Yeah, yeah, everyone should be nice and honest and kiss puppies. But in reality they're greedy, conniving, and power-hungry sons-of-bitches. And if you want to have power and keep it in a world like this, there are certain things you should do."

According to *The Prince,* here are some things you should do if you find yourself in a position of power:

1. Destroy your enemies completely. Then kill their families.
2. Have a long-term plan, but keep it secret.
3. Build alliances, but be ready to betray your allies if it's in your interest.
4. Take control of the levers of power and control the political process.
5. Be stingy. Especially with your friends. Always withhold affection.
6. Lie whenever you have to, and break your word when it suits your interests.
7. Be feared.
8. Be cruel when necessary.
9. Ask your subordinates to do ugly, cruel, unpopular things, and

then get rid of them (even kill them) when they accomplish the job you asked them to do. Then disown them publicly and take credit for saving everyone from the monsters you created.

Machiavelli isn't speaking hypothetically. He cites numerous and multiple examples from ancient and contemporary history to support his arguments. Unlike most philosophers, he's speaking from first-hand personal experience in governance. Plato famously went to Syracuse to try to implement his ideas and create the ideal state. He failed. Repeatedly.

Machiavelli was good at his job until he lost it. A lot of people think that *The Prince* is basically a job application. Machiavelli worked in the Florentine government, and when the Medici family came to power late in the 15th century, Machiavelli found himself out of work. The new regime even took some time to torture him. But Machiavelli didn't hold that against them. He was still a relatively young man, so he wrote the Medici family this book, sort of as a way of saying, "Look, no hard feelings on the torture—I know how to govern, I know how power and government works, and you should hire me and let me help you run things."

The most famous line from *The Prince* is probably this one:

It is better to be feared than loved.

It's nice to be loved, and it's nice to be both feared *and* loved, but if you can only pick one, choose to be feared. Love is fickle. Fear is a bit more permanent. People may fall out of love with you. They probably won't stop fearing you.

The Prince is not some kind of meditation or theoretical work, in the way that Plato's *Republic* is. It's a handbook. It's a practical manual. You can use it yourself to run anything. I have absolutely used this book in a practical way, and I know others in executive positions who have done the same.

A lot of people think that Machiavelli said, "the ends justify the means." But it's a bit more complicated than that. Above all else, *The Prince* is a book about the importance of *order*. People say they want freedom, liberty, and prosperity—and all that may be true. But whether it's true or not, none of those higher goods are possible without order.

I'll give you a small example. A few years before you were born, there was a national obsession with nanny shows. All the shows essentially worked like this: upper-middle-class parents have two children who are out of control. The kids refuse to eat their vegetables. They throw tantrums, they throw toys at their parents. They scream, fight, bite, and generally behave like monsters. The parents don't know what to do. So they call in a stern British nanny to come in and assess the situation. The British nanny comes in and looks around for five minutes, and she diagnoses every house the same way: the parents have lost control. There is zero discipline. So the British nanny imposes some law and order in the house. She doesn't give in to the children. The kids throw tantrums. They scream themselves to sleep. When they don't eat the food that's offered to them, the nanny lets them go hungry. She punishes them. She forces them to clean up their messes. The parents are skeptical of all this. They think the nanny's being cruel.

Two days later, they're shocked by the results. The children are like different people. They're well behaved and loving. They clean up all their toys without asking. They eat their vegetables. They go to bed without a fuss. The parents have reestablished control and respect, and the nanny leaves, sure that Chris and Mary from Cincinnati are going to be just fine, now that order's been restored.

In any political situation—in your family, school, job, or nation—*order* must come first.

In America, we pay a lot of lip service to *freedom*. We claim that freedom is the ultimate virtue, and that people around the world "crave freedom." But what do Americans really mean by freedom? Do we mean freedom to pursue our dreams, freedom from burdensome government regulations, freedom to live as we choose, say what we want, and worship how we please?

We turn on our faucets and clean water comes out; we flick our light switches and the power goes on. Our roads are maintained. Our trains operate on time. We take those things for granted, and we become outraged by relatively minor inconveniences. In the wake of big storms, we become frustrated when our power fails for more than a few hours, or when the streets are not immediately cleared of snow.

Do we even think about freedom from invasion, or from foreign occupation, or from civil anarchy? We don't live under the fear that a foreign power can march ashore and bring the continental United States under its military dominion, or that our entire national infrastructure can be crippled in an afternoon. Machiavelli could not take such order for granted, and still today, there are many countries that cannot, either. Do these countries crave freedom of the press, or do they first desire freedom from assault, torture, imprisonment, and starvation?

You can't have civil liberties and economic prosperity until there is some semblance of order. When things are chaotic, a strong and ruthless figure must establish order. And in a chaotic state, that person may need to be brutal and duplicitous. Forget morality and justice. In a chaotic state, there is no morality, and no justice—the *only* virtue worth pursuing is order.

So cruelty is okay, so long as you're doing it to establish order in a chaotic situation. And Machiavelli makes it quite clear that it's *not* okay to be cruel for cruelty's sake. Machiavelli also did not believe that a state should (or would, or even could) remain under ruthless and authoritarian conditions forever. He believed that free republics were superior and more advanced forms of government than tyrannies—but that free republics could only emerge once order had been established. And often, it takes a tyrant to do that. In fact, Machiavelli shows us there's a cycle to our government—that we begin under tyranny, advance to republics, and then slide back to tyranny, which then leads us back to the republic.

Free republics are complicated, and you can't institute one in a state of chaos. They take time to evolve. You can't simply walk into a chaotic state and say, "All right, now we're going to have a hugely complex system of government that relies upon civic virtue to succeed." That's doomed to fail. In a chaotic state, there is no reservoir of civic virtue to draw upon. Anarchy reigns, because people cannot be animated by any larger purpose than their own survival. The traditions and culture are corrupt and lawless. First, you must create the conditions for the higher form of government to flourish. And even if you are perceived as cruel in doing so, in the long run, you will actually be pursuing the just course.

In *Discourses on Livy,* Machiavelli uses the Roman Republic as an example. The Roman Republic would not have existed without first going through an authoritarian period. That authoritarian period lasted for centuries. But after things were sufficiently calm, and the people were virtuous, then a free republic naturally emerged. The king was expelled, and people set up a more advanced form of government: the Roman Republic, with its representative nature, its civil liberties, and its complicated judicial and legislative systems. That system also endured for centuries, but then fell victim to its own inherent deficiencies, and the Roman Republic became the Roman Empire.

Some might argue that the circumstances don't matter—that it's morally wrong for a ruler to be cruel no matter what his or her justification might be. But that depends upon how you define "morality," and if you look at morality over the long term, then the picture becomes much murkier. What is "cruel" in the short term may be "kind" in the long term—like the nannies imposing discipline in the house. Cruelty (or discipline) is applied to achieve the conditions of peaceful life.

There are plenty of modern examples of this, such as the American Civil War. In the Civil War, Sherman introduced the concept of "total war" to the South on his March to the Sea. Sherman's army set out to totally destroy the *will* of the South by rampaging across the Southern states. He destroyed both the capability and the *will* of the people to wage war. He destroyed factories, farms, ports, everything he could, until he achieved unconditional surrender. He was viewed as a monster.

The same thing happened in World War II, with the atomic bombings of Hiroshima and Nagasaki. These acts were far more "cruel" than anything Machiavelli could've imagined. But the goal of these bombings was not necessarily to destroy Japanese capacity; it was to break the *will* of the Japanese people.

Were there alternatives? Maybe everyone could've sat down and discussed things? Not so much. And what were the moral qualities of the slaveholding South, or Imperial Japan? Were these morally virtuous cultures? After the application of a great amount of cruelty, the Union was preserved and Japan surrendered. What happened to the conquered states in these examples? Eventually, over time, they became prosperous, free, and virtuous. After the Civil War, slavery was abolished, civil rights emerged, and the South even became dominant in American politics. In the case of World War II, Japan, Germany, and Italy rejected totalitarianism, and eventually became prosperous republics and loyal friends of the United States.

Machiavelli argues that you have to look at cruelty in this big, long context. Sherman himself understood this, as he said in a letter to the city council of Atlanta in 1864:

War is cruelty, and you cannot refine it; and those who brought war into our country deserve all the curses and maledictions a people can pour out. I know I had no hand in making this war, and I know I will make more sacrifices today than any of you to secure peace. But you cannot have peace and a division of our country. If the United States submits to a division now, it will not stop, but will go on until we reap the fate of Mexico, which is eternal war.

In 2003, we invaded Iraq under many pretenses, but one of the arguments we made was that we were "liberating" the people from a tyrant. We found the tyrant, and the Iraqi people promptly hung him in a public square. Iraq had been "liberated" and we "gave the people their freedom."

Was Justice served? Maybe. Were the Iraqi people better off? Not necessarily. After the initial period of conflict that removed the tyrant, we, as occupiers, allowed order to break down. The results were predictable: chaos, rampant corruption, and anarchy. People got blown up drinking coffee. There was no electricity, no running water. In a country with some of the largest oil reserves on the planet, nobody could get any gasoline. Buildings were looted, the infrastructure was picked clean by scavengers, and even the country's cultural treasures (some tracing back to the very origins of human civilization) were stolen or destroyed. Once the conditions of chaos took hold, they proved very difficult to reverse. However odious Saddam Hussein might've been, we replaced order with chaos, and in this chaotic environment, we set out to establish an advanced, representative system of government. It failed. After a decade of war, trillions of dollars, and hundreds of thousands of deaths, The United States finally withdrew. Shortly afterward, extremists seized control of much of the country, imposed horrifically brutal religious law, and began committing genocide. Now the Iraqi people were worse off than they had been under Hussein, and the United States was less secure as well. We had created a resource-rich haven for our worst enemies.

So you have to put men like Machiavelli, Sherman, and Alexander in context, Violet. You have to look at the *long-term good*, not just the short-term suffering.

> *Therefore a prince, so long as he keeps his subjects united and loyal, ought not to mind the reproach of cruelty; because with a few examples he will be more merciful than those who, through too much mercy, allow disorders to arise, from which follow murders or robberies, for these are wont to injure the whole people, while those executions which originate with a prince offend the individual only.*

The person who sets out to establish order is in the most dangerous position of anyone.

> *And it ought to be remembered that there is nothing more difficult to take in hand, more perilous to conduct, more uncertain in its success, than to take the lead in the introduction of a new order of things. Because the innovator has for enemies all those who have done well under the old conditions, and lukewarm defenders in those who may do well under the new.*

That person cannot be neutral; they should take strong positions and they should fight for them. They can't please everyone. They shouldn't fear making enemies, as long as they're prudent enough not to offend the *most* powerful. People will always resist change, but with hard work and a few successes, you will not only overcome your enemies, you might even win them over.

And yeah, if you can only choose to be feared *or* loved, it's better to be feared—but Machiavelli also takes great pains to stress that a ruler must not be *despised*. It's all right if people know you're a badass, but you'd better avoid being hated. That's how you wind up with a bullet in your skull, or hung up on a meathook in the town square. Don't be cruel for cruelty's sake, or because you're a sadist, but always with an eye toward establishing order.

So did Machiavelli argue that the ends justify the means? No. He argued that the ends justified the means *sometimes*—but it depends entirely on the ends.

This brings me back to Kristin, and to my own life, and the state of chaos I once lived in. I take no pleasure in telling you about that period in my life, Violet, and I hope that you never find yourself as lost as I once was. I hope that you never have to be cruel to people.

But if you're anything like me, and there's some dark part of you that's attracted to chaos, please be careful, Violet. It can drag you down quickly, despite your best intentions. I know now that I could not have changed Kristin. She was just bad news. She was chaos. I needed to avoid her, and everyone like her. I needed to change my life, and establish some order.

When I made this decision, it meant taking an honest, brutal assessment of myself, and it meant making some harsh decisions. It meant leaving my job and even my home, so I could start over. It meant abandoning people I considered my friends. I took a big risk and left that life behind me. It was a life that, for all its numerous faults, was familiar to me. I created some structure and boundaries in my personal life, and I did not let people cross them, regardless of my personal feelings. Old friends called me in desperate need. I abandoned them. And when I saw myself about to slide back, I acted swiftly, and with cruelty, to ensure that it would not happen again.

It was only then, after I got my shit together, that I was ready to meet your mom. All the good things in my life—your mom, you, and your brother—were not possible until I instilled some discipline and order in my own life.

So if you ever find yourself in a chaotic state in your life, Violet, and you don't know what to do first—if you're lost and desperate and terrified—then before you do anything else, before you *can* do anything else, you have to establish order. Everything else flows from that.

CHAPTER 15

WHAT'S YOUR MAJOR?

MONTAIGNE
Of the Education of Children

———◦◦◦◦———

E very few years some guy in a suit comes into the White House and decides he knows exactly how to fix America's "broken" educational system. For George W. Bush, the problem was "accountability," and the "soft bigotry of low expectations." We needed uniform test scores for everyone across the board. If public schools couldn't meet scores, then they needed to be shut down completely and replaced with private schools. The private sector could do everything better.

After "No Child Left Behind" ended in abject failure, Barack Obama was elected, and his team decided that the problems were "standards" and "incentives." We needed to "train the 21st-century workforce," so we could "compete in the Global Marketplace." A bunch of committees developed the "common core" standards, and they created financial incentives for pursuing their educational agenda. If we just taught everyone the same set of skills, and incentivized them properly, then everything would work like clockwork. We really needed to emphasize STEM: science, technology, engineering, and mathematics.

Common Core is proving just as disastrous as No Child Left Behind.

I'm sure the next administration will come up with yet another grand policy and another acronym that costs a fortune, pisses off teachers, and fails students comprehensively.

Montaigne believed that the most important thing we should teach children is *virtue*. An expectant mother asked Montaigne to explain the best way to educate a child. Humbled by the request, Montaigne began by reflecting on his love of the classics.

> *I never seriously settled myself to the reading any book of solid learning but Plutarch and Seneca, and there, like the Danaides, I eternally fill.*

He does more than make a show of humility to these writers—he acknowledges the complete superiority of their talents and their work.

> *[I] see myself so weak and so forlorn, so heavy and so flat, in comparison of those better writers, I at once pity or despise myself ... and that I go in the same path, though at a very great distance, and can say, "Ah, that is so," I am farther satisfied to find, that I have a quality, which every one is not blessed withal, which is, to discern the vast difference betwixt them and me; and notwithstanding all that suffer my own inventions, low and feeble as they are, to run on in their career, without mending or plastering up the defects that this comparison has laid open to my own view.*

So why does he keep writing, if he knows he will never equal those he admires?

> *I know very well how audaciously I myself, at every turn, attempt to equal myself to my thefts, and to make my style go hand in hand with them, not without a temerarious hope of deceiving the eyes of my reader from discerning the difference; but withal, it is as much by the benefit of my application, that I hope to do it, as by that of my invention or any force of my own.... For these are my own particular opinions and fancies, and I deliver them as only what I myself believe, and not for what is to be believed by others. I have no other end in this writing, but only to discover myself, who, also,*

shall, peradventure, be another thing tomorrow, if I chance
to meet any new instruction to change me.

Montaigne believes in the pursuit of wisdom and self-knowledge.
He knows that education is one of the most important functions of
a civilized society, and yet we often fail miserably. Our first mistake
is to try to make kids do things they're not individually suited to do.
We teach children to obey and trust authority too much. Worst of
all, we teach children to simply spit back what they have learned,
rather than to synthesize and use what they have learned to think
for themselves.

> *'Tis a sign of crudity and indigestion to disgorge what we eat*
> *in the same condition it was swallowed. The stomach has not*
> *performed its office unless it have altered the form and condi-*
> *tion of what was committed to it to concoct.*

We should teach children to be skeptical and question authority.
We should teach them to *doubt,* so that they have the ability to
invent new knowledge and new ways of thinking. He compares
education to the work of bees, which gather pollen and nectar but
then transform the raw materials into honey, which is solely their
own creation.

> *To know by rote is no knowledge, and signifies no more but*
> *only to retain what one has entrusted to our memory.*

Children should learn the value of humility, and that it's often better
to remain silent than to speak about things they might not know.
If they do speak, they should embrace brevity, and not adorn their
speech with all sorts of fancy words or rhetoric. And it's crucial that
children learn to admit mistakes.

> *Make him understand, that to acknowledge the error he*
> *shall discover in his own argument, though only found out*
> *by himself, is an effect of judgment and sincerity, which are*
> *the principal things he should seek after; that obstinacy and*
> *contention are common qualities, most appearing in mean*
> *souls; that to revise and correct himself, to forsake an unjust*

argument in the height and heat of dispute, are rare, great, and philosophical qualities.

Kids should also learn not to be fooled by the appearance of greatness, or be swayed by the power of class. They should study history, especially the heroic souls and individuals of past ages. And by so doing, they are not only learning how to act, they are also getting some badly needed perspective.

Who is it, that seeing the havoc of these civil wars of ours, does not cry out, that the machine of the world is near dissolution, and that the day of judgment is at hand; without considering, that many worse things have been seen, and that, in the meantime, people are very merry in a thousand other parts of the earth for all this?

When 9/11 happened, Violet, I thought the world was coming to an end. I'm sure Americans felt that way when the Japanese bombed Pearl Harbor, or when the stock market crashed in 1929, or when the Confederacy attacked Fort Sumter, or when the British looked like they were going to win the Revolutionary War. I can't imagine what people thought when they saw the Mongol horde approaching their cities, or when they dealt with the Black Plague, or when the western half of the Roman Empire collapsed. Every age thinks they're in the end-time. Somehow the world keeps on going. Bad as it might get, don't worry about doomsday. Bad things are going to happen. It's been worse, I promise.

Montaigne really hopes that children, by learning all these things, will learn what it is they want; where their natural talents lay, and what profession they should pursue naturally. They shouldn't just be thrown into some trade or profession; they should choose their own path in life—but only after they've been given the necessary tools to make that decision.

What it is to know, and what to be ignorant; what ought to be the end and design of study; what valor, temperance, and justice are; the difference betwixt ambition and avarice, servitude and subjection, license and liberty; by what token a man may know true and solid contentment; how far death, affliction, and disgrace are to be apprehended.

Look inward first; get to know yourself. Be honest with yourself. Try to be better as much as you can, but learn to admit your own unique strengths and limitations.

Don't be intimidated by anything, either. If something interests you, look into it. In Montaigne's day (just like today) the study of philosophy was set up to seem daunting and unpleasant. It doesn't have to be that way. Instead of being serious all the time, you should try to be cheerful.

The most manifest sign of wisdom is a continual cheerfulness; her state is like that of things in the regions above the moon; always clear and serene.

Don't compound misfortune by embracing misery. Sometimes you're successful, sometimes you fail. And I hate to tell you this, but a lot of times you don't have much say in the matter, so why not accept the difficulties in your life as simply a different experience, and be happy about them?

Don't get too caught up in the pursuit of sensual pleasures. Pleasure's a part of life, so don't ignore it, but if you indulge yourself too much, or you make pleasure the object of your life, you're going to be unhappy in the end.

The gods have planted more toil and sweat in the avenues and cabinets of Venus than in those of Minerva.

The important thing to learn is the same thing Aristotle taught Alexander the Great: *virtue.* Aristotle did not teach Alexander facts and figures; he taught him "good precepts," including prudence, justice, and courage. Alexander used these tools to conquer the world.

Make virtue the object of your study, Violet. Enrich your character. Become a better person. Everything else is just information.

CHAPTER 16

IS AMERICA EXCEPTIONAL?

MONTAIGNE
Of Cannibals

———=◦◦◦=———

Y ou were born during the wars in Iraq and Afghanistan. It's barely discussed today, but when America was gearing up for these conflicts, we were told (and we believed) that these affairs would be quick, cheap, and easy. Our armed forces would instill "shock and awe" in these "backward" countries. Regarding Iraq, Donald Rumsfeld, the secretary of defense, told our European allies, "It could last six days, six weeks. I doubt six months." The war would cost "somewhere between $50 and $60 billion."

None of these predictions proved remotely close to the truth, but I believe the people who made them believed what they were saying. I think our policymakers actually believed that once we'd installed a "model democracy" in the Middle East, it would result in a cascade of democratic movements across the Muslim world, which would transform the region into a block of secular and rational nations, loyal and grateful to the United States.

Democratic movements *did* sweep over the region, and tyrants who had been installed or tolerated by the US were hung, shot, and dragged through the streets. But in their place the people of these countries—who had curiously not forgotten decades of American interventions—*democratically* chose to install militant theocracies hostile to America. The legacy of our invasions—both of which turned out to be hugely expensive, decadelong fiascos—was that we had made this region, remarkably, *more* hostile to the United States.

We also played right into our enemy's hands. When al-Qaeda attacked the World Trade Center on 9/11, their goal was to bait the United States into massively expensive and politically suicidal wars in the Middle East. That's not my analysis—it's Osama bin Laden's. Osama bin Laden *wanted* us to invade Afghanistan, and he would've been absolutely thrilled if we invaded other Muslim countries like Iraq. He didn't even try to conceal this strategy. He broadcasted it to the world in 2004, in a message broadcast by Al Jazeera:

> *All that we have to do is to send two mujahedeen to the furthest point east to raise a piece of cloth on which is written al-Qaeda, in order to make generals race there to cause America to suffer human, economic and political losses without their achieving anything of note other than some benefits for their private corporations.*

Obviously, I'm not a fan of Osama bin Laden. Nevertheless, his predictions proved far more accurate than those of America's political elite.

At the very least, why didn't we at least pay attention to what the enemy was saying?

—◆—

The Greeks coined the term *barbarian*, which was first a linguistic distinction. They called all sorts of people who didn't speak Greek "barbars," because to the Greeks, that's what they sounded like when they talked: *"Bar bar bar."* The Greeks thus reduced the entire non-Greek-speaking world to a homogenous lump of ignorant savages. And that included the young state of Rome.

Of Cannibals starts with a quote from the great Greek general Pyrrhus, who was sent into Italy to confront the Romans.

> *"I know not," said he, "what kind of barbarians" (for so the Greeks called all other nations) "these may be; but the disposition of their army that I see has nothing of barbarism in it."*

Rome incorporated Greece into its massive empire only to experience a similar arrogance centuries later. And one day in some history class you will be told that a gang of marauding barbarians flooded over the Italian border in the 5th century and "sacked" Rome. The image painted for you will be that of a horde of filthy savages in bearskins, wearing horned helmets, wielding clubs and huge axes, and dragging away women by their hair in acts of senseless violence.

But, in fact, the people who sacked Rome were not "uncivilized," even by Roman standards. They were neither dirty nor stupid. They had well-educated generals who outwitted and outfought the Roman armies. They also had plenty of reasons for doing what they did, and they were not senseless, pitiless monsters. Rome had actually *invited* them to live within the borders of their empire, because in the 4th and 5th centuries, Rome needed more troops to defend its borders. Rome actually *created and subsidized* the mercenary army that would one day destroy it. Many of the people who "sacked" Rome in the 5th century had families who had resided inside the Roman Empire for generations. The armies that "sacked" Rome were actually made up of people living inside the Roman Empire— disaffected, marginalized people who assaulted a legally suspect and morally bankrupt empire reeling from centuries of decline, corruption, and abuse.

And yet, as Montaigne reminds us, the Romans were not always such easy targets.

After the fall of Rome, the next great European world powers would reach a zenith of sorts during Montaigne's lifetime, which coincided with the Age of Discovery. The European powers were busy "discovering" the New World and colonizing it ferociously. After repeated voyages of discovery that took place in the late 15th century, all the Atlantic powers got into the New World business. And there they encountered a people they did not understand, and which they ultimately annihilated: the Native Americans.

Montaigne didn't think there was anything inferior about the Native Americans. In fact, he believed they were superior to Europeans in many ways.

I find that there is nothing barbarous and savage in this nation, by anything that I can gather, excepting, that every

*one gives the title of barbarism to everything that is not in use
in his own country.*

Actually, Montaigne argues they might be of better character
than the Europeans, and he uses Plato's *Laws* to justify his initial
reasoning.

*All things, says Plato, are produced either by nature, by
fortune, or by art; the greatest and most beautiful by the one
or the other of the former, the least and most imperfect by
the last.*

He also compares the society of the Native Americans to the "ideal"
state described by Plato, and the admired state of ancient Sparta,
founded by Lycurgus.

*I am sorry that Lycurgus and Plato had no knowledge of
them; for to my apprehension, what we now see in those
nations, does not only surpass all the pictures with which
the poets have adorned the golden age, and all their inventions in feigning a happy state of man, but, moreover, the
fancy and even the wish and desire of philosophy itself; so
native and so pure a simplicity, as we by experience see to
be in them, could never enter into their imagination, nor
could they ever believe that human society could have been
maintained with so little artifice and human patchwork....
How much would [Plato] find his imaginary Republic short
of his perfection ... men fresh from the gods, these were the
manners taught by nature.*

Montaigne provides numerous examples of the bravery, generosity,
ingenuity, and industry of the Native Americans. He describes how
healthy the Natives are, and how there are very few old or infirm
among them. They have plenty to eat, and they rise with the sunrise
and go to bed after sunset. They're happy and reverent to their
gods, they spend their free time dancing, and they have luxuries,
such as an intoxicating drink made from some kind of root. They're
generous and hospitable to strangers. They are also exceedingly
loyal and brave.

*All their ethics are comprised in these two articles, resolution
in war, and affection to their wives.*

He isn't rosy-eyed about the Native Americans. He understands that
they have flaws. He just doesn't believe they're any worse than Europeans. For example, he notes that the wives encourage their husbands
to sleep with other women. Then again, this doesn't seem to cause
any strife among them. Besides that, this kind of "sleeping around" is
hardly uncommon in Europe, though Europeans are hypocrites about
it. He notes that the Natives are also exceedingly violent, and that
they kill their prisoners of war. But he wonders if this might be preferable to the European custom of imprisoning and torturing enemy
soldiers. He also describes how they eat the dead for nourishment,
but that this practice had occurred in the Western past—and besides,
Western doctors commit all sorts of blasphemies upon corpses.

*I am not sorry that we should here take notice of the barba-
rous horror [of the Natives'] cruelty, but that, seeing so clearly
into their own faults, we should be so blind to our own.*

As to the subject of being killed by the enemy, he notes that captured
Native soldiers willingly submit to death, and that they see it as an
act of defiance. They don't submit to the enemy, they are simply
killed by them.

He is killed, not conquered.

And what do the Natives have to say about the Europeans and their
way of doing things? Montaigne gives us their assessment.

*They said, that in the first place they thought it very strange,
that so many tall men wearing beards, strong, and well armed,
who were about the king ('tis like they meant the Swiss of
his guard) should submit to obey a child, and that they did
not rather choose out one amongst themselves to command.
Secondly ... that they had observed, that there were amongst
us men full and crammed with all manner of commodities,
whilst, in the meantime, [others] were begging at their doors,
lean, and half-starved with hunger and poverty; and that they*

thought it strange that these necessitous [men] were able to suffer so great an inequality and injustice, and that they did not take the others by the throats, or set fire to their houses.

Ouch.

CHAPTER 17

WHY AM I AFRAID?

MONTAIGNE

*That the Relish of Good and Evil Depends in Great Measure
Upon the Opinion We Have of Them*

⸺⸺◦◦◦⸺⸺

During the first two years of your life I had three different job
titles, and right after your second birthday, I changed jobs yet
again. For some reason, your birth coincided with the most tumul-
tuous period in my career.

For more than a decade prior to your birth I'd held a stable job.
I'd always been successful at work. This uncertainty was new to
me, and I didn't know how to handle it. If I slept—and mostly I
didn't—I woke up every morning believing that by the day's end I
might be unemployed. One of the organizations I went to work for
experienced a massive financial crisis, and I found myself struggling
just to keep the organization solvent. I had not created the crisis,
and I couldn't really control it—but I was in charge, and my job was
threatened regularly.

At first I believed that it must be me. I had done something wrong,
something to deserve this. It was my fault. And if that was true, then
I could correct the problem. I could work harder, I could raise more
money, and I could navigate the politics. I remembered what my boss
had told me in Chicago—that I had to shape the shape. And I tried
as hard as I could.

But then, even as I succeeded, the problems didn't stop. And after
a lot of self-examination and constant self-criticism, I realized that
all this really didn't have much to do with me. There were simply

some factors I could not control.

This didn't help my anxiety. After all, if I could *not* control the situation—if it was simply a matter of bad timing, personalities, and luck—then what control did I have? It didn't matter how much money I raised, how many hours I worked, or what kind of political alliances I lined up behind me. In the end, I was really not in control of anything.

I felt suffocated, exhausted, and hopeless. I thought my professional life was never going to get any better. This would be the rest of my life, always teetering on the edge of unemployment. My stomach hurt from fear. I couldn't sleep, I stopped eating right, I fought with your mom about stupid things, I brought all anxieties home, and they infected every corner of my life.

What was I going to do?

Men (says an ancient Greek sentence) are tormented with the opinions they have of things and not by the things themselves .... We hold death, poverty, and pain for our principal enemies.

So begins *That the Relish of Good and Evil Depends in Great Measure Upon the Opinion We Have of Them.* Socrates wondered if death might actually be the best thing that could ever happen to him, and Montaigne echoes that sentiment.

Now, this death, which some repute the most dreadful of all dreadful things, who does not know that others call it the only secure harbor from the storms and tempests of life, the sovereign good of nature: the sole support of liberty, and the common and prompt remedy of all evils?

For many people, life is actually worse than death. And there are many instances where faith, virtue, and pride all allow people to accept death happily.

Should I produce a long catalogue of all those sexes and conditions and sects, even in the most happy ages, who have either with great constancy looked death in the face, or voluntarily sought it, and sought it not only to avoid the evils of this life, but some purely to avoid the satiety of living, and others for the hope of better condition elsewhere, I should never have done.

Pain, Montaigne reasons, is what we actually fear about death and poverty. Pain is a symptom of both conditions—we fear the physical pain of death, and the pains of poverty: cold and hunger, but also humiliation. But there are many examples of people bearing pain with great ease.

The pains of childbirth, said by the physician and by God himself to be very great, and which women keep so great a clutter about—there are whole nations that make nothing of them.

Then there are the martyrs, who endured enormous amounts of suffering for the sake of their faith. And of course, the faithful in general:

But do we not, moreover, every Good Friday, in various places, see great numbers of men and women beat and whip themselves till they lacerate and cut the flesh to the very bones?

Besides that, a painful life seems to be the life we should actually aspire to.

A man should most covet to perform that wherein there is greater labor and pain.

Pain in all its forms is actually an essential part of life. And no life is without it. Live long enough, you will feel pain—physical, emotional, financial, it doesn't matter. What matters is how you feel *about* pain. If you're terrified of getting hurt, you're never going to do anything worthwhile. What great thing was accomplished without pain?

And that brings us to the conclusion of Montaigne's essay, which takes a surprising turn. The essay concludes with a discussion about money. I thought this was going to mostly be a lesson about facing down death (and in many ways, it is), but for me, the more profound discussion concerned money.

Montaigne explains that he lived in three different stages throughout his life. In the first stage, when he was young, he had no money. So when he got money, he spent it. He went into a great deal of debt. He didn't worry about it.

In the second stage of his life, he started earning money, and soon he discovered he had loads of it. But something changed. He became terrified about *losing* it. He became miserly and obsessed with his money. He worried about fortune taking his money away. What if there was some accident, some calamity, and he couldn't make a living anymore?

For what, said I, if I should be surprised by such or such an accident?

Money began to change him as a person.

I kept it very close, and though I dare talk so boldly of myself, never spoke of my money, but falsely, as others do, who being rich, pretend to be poor, and being poor, pretend to be rich, dispensing their consciences from ever telling sincerely what they have: a ridiculous and shameful prudence. Was I going a journey? Methought I was never enough provided: and the more I loaded myself with money, the more also was I loaded with fear, one while of the danger of the roads, another of the fidelity of him who had the charge of my baggage .... My mind was eternally taken up with such things as these, so that, all things considered, there is more trouble in keeping money than in getting it .... I reaped little or no advantage by what I had, and my expenses seemed nothing less to me for having the more to spend .... Necessity must take you by the throat before you can prevail upon yourself to touch it .... Men still are intent upon adding to the heap and increasing the stock, from sum to sum, till at last they vilely deprive themselves of the enjoyment of their own proper goods, and throw all into reserve, without making any use of them at all.

When I was younger, I didn't have any money at all. I never thought I would. There was no money in the theater, and there was even less in literature. Even if I was a success as a writer, I knew that success would not mean long-term financial security. Very few writers achieve this kind of financial success, and since I worked for an association serving tens of thousands of writers, I understood just how unlikely that was—and that it really wasn't a question of work ethic, talent, or skill. Lots of great, hard-working writers have died poor. Financial success was mostly a matter of luck—of catching the right subject, the right way, at the exact right cultural moment, and then getting the right publisher and promotion.

So I didn't worry about money, and I had the best time in my life. I didn't care if the place I lived was shabby, or the clothes I wore were old. I didn't care about eating cheap food. I can honestly say this was one of the happiest times in my life.

But then something happened. Somehow, I started to have a *career.* I started earning all this money. It was not a fortune, but it was certainly more than I needed. And the money kept increasing. I started amassing savings and a retirement fund. I bought a house, I started investing, and that's when the worry began to set in, exactly as Montaigne describes. The more I earned, the more money I had stashed away, the more I worried about losing it all. Whenever we wanted to buy something nice, or take a trip, I worried about how much it cost. I watched my retirement fund and investment portfolio daily, tracking every little increase or loss. Every extra nickel I made, I put into the bank, terrified of what would happen if I lost my job, or if some accident befell me. I was terrified about returning to the state of life I had so thoroughly enjoyed. And I was miserable.

So I was interested in Montaigne's third stage of life.

I live at the height of my revenue; sometimes the one, some-times the other may perhaps exceed, but 'tis very little and but rarely that they differ. I live from hand to mouth, and content myself in having sufficient for my present and ordi-nary expense; for as to extraordinary occasions, all the laying up in the world will never suffice. And 'tis the greatest folly imaginable to expect that fortune should ever sufficiently arm us against herself; 'tis with our own arms that we are to fight her.

Machiavelli argued that a prudent man prepares himself for bad fortune, as a village might build levies and dams to anticipate a flood. There is some logic to that, and it's good to have a safety net. But if you obsess about disaster and worst-case scenarios, you're wasting your time. You can't really prepare for the worst life has to throw at you. You'll find that you deal with it as best as you can. You will get through it. It might even be fun.

I was living in a state of fear, and I wasn't terrified of the loss of money, I was terrified by the *prospect* of losing it. I was terrified about losing my job, and losing my income, even though your mom had a very secure job, and even though we had saved enough money to live comfortably for at least a couple of years. Hadn't I concluded that it was out of my control? If that was the case, why should I be terrified? What purpose did my fear serve? The fear was hurting me more than the thing itself. So these words, which conclude Montaigne's essay, resonated with me greatly:

He who neither has the courage to die nor the heart to live,
who will neither resist nor fly, what can we do with him?

CHAPTER 18

WHAT *DON'T* I KNOW?

MONTAIGNE

That It Is Folly to Measure Truth and Error by Our Own Capacity

———◦◦◦◦———

When I was a kid, it was a well-known fact that modern humans and Neanderthals had never coexisted. Human evolution had progressed in a neat and tidy line, from chimpanzees to *Homo erectus* ("upright man"), to *Homo habilis* ("man with ability"), to Neanderthals, to *Homo sapiens*. You could put all the "protohumans" in segments along the line, and each enjoyed their time as the dominant species, until they were suddenly supplanted by the newer model. I was taught that Neanderthals were grunting savages, little better than apes.

But now we know that not only did modern humans coexist with Neanderthals, but that we actually interbred with them. Neanderthals and modern humans lived together for tens of thousands of years, and not only that, we may have shared the planet with *other* hominids, including a strange race of "hobbits" who lived in Indonesia, and who might have been around as recently as 12,000 years ago. And Neanderthals weren't dumb. They actually had larger brains than we do. They used tools, they had a language, they made art, and they had complex societies.

That's conventional wisdom for you, Violet. The future is not nearly as mysterious as the past. For a species whose chief evolutionary advantage is our ability to communicate and think rationally, it's amazing how little we understand our own past. We barely comprehend what happened 20 minutes ago, let alone 5,000 years ago, and never mind 50,000 years ago.

And yet, human beings may still retain faint memories of our ancient relatives, which may have been preserved in the oral tradition. We still teach children that ancient myths were nothing but nonsense—fictions invented by an ignorant people to explain natural phenomena. Yet many legends from antiquity have nothing to do with natural phenomena, transmitting instead very human tales of war, suffering, disaster, and heartbreak. Many ancient legends (such as the Trojan War) were once believed to be complete fantasy, but have now been supported by archaeological evidence.

The ancient mind was different from our own. In the past, human beings were capable of intellectual feats that would stagger the modern imagination. For example, in antiquity, it was possible for some human beings to recite a thousand pages of poetry from memory, verbatim, without committing a single mistake.

How could they do this? The Greeks developed complex mnemonic devices in poetry to train the memory, including refrains, meter, and rhyme. These devices weren't just used to make pretty sounds, and recitation was hardly a useless skill. Before the advent of accessible print technology, this was how stories were passed down from generation to generation. This was how people remembered what happened before they were born. They gathered together to hear stories of the distant past. A single poet would recite an epic, taking on the voices and aspects of the different characters. In this way, the past was preserved.

The Greeks weren't "primitive" (a modern euphemism for "stupid"), and they weren't blind to the importance of history. That's why they invented it. Imagine being born into an America with absolutely no knowledge of the Revolutionary War, the Civil War, World War I, or World War II—or any event that occurred more than 50–60 years prior to the present moment. How could such a society function? How could it understand itself, or ever make any progress?

These poems could be transmitted to the next generation, and because of their structure, they maintained their integrity. They may have been altered slightly by successive generations of skilled poets, but they would still preserve essential truths from the remote past. The epics of Homer (the *Iliad,* the *Odyssey*) were preserved this way.

We don't even know if there *was* a Homer, or if Homer was simply an amalgamation of successive generations of oral poets. Herodotus believed that Homer lived in the ninth century BCE, but the events in the *Iliad* took place 300 years prior to that. Since we know that the poems contain clear anachronistic elements from the ninth century BCE, *and* we know that the Trojan War did actually take place in the 12th century BCE, in the location where Homer said it took place, with at least *some* of the elements described by Homer (the burning of Troy, for example), we must concede that the oral tradition was capable of preserving actual events that occurred in truly archaic, "prehistoric" times. Yes, there are gods and monsters and the rest—but there was also a real war, with real people, waged in a real place.

There are far too many strange coincidences in the ancient legends of disparate peoples to simply dismiss them as superstitious tales to explain natural phenomena. The most obvious example is the flood myth, which occurs in dozens of ancient legends, despite the fact that many of these civilizations had no commerce with each other. The Greek flood myth is remarkably similar to the story found in the Old Testament of the Hebrews, which is remarkably similar to the story preserved in the Sumerian epic *Gilgamesh*. There are differences, of course, but the core elements (the gods sent a divine flood to punish man for his wickedness, the flood destroyed all mankind, except one guy, forewarned by the gods, who survived in a huge boat) remain consistent.

Many ancient oral epics from different civilizations refer to previous ages of man, which were characterized by the existence of "giants." In these remote *golden ages*, man was at harmony with nature, and it was common for people to live impossibly long lives.

One extremely ancient myth from Greece concerning the mythical hero Theseus describes a war between the Lapiths (a pre-Greek people), and the "centaurs." In the account preserved by the Roman poet Ovid, which was taken from a much more ancient source, the "centaurs" do not seem like the half-man, half-horse creature we imagine today, but rather some kind of crude—but physically massive—hominid. The Lapiths kill many of these creatures in the course of the war, and exile the remainder of them to the remote north. The age of this legend is impossible to determine, but it likely survives from the very dawn of Western civilization—if not before it. Like a game of telephone played across thousands of years, could this story be a garbled memory of an actual conflict between Homo Sapiens and Neanderthals?

At the same time we ridicule ancient legends as "ignorant superstition," we also scoff at the possibilities of the future. No, we will never achieve interstellar travel, some say. The technical barriers are simply too great.

I wrote this for you to read when you turned 18. When I was that age, nobody owned a cell phone, or an email account. The second-generation cell phones that came onto the market by the time I graduated from college looked very much like the communicators from the 1960s *Star Trek* television show. They were small and black, and they even flipped open.

And you? You will always live in a world where you can be reached anywhere at any time, and you will always have every single bit of information ever produced in recorded history at your instant disposal.

People who say that something's impossible simply lack imagination. Nearly 500 years ago, in his essay *That It Is Folly to Measure Truth and Error by Our Own Capacity,* Montaigne thought exactly the same thing.

> *'Tis a foolish presumption to slight and condemn all things for false that do not appear to us probable ... If we give the names of monster and miracle to everything our reason cannot comprehend, how many are continually presented before our eyes?*

Imagine what it was like to live in the 16th century. A literal new world had been discovered. The only comparable discovery would be if we discovered intelligent life beyond our solar system, and we actually made fact-to-face contact with it. Wouldn't we cast aside all of our religious and scientific assumptions? This was the case in the 16th century, in the wake of the discovery of the Americas. Here was a race of people who organized themselves in a completely unknown manner. They had different gods, different customs, different political systems, different animals, and different diets. They had wonderful and strange new luxuries, to Europeans—tobacco, coffee, and chocolate. There was so much gold in South America that the value of it plummeted worldwide. These people got along for a long time without the benefit of Jesus Christ. And everything was now open for debate.

This included strange reports from antiquity, including accounts from venerable authors such as Plutarch and Pliny, in which the authors report that news of battles spread hundreds of miles almost instantaneously. On the one hand, Montaigne doesn't see how this could be possible, but on the other, the authors themselves are of such character and virtue that he can't dismiss them out of hand.

> *Is any man living now so impudent as to think himself comparable to them in virtue, piety, learning, judgment, or any kind of perfection?*

There are limits to our imaginations; what we think we know is really limited by our own experience.

> *He that had never seen a river, imagined the first he met with to be the sea ... 'Tis a presumption of great danger and consequence, besides the absurd temerity it draws after it, to contemn what we do not comprehend.*

I also can't help but think about Plato's oddly compelling account of Atlantis, which can be found in the *Timaeus* and *Critias*. In Plato's account, there once existed a highly advanced civilization called Atlantis, which ruled the world. Atlantis was reportedly enormous—practically another whole continent—and it resided in the Western Ocean, "beyond the Pillars of Hercules," which means it resided west of Africa, outside the Strait of Gibraltar. Plato also describes "an opposite continent on the other side of the world" that was well known in the distant past, and which was visited frequently by ancient mariners before a cataclysm prevented navigation of the Atlantic Ocean.

According to Egyptian priests, Atlantis was destroyed in a great seismic catastrophe 12,000 years ago, when it sank beneath the ocean. Atlantis was opposed by an ancient European civilization headquartered in Athens—a civilization so ancient that even the Athenians themselves do not remember its existence.

Socrates explains that he learned all this from the Greek philosopher Solon, who had occasion to visit the mysterious Egyptian priests of Saïs. In *Timaeus,* Plato recounts that Solon tried to impress the Egyptian priests with his knowledge of the past, recounting Greek history as far back as he could reckon, all the way back to a legendary flood that marked the beginning. The Egyptian priests humor Solon, and then they laugh at his ignorance. In doing so, they reference the story of Phaethon, the human child of the god Helios, who attempted to drive the chariot of the sun. In the account of this myth preserved by Ovid in Book II of the *Metamorphoses,* the path of the sun is described in disturbingly precise astronomical terms, and when Phaethon loses control of the chariot, literally bringing the sun down to the ground, it causes unimaginable catastrophe, "destroying huge towns and walls / whole regions and their peoples." Volcanoes around the world erupt, rivers are either vaporized or set on fire, and massive environmental change occurs instantly. ("It was then that Libya became a desert, all her moisture dried.") The calamity is followed by a period of total darkness, during which all remaining life on earth "withdraws into the deepest caves."

If you read the story of Phaethon today, it's hard *not* to read it as an eerily accurate description of an actual astronomical event, such as an asteroid impact. All the events described would have actually occurred if an asteroid hit the earth—vast destruction, sudden and violent volcanic activity, instant environmental upheaval, and a period of darkness resulting from the ash cloud. But this can't be. Surely we could not have preserved any memory of such an event— could we? Remarkably, the Egyptian priests suggest that such things have happened repeatedly in the remote past.

O Solon, Solon, you Hellenes [Greeks] are never anything but children, and there is not an old man among you. Solon in return asked him what he meant. I mean to say, he replied, that in mind you are all young; there is no old opinion handed down among you by ancient tradition, nor any science which is hoary with age. And I will tell you why. There have been, and will be again, many destructions of mankind arising out of many causes; the greatest have been brought about by the agencies of fire and water, and other lesser ones by innumerable other causes. There is a story, which even you have preserved, that once upon a time Phaethon, the son of Helios, having yoked the steeds in his father's chariot, because he was not able to drive them in the path of his father, burnt up all that was upon the earth, and was himself destroyed by a thunderbolt. Now this has the form of a myth, but really signifies a declination of the bodies moving in the heavens around the earth, and a great conflagration of things upon the earth, which recurs after long intervals; at such time those who live upon the mountains and in dry and lofty places are more liable to destruction than those who dwell by rivers or on the seashore. And from this calamity the Nile, who is our never-failing savior, delivers and preserves us. When, on the other hand, the gods purge the earth with a deluge of water, the survivors in your country are herdsmen and shepherds who dwell on the mountains, but those who, like you, live in cities are carried by the rivers into the sea. Whereas in this land, neither then nor at any other time, does the water come down from above on the fields, having always a tendency to come up from below; for which reason the traditions preserved here are most ancient.

The fact is, that wherever the extremity of winter frost or of summer sun does not prevent, mankind exist, sometimes in greater, sometimes in lesser numbers. And whatever happened either in your country or in ours, or in any other region of which we are informed—if there were any actions noble or great or in any other way remarkable, they have all been written down by us of old, and are preserved in our temples. Whereas just when you and other nations are beginning to be provided with letters and the other requisites of civilized life, after the usual interval, the stream from heaven, like a pestilence, comes pouring down, and leaves only those of you who are destitute of letters and education; so you have to begin all over again like children, and know nothing of what happened in ancient times, either among us or among yourselves. As for those genealogies of yours which you just now recounted to us, Solon, they are no better than the tales of children. In the first place you remember a single deluge only, but there were many previous ones; in the next place, you do not know that there formerly dwelt in your land the fairest and noblest race of men which ever lived, and that you and your whole city are descended from a small seed or remnant of them which survived. And this was unknown to you, because, for many generations, the survivors of that destruction died, leaving no written word.

Solon—who was born 2,700 years ago—is himself counting back thousands of years. But the Egyptians are not impressed; they inform Solon that the Great Flood he imagines to be the beginning of time was merely the *most recent* flood in a long, recurring sequence of disasters. In reality, the world of man is much, much more ancient.

The experts will tell you that this is not true, either. They'll say that it's impossible; that it's just a fairy tale. They'll say that no advanced civilization could've possibly existed more than 7,000 years ago. Scholars will say that Atlantis was simply an allegory—a fable concocted by Plato to prove some sort of philosophical point. The smart people could be right. But they haven't exactly batted a thousand, Violet.

The impossible is possible. Keep an open mind.

CHAPTER 19

WHAT IF LIFE IS MEANINGLESS?

WILLIAM SHAKESPEARE
Hamlet

———◦◦◦———

Why, look you now, how unworthy a thing you make of me!
You would play upon me; you would seem to know my stops:
you would pluck out the heart of my mystery.
—Hamlet, Act III, scene ii

When I was 22 I moved to Hollywood with grand ambitions of becoming a screenwriter. Before I moved, my dad—who is not an outdoorsy type—took me on a weeklong rafting trip through the Grand Canyon. For a week, my dad and I slept on warm sands at the bottom of the Grand Canyon, staring up at the stars.

Our rafting guide was a rugged, bearded man named Mike. Mike had a sidearm for snakes. The guy was in his mid-40s, and his black hair was starting to turn gray underneath his beat-up ball cap. The portion of the Colorado that runs through the Grand Canyon isn't the most dangerous river you can find, but there are serious patches. Mike and his team did the heavy lifting—they cooked, they cleaned, they even hauled out our trash and our waste. The rest of us had paddles, but we did what the guides told us.

One evening as we made camp, I saw Mike hike up a few rocks to get a look at a dangerous stretch of river that awaited us the next morning. I walked up next to him to see it, too. It looked like a churning whirlpool of death. There was a steep drop in the river, and the water—whose temperature never rose much above 40 degrees—crashed violently on rocks beneath it. It was by far the most dangerous stretch we'd navigate on the trip.

Mike took stock of the rapid, and then he nodded and turned to me.

"What do you think?" he asked, as if I could offer anything helpful.

"We're going down *that?!*" I asked.

He nodded.

"You scared?" he asked.

"Uh...kinda."

"Yeah, well," he said, patting me on the shoulder. "That's called intelligence."

That evening, my dad and I were drinking beers and smoking cigarettes. We talked about his career, about our family, about politics. We were just chatting. And then he told me that he believed that when you die, it's the end of your existence.

"I think it's like a light switch just goes off," he said. "And that's it."

We made it down the rapid. After we put in at Lake Mead, they packed us on a bus and drove us straight to Las Vegas. After more than a week in the Grand Canyon, Vegas seemed obscene and preposterous, with its facsimile Great Pyramid, Eiffel Tower, and Empire State Building; its neon pollution everywhere, its garish shows, and the free buffets overflowing with rich, fatty food. Everything about it seemed artificial and sickly, a huge monument in the desert to greed and lust, and all to be torn down next week for another, bigger, and more spectacular monument. I could not help but recall Shelley's famous poem "Ozymandias."

> I met a traveller from an antique land
> Who said: "Two vast and trunkless legs of stone
> Stand in the desert . . . Near them, on the sand,

Half sunk, a shattered visage lies, whose frown,
And wrinkled lip, and sneer of cold command,
Tell that its sculptor well those passions read
Which yet survive, stamped on these lifeless things,
The hand that mocked them, and the heart that fed:
And on the pedestal these words appear:
'My name is Ozymandias, king of kings:
Look on my works, ye Mighty, and despair!'
Nothing beside remains. Round the decay
Of that colossal wreck, boundless and bare
The lone and level sands stretch far away.

I couldn't sleep at the hotel. It was too weird after spending the week in the Grand Canyon, listening to the air conditioner turn on, and then off. Too cold and too clean. In the middle of the night I went out to have a cigarette. It was a Vegas hotel, and you could smoke by the elevators, so I sat down on a bench in front of them. There was a suit of armor on a stand next to me. Every so often the doors would open, and out would tumble young drunks, or stately old couples. In that moment, it all seemed so ridiculous to me.

I was bothered by what my dad told me. I wanted him to believe life was *not* meaningless, even though at the time, I thought he was absolutely right. I believed that when we died, there was nothing waiting for us. And if anyone should know what death is really like, wouldn't it be a man like my father? He was a doctor, a medical man, a man of science. He saw death firsthand. He'd been educated by Jesuits and raised Roman Catholic. He'd been told all the same stories I was told, and he even took me to church. I wondered why he would do that, if he believed it was all nonsense? Why did it bother me so much that he believed the same thing I did?

﹃﹄

We know that William Shakespeare's version of *Hamlet* was performed as early as 1603, and possibly a year or two before that. We also know that in 1597, William Shakespeare's only son, Hamnet, died from the Bubonic Plague at the age of 11.

I do not think that the timing is a coincidence.

During the time of its production, *Hamlet* was simply another "revenge tragedy." Many plays with similar plots existed at the time, in which a protagonist seeks vengeance for some crime against them, only to be destroyed by their own pursuit of vengeance. Such plots were not even new to the Elizabethans. Similar plays had already existed for nearly two thousand years, since the advent of Greek drama. Aeschylus's *Oresteia,* for example, bears many striking resemblances with *Hamlet,* and other plays like it.

The story goes like this:

Prince Hamlet returns from studying abroad because his father, the king, has died suddenly. Upon returning, Hamlet discovers that his mother, Gertrude, has quickly become remarried, to Claudius, Hamlet's Uncle. Hamlet is depressed, and he grieves for his father. He is angry with his mother for remarrying so quickly. He doesn't like Claudius, whom he believes to be a man of low character. Suddenly, Hamlet's good friend Horatio reports that he and the castle guards have seen the King's ghost wandering at night. Hamlet keeps watch, and he, too sees the ghost. The ghost tells Hamlet (and only Hamlet) that his death was no accident: the king claims that he was poisoned by his own brother, Claudius, who has now married the queen. The King's ghost commands his son to avenge his murder. Hamlet agrees to do so.

But then Hamlet dawdles. He doesn't kill Claudius right away. He blames his inaction on the fact that he can't truly know if the ghost was *actually* his father, or rather a demon sent to trick him. So he concocts an elaborate scheme to test the ghost's story. He pretends to be insane, and then he stages a play based on an old legend. In the play, a king is murdered by his nephew, who pours poison in the king's ear while he naps. This is precisely how the ghost described his own murder. Claudius is visibly shaken while watching the murder scene, and Hamlet has his proof.

But even then, Hamlet *still* doesn't kill him. He finds his uncle alone, unguarded, and he assumes that Claudius is begging forgiveness for his sins. (In fact, Claudius is simply confessing to the audience, and also plotting Hamlet's murder). Hamlet resolves to catch Claudius in bed with his mother, whereupon he will feel absolutely justified in killing him. Then Hamlet goes to see his mother. While spitting unfounded accusations at his mother, Hamlet hears the ghost again, who admonishes him for the delay. Hamlet then hears something behind the curtain, and assumes that it's Claudius. Mistakenly,

Hamlet kills Polonius (his girlfriend's father), after which he is seized and sent away, ostensibly to be murdered by two of his friends.

After a short absence, Hamlet returns, having escaped the plot to kill him. When he returns, he discovers that his girlfriend has killed herself out of grief over her father's murder. Her brother, Laertes, challenges Hamlet to a duel. Hamlet accepts. In secret, Claudius meets with Laertes and they conspire to poison Laertes's dueling sword. If Laertes can simply scratch Hamlet during the duel, Hamlet will die. But just in case that doesn't happen, Claudius fills a goblet with poison, so when Hamlet is thirsty from the fight, he'll take a big drink and die.

Laertes does manage to scratch Hamlet during their duel, and Hamlet responds by kicking his ass. Somehow the swords get mixed up and Hamlet scratches Laertes in return. At this point the queen raises the poisoned chalice to salute Hamlet's victory. She drinks the cup of poison meant for her son, and she seems to finally realize the truth. Hamlet *finally* kills Claudius. But Hamlet is doomed as well, and he dies from the poison.

Now that the stage is littered with corpses, an invading army promptly enters the throne room, led by Fortinbras of Norway.

The end.

That's the plot of *Hamlet*. But that's not what it's about. It's about what my dad confessed to me that night in the Grand Canyon.

Hamlet is not simply "just another revenge tragedy." There's a reason we all know *Hamlet* and very few of us remember *The Spanish Tragedy*. No other piece of English literature has attracted as much debate, criticism, controversy, love, and even hatred as *Hamlet*. T.S. Eliot, perhaps the greatest poet of the 20th century, once famously called *Hamlet* "an artistic failure" because of its inscrutable nature. *Hamlet* may be a simple play with a derivative plot—and yet, the more one examines it, the more the play changes. At a certain point, you realize that you can never pluck out the heart of its mystery.

Is Hamlet right or wrong? Has he accomplished the impossible, or has he achieved nothing? Why didn't he just kill Claudius? Is he sane or insane? Why did he pretend to be crazy? Or was he *actually* crazy the whole time? Or was he sane at one point and then crazy at another?

These are not small questions in a play. We are supposed to root for a central character. At the very least, we are supposed to understand the events that transpire. We *do* root for Hamlet, and we also understand the events. We can describe them all just fine. But we don't know what those events add up to. And even as we root for Hamlet, we also watch a man who commits monstrous, unforgiveable crimes. Hamlet is absolutely merciless to Ophelia, and then he murders her father simply by accident. And he doesn't regret it, either. Ophelia understandably goes nuts and kills herself, damning her soul for eternity because the church won't give a suicide a proper burial. At her burial, Hamlet ridicules the suffering of her poor brother, Laertes, who has now lost his entire family due to Hamlet's carelessness.

In the end, were the wicked punished? Yes. Maybe. I don't know. Did "good" triumph? No? Yes? Hamlet, at the center of everything, is the embodiment of noble perfection, but he is also a flawed and brutal, and perhaps even an insane psychopath.

So why do we root for him?

Because at some point, perhaps our lowest point, every one of us has *been* Hamlet. Every one of us, in secret or otherwise—has entertained the question that consumes and tortures Hamlet:

What if it all means nothing?

There are two very famous scenes in *Hamlet,* and both deal with this question. Consider how Hamlet views the accomplishments of great men like Alexander and Caesar. Upon his return to Denmark, Hamlet is at the cemetery with his buddy Horatio when he stumbles upon the skull of his former court jester, a man named Yorick. He holds the skull in his hand, and he reflects on Yorick's pointless existence.

Hamlet

Alas, poor Yorick! I knew him well, Horatio; a fellow of infinite jest, of most excellent fancy. He hath borne me on his back a thousand times; and now, how abhorred in my imagination it is! My gorge rises at it. Here hung those lips that I have kissed I know not how oft. Where be your gibes now? Your gambols? Your songs? Your flashes of merriment, that were wont to set the table on a roar? Not one now, to mock your own grinning? Quite chapfallen ... prithee, Horatio, tell me one thing.

Horatio
What's that my lord?

Hamlet
Dost thou think Alexander looked o'this fashion i'the earth?

Horatio
E'en so.

Hamlet (putting down the skull)
And smelt so? Pah!

Horatio
E'en so, my lord.

Hamlet
To *what base uses we may return*, Horatio! Why may not imagination trace the noble dust of Alexander, till he find it stopping a bunghole ... Alexander died, Alexander was buried, Alexander returneth into dust; the dust is of earth; of earth we make loam; and why of that loam, whereto he was converted, might they not stop a beer-barrel?
    Imperious Caesar, dead and turn'd to clay,
    might stop a hole to keep the wind away.
    O, that the earth, which kept the world in awe,
    Should patch a wall to expel the winter's flaw.

Our whole lives we're striving for things—money, power, love, glory—and yet even if we conquer the whole world, we will wind up as stinking corpses in the dust. In such an indifferent universe, the question isn't *how* we should live: it's *why*. To live is to suffer. Why shouldn't we just kill ourselves? Which brings us to the other famous scene.

Hamlet
To be or not to be—that is the question:
Whether 'tis nobler in the mind to suffer
The slings and arrows of outrageous fortune
Or to take arms against a sea of troubles,

157

And by opposing, end them. To die—to sleep
No more; And by a sleep to say we end
The heartache, and the thousand natural shocks
That flesh is heir to. 'Tis a consummation
Devoutly to be wish'd. To die—to sleep.
To sleep, perchance to dream: ay, there's the rub!
For in that sleep of death what dreams may come
When we have shuffled off this mortal coil,
Must give us pause. There's the respect
That makes calamity of so long life.
For who would bear the whips and scorns of time,
Th' oppressors wrong, the proud man's contumely,
The pangs of despis'd love, the law's delay,
The insolence of office, and the spurns
That patient merit of the unworthy takes
When he himself might his quietus make
With a bare bodkin? Who would these fardels bear,
To grunt and sweat under a weary life,
But that the dread of something after death—
The undiscover'd country, from whose bourn
No traveler returns—puzzles the will,
And makes us rather bear those ills we have
Than fly to others we know not of?
Thus conscience does make cowards of us all,
And thus the native hue of resolution
Is sicklied o'er with the pale cast of thought,
And enterprises of great pith and moment
With regard their currents turn awry
And lose the name of action—soft you now!
The fair Ophelia! Nymph in thy orisons
Be all my sins remembered.

Hamlet's world is absolutely corrupt. *Everyone* betrays him: his friends, his lover, his advisors, his king, and maybe even his own mother. He is truly alone. The state, the family, and the bonds of friendship and love have all broken down.

But even if all was going well for Hamlet, the question would still remain: *so what?* So what if I make a million dollars, or I become king, or I fall in love? It is not that I fear death—it is that I fear the *absence of meaning*. I fear a universe in which nothing has any purpose—not love, power, riches, or glory. And all my fictions—my religion, my romances, and my state—are mere contrivances to paper over the void I know, deep in my soul, is waiting for me. I try to hide my fear; I pretend it doesn't exist, I pretend that death has meaning; I invent gods and heavens and hells. But death is waiting, and as hard as I try to believe otherwise, I fear there is nothing beyond it.

The switch goes off, and everything goes black.

Hamlet gives the most eloquent expression of our most basic human fear: that each of us is merely a machine, or a "piece of work," in a nonsensical, random, and irrelevant universe. Our lives have no meaning, and neither do our accomplishments. We could cure cancer or enslave the world. It wouldn't matter either way. In the end, we are to be stripped naked, stuffed into a hole, and forgotten.

These aren't feelings we talk about at happy hour. You don't turn to Sally on Friday night and say, "You know, Sally, there's no point to my existence." Sally would be concerned. Sally might have you committed. Maybe Sally would take you to church with her, where you could hear all the nice stories about an afterlife in the clouds, with flying cherub harpists. You would be told to pray a little faster, and commit to a strange financial scheme to carry your soul to paradise. Or perhaps Sally would tell you what you need is a plan: what you need to do is to focus on your work fixing pipes or selling widgets; yes, get ahead, and acquire titles and lands that you can't take with you. Perhaps what you need is a torrid affair that will be over when the sun rises. Maybe you need a stiffer drink to help you forget.

But deep down, even if she can't articulate it or admit it, Sally's scared, too.

When we watch *Hamlet*, we realize that we are not alone with our terror. Others feel it too. And as the Greeks knew so well, a simple play can unite us as human beings, across all cultures and all divides. For a brief time, we are simply free to be afraid, and to seriously consider our fear. So what should we do? What does Hamlet do?

Despite his fear, Hamlet refuses to give up. Hamlet, in the face of an indifferent universe, does the just and honorable thing—the thing that *must* be done to restore moral and legal order—even if it means he will be remembered as a murderer, a traitor, and an assassin.

I didn't understand what compelled my dad to take me down the Grand Canyon until years later. I was young, and I craved fame and fortune. My dad wanted to show me that these things were not important in the grand scheme of things. My dad was wealthy, powerful, and respected. He was (and is) a great man. But what did any of that mean to the Grand Canyon? What did it care? It was there before us, and it would be there long after we were dead and gone. That rapid didn't care if we lived or died, or if we were famous or anonymous. We were just bits of matter traveling down its waters. My dad was telling me not to take myself or my ambition too seriously. But he still wanted me to go out and see the world, and have adventures, and enjoy my life.

That's what my dad did. He came from very humble origins, moved all around the country earning his education, and then he rose to prominence, raised a large family with my mom, and traveled the world. Anybody who knows the man would tell you: my dad's a guy who loves living. He loves his family, he loves to travel, to ski, to garden, and to sail. At the end of a day he's been known to enjoy a glass of whiskey.

I don't think my dad believes that life is meaningless. I think he believes that it's *precious*.

I think that's what Shakespeare thought, too. I think William Shakespeare was wrestling with some pretty serious demons in the aftermath of his only son's horrific death. I think that at one point, he asked, "How can I live with this pain? Why shouldn't I just kill myself? What's the point?" And I think he decided that he just loved life too much.

In *Hamlet*, William Shakespeare asks and answers the question that terrifies every human being. What if it's meaningless? What if this life is all there is? Well, if that's true, then life is extremely precious. I think Hamlet feels that way. He admires men like Alexander, and Caesar, but in the end, all he really wants is to live a normal life. He wants to go to college, joke with his friends, and romance a beautiful woman. In due time, he wants to take up the family business. Claudius takes all that away from him. Now Hamlet's gotta kill him, and worse, he knows he has to give up his own life to do it. And Hamlet *doesn't want to*. *Nobody* would want to. So he hems and haws about it, he gripes about the futility of life, he tries to talk himself out of it, and he may even drive himself insane trying to avoid his fate—but in the end, he fulfills a noble purpose: he restores justice and order to his kingdom, and he dies.

When Hamlet collapses, his good friend Horatio cradles him in his arms. Sick with grief at his best friend's impending death, Horatio reaches for the goblet of poison, with the intention of killing himself. With the last of his remaining strength, Hamlet wrestles the cup from Horatio's hands.

> *Hamlet*
> *As th'art a man,*
> *Give me the cup. Let go! By heaven, I'll ha't.*
> *O Good Horatio, what a wounded name*
> *(Things standing thus unknown) shall live behind me!*
> *If thou didst ever hold me in thy heart,*
> *Absent thee from felicity awhile,*
> *And in this harsh world draw thy breath in pain,*
> *To tell my story.*

Live, he begs us, and live honorably. The rest is silence.

CHAPTER 20

WHAT IS GOVERNMENT FOR?

JOHN LOCKE

*Concerning the True Original Extent
and End of Civil Government*

The decade before you were born was terrifying, Violet. I was at Oxford on 9/11. I'd just met your mom the previous month, and she was living about a mile away from the Pentagon. I was on my way home from a seminar, walking past a pub. A chalkboard sign was set up on the sidewalk that read, "NEW YORK, WASHINGTON ATTACKED." One of the exchange students I was with had a brother who worked at the World Trade Center. He wept inconsolably as he tried to reach his brother, without success. I tried to get a hold of your mom, but the phones were down. The Internet (which was still very new then) was down. Nobody knew what was happening or what was next—there was so much misinformation and confusion. I heard that the entire city of Washington had been evacuated. I heard there were more planes headed for the White House and the Capitol. More attacks were expected in the next few days, as the United States of America literally shut down. The New York Stock Exchange closed, and for the first time in the history of aviation, every airplane in America was grounded.

Everyone who lived through 9/11 knew that the world was now fundamentally different from the day before. But in that moment, which was fraught with so much fear, confusion, anxiety, and rage, there was also a strange and wonderful feeling. As I stared slack-jawed at the television set, watching the towers collapse, the British bartender handed me a pint of beer that I had not ordered. He knew I was an American.

"We're with you, mate. Shoulder to shoulder," he said.

I was moved to tears when, during the changing of the guard at Buckingham Palace, the band played *The Star Spangled Banner.* The world's leaders expressed solidarity with the United States. A French newspaper echoed John F. Kennedy with the headline "We are all Americans." At home, all the vicious partisan debates vanished immediately. In that moment, we faced a truly momentous opportunity as Americans. What we did then would determine our nation's course for decades, and, as the world's only superpower, it would change the world, too.

We were ready to make the right choice. All Americans—rich, poor, weak, and mighty—were willing to sacrifice everything for one another. The entire world was united behind us. Business was on board. Our political leaders could've asked us for higher taxes, for thriftiness, for prudence, and patience. They could've asked us to reduce our energy consumption. They could've reinstated the draft, or implemented some other form of national service.

We were willing to listen, and we were willing to have a frank conversation about America's place in the world, because we all wanted to understand what could've possibly driven these madmen to do something so despicable, and so brutal. *Why did they hate us so much?*

Finally, the president told us what we could do. We could go about our lives as if nothing had happened. We could go shopping, and go to the movies, because doing so meant "not letting the terrorists win." As for the motives of the terrorists, we were told there was no why, and there was no sense in even asking that question; our enemies were simply fanatic cultists who hated us for our freedoms. Their leader was a comic book supervillain: rich beyond imagination, preternaturally cunning, and certifiably insane. As for the freedoms our enemies despised so much, those would need to be suspended and modified now, because the enemy was everywhere, lurking in unknown sleeper cells across America. The enemy could be next door, or in your place of business, ready to detonate a nuclear device. The enemy could have a bomb in his underpants, or in his shoes. We should be vigilant, and report any suspicious behavior. We should take our shoes off at the airport. We should buy duct tape and bottled water. We should allow our intelligence services and military to "take the gloves off," and "work in the shadows." We would need to build massive new surveillance systems, so that our protectors could "connect the dots." Red tape needed to be eliminated so that the government could move with great speed and massive force, whatever the cost. We should wage war, which would be cheap, and over quickly, and we should all get a tax cut.

Like a lot of people, I was scared and angry after 9/11. I wanted to get those sons of bitches. I wanted us to find the man responsible, and I wanted him killed as horribly as could be arranged. I read that a man named Cofer Black, a leading US counterterrorism official, traveled to Afghanistan following 9/11 with a box of dry ice meant to hold bin Laden's head. "When we're finished," he was said to have remarked to the president, "the flies will be crawling on their eyeballs." I thought, *That's awesome.*

I wanted guys like Cofer Black to do whatever was necessary to kill those people and keep us safe. Whatever it took. That's what the government was for.

The concept of rights was not new in the 17th century. Roman citizens had rights, even under the empire. But in the centuries between the fall of the Roman Empire and the rise of constitutional republics, the dominant form of political system in the West had been monarchy. And in the monarchical system, the sovereign was absolute. Kings (and in some cases queens) had a *divine right*, which meant that their power came from God, and not the people. Perhaps the most famous expression of this kind of power was articulated by Louis XIV of France, who remarked *"L'etat, c'est Moi"* ("I am the state.")

But around the time that John Locke lived (1632–1704), people were starting to have serious problems with monarchy, and the reason was pretty simple: over time, the interests of the monarchs began to diverge from the interests of the people.

Between 1642 and 1651, a civil war in England raged between Royalists (those supporting the King) and Parliamentarians (those who supported the legislative body). The Parliamentarians came out on top, and the result was a sharp decline in royal power in

England. In 1688, King James was overthrown and parliament essentially seized control of political power in England. In 1689, the English parliament produced a "Bill of Rights," and the intention of this bill was to expressly limit the authority and power of the king. The English Bill of Rights laid out a series of things the king could *not* do:

- The king couldn't set up courts, or act as a judge
- The king couldn't levy new taxes by decree
- The king couldn't keep a standing army without the consent of parliament
- The king couldn't keep people from owning weapons
- The king couldn't restrict freedom of speech
- The king couldn't interfere with parliamentary elections

The founders of our own country believed that the King of England had violated their *existing rights as English citizens*. They were not claiming to possess new rights. And they looked to John Locke's *Concerning Civil Government* for inspiration and moral defense.

Concerning Civil Government begins by debunking divine right, the idea that the monarch gets his or her power directly from God. First, Locke says, according to the Bible, Adam (the first man) didn't have divine right over his children, and even if he did, he didn't really have any authority over the world to begin with. Even if he *did* have authority over his children and the world, his children didn't necessarily inherit it. And even if Adam's children inherited dominion over the world, there is no way now to determine *who* is descended from Adam and thus would have a legitimate claim to that inheritance. So divine right is a sham.

Locke then defines political power:

Political power, then, I take to be a right of making laws, with penalties of death, and consequently all less penalties for the regulating and preserving of property, and of employing force in the community in the execution of such laws, and in the defense of the commonwealth from foreign injury, and all this only for the public good.

Essentially, this is what Americans believe to be the powers of our government. We think the government (and only the government) has the right to make laws, both civil and criminal, and we allow the government to have the authority to use force to execute those laws. We also believe the government should provide for the common defense. And strangely, the most important thing the government does is to protect our property.

John Locke's concept of "property" is essential to understanding the American political and economic framework. Just like Athens, our commitment to private property is at the core of our political and economic beliefs. According to Locke, man is born into **the State of Nature,** and in the State of Nature, we're all essentially equal. Not *exactly* equal, mind you—some people have gifts that others lack—but in general, we're all basically living in a state of equal power and equal agency with one another. In the beginning, before there were governments, you could roam wherever you wanted, take whatever you wanted, and do whatever you pleased.

Now, some would argue that in the State of Nature, every person would simply be out for him or herself. Every individual would take as much as they could, kill indiscriminately, and so on.

Because of this, there would be constant war and struggle. But Locke argues that this isn't the case, because in the State of Nature every man would want to secure every possible advantage for himself. In this environment, every man would only want to receive good from others. People wouldn't go out looking for fights and enemies. They'd want (and need) friends and allies. Consequently, in the State of Nature, we would actually try to do good for others, to the extent it would benefit us.

> *If I cannot but wish to receive good, even as much at every man's hands, as any man can wish unto his soul, how should I look to have any part of my desire herein satisfied, unless myself be careful to study the like desire?*

In this way, the Golden Rule is basically a selfish principle—we "do unto others as we would have done unto us" in the expectation that if we do good to others, we will receive good in return. We share our extra food with others, understanding that there may come a day when we need others to share with us.

Is it really in our interest to destroy one another? Well, look at *Hamlet* and the concept of revenge. If we go out and murder somebody, what happens? We can expect that person's family or friends will try to murder us. Blood will have blood, and once begun, the cycle of vengeance is very difficult to stop. So even in the supposedly anarchic State of Nature, we're not necessarily always fighting one another or stealing from one another. In fact, the opposite may be true: we may have cooperated with one another.

But in the State of Nature, we also have innate notions of justice. If someone comes and steals our stuff, we would have the right to retaliate against that person. If someone tries to kill us, we can kill that person in self-defense—and everyone would naturally understand this.

In the State of Nature, each man is his own judge, jury, and executioner. The problem arises when the "wrong" that is committed is not so clear. In these instances, we need an arbiter, or a *magistrate*, to sort out who's right and who's wrong, and to determine the proper remedy.

Who can serve as such a magistrate? Well, monarchs can never be impartial arbiters, and the exercise of **arbitrary power** is always unnatural:

> *Remember that absolute monarchs are but men; and if government is to be the remedy of those evils which necessarily follow from men being judges in their own cases, and the state of Nature is therefore not to be endured. I desire to know what kind of government that is, and how much better it is than the state of nature, where one man commanding a multitude has the liberty to be judge in his own case, and may do to all his subjects whatever he pleases without the question or control of those who execute his pleasure?*

Moreover, we *always remain* in a State of Nature:

> *But I, moreover, affirm that all men are naturally in that state, and remain so till, by their own consents, they make themselves members of some politic society.*

Government's power does not come from God—it comes from our *consent,* and we grant that consent every second of our existence as citizens. At any moment, we may *withdraw* that consent, thereby rendering the government illegitimate.

But why would we consent in the first place? Why would we give up our freedom to some anonymous government bureaucracy? Well, first we need to understand what *freedom* is.

> *Freedom then, is not what Sir Robert Filmer tells us, "A liberty for every one to do what he lists, and to live as he pleases, and not to be tied by any laws"; but freedom of men under government is to have a standing rule to live by, common to every one of that society, and made by the legislative power erected in it.*

Government does not exist to *restrict* our freedom, but rather to *protect and enlarge* our freedoms. And we do that by agreeing on a common set of laws and rules—rules that everyone, including the magistrates (or even especially the magistrates) live by.

Locke argues that just as we have the natural right of self-defense, we also have a natural right to property. Locke defines property as "the appropriation of something in nature with which an individual mixes their labor."

Think of it this way: let's say a tiny island pops up in the Atlantic Ocean. It's a rocky and useless piece of land. You row a boat to the island, and you plant some apple trees. You nurture the trees for years. You water them, you spread fertilizer down to help them grow, you pull the weeds out. Eventually, the trees begin to produce apples. You—and only you—have a right to that fruit, because it is, quite literally, the fruit of your labor. The fruit would not exist without you. You have combined your labor with the land, and it has produced fruit.

But one day somebody else sails ashore, and they try to steal your fruit. We would all find that to be naturally wrong. *Innately* wrong; it wouldn't matter if this happened long before any government existed. That person didn't work for it. There was no labor involved.

But then again, let's say your trees start to produce too many apples for you to harvest, and a bunch of that fruit simply falls the ground and rots. A starving man sails ashore and begins eating the apples that are going to waste. In this case, we would *not* say you had a right to the apples, because you weren't doing anything with them.

> *As much as any one can make use of to any advantage of life before it spoils, so much he may by his labor fix a property in. Whatever is beyond this is more than his share, and belongs to others. Nothing was made by God for a man to spoil or destroy.*

This problem of surplus leads to a natural system of barter and exchange: therefore, the economy *precedes* government. This is a big, big change, Violet. To a large degree, this simple distinction is what separates the modern period from the premodern period. Aristotle believed it was the other way around; that man was first and foremost a *political animal,* and not an *economic one.* For nearly 2,000 years, the economy was seen as secondary or subservient to the state, and political systems (e.g., monarchies, civic republics) and economic systems (e.g., feudalism, mercantilism) were designed accordingly.

Now that notion is flipped around. Political systems now become secondary to the economy, so the *individual,* not the state, becomes supreme. Class systems would be destroyed, individual rights would emerge, and absolutist states would give way to representative governments that embrace capitalism.

Back to our apple tree. Sure, you've got tons of apples. But you also need other things: shoes, clothes, shelter, and other kinds of food. So you take your surplus fruit and trade it for something else you need, or you sell it for gold or silver. Now that fruit isn't simply wasting on the ground. It has been put to use. You have "stored" its value—not the value of the fruit, but the value of your labor. This is what money is: stored labor. And it's perfectly fine to acquire wealth through your labor.

> *And if he also bartered away plums that would have rotted in a week, for nuts that would last good for his eating a whole year, he did no injury ... and thus came in the use of money; some lasting thing that men might keep without spoiling, and*

that, by mutual consent, men would take in exchange for the truly useful but perishable supports of life.

We grant the state limited powers for the sake of expanding our freedoms, but we never grant it our blind obedience.

It is one thing to owe honor, respect, gratitude, and assistance; another to require absolute obedience and submission.

In fact, when the state overreaches, and demands too much in return for your consent, then you reserve the right to disobey. Actually, Locke would argue, you have a *duty* to disobey. During the Enlightenment, this is what happened to monarchies all across Europe.

In the monarchical system, where there is one divine ruler, everything works pretty well at first. But over time, the monarch's interests diverge dramatically from those of the people. One day an heir emerges who is incompetent, or the monarch abuses his power. When this happens, the people naturally rebel, because they seek competent government, and more importantly, they seek to be free from arbitrary power.

Yet when ambition and luxury, in future ages, would retain and increase the power, without doing the business for which it was given, and aided by flattery, taught princes to have distinct and separate interests from their people, men found it necessary to examine more carefully the original rights of government, and to find out ways to restrain the exorbitances and prevent the abuses of that power ... for there are no examples so frequent in history, both sacred and profane, as those of men withdrawing themselves and their obedience from the jurisdiction they were born under.

The state exists to do three things, and in this order of importance:

1. Defend the property of its citizens
2. Serve as an impartial arbiter in disputes, both criminal and civil, and execute judgments under the law
3. Provide for the common defense

It is granted power to perform these functions *only for the public good*. To the extent the state performs these three functions well, the state guarantees our freedoms; it does not take them away. This is the reason why we agree to surrender our individual sovereignty.

But when the state exceeds its mandate, abuses its powers, or fails in its obligations, then we can withdraw our consent from the state. The questions that we should constantly ask the government are:

1. Am I free from arbitrary, illegitimate power of any kind?
2. Do I trust that my government can be an impartial mediator in disputes?
3. Is my private property secure?

And perhaps most importantly:

4. Is the government using the limited power I have granted it for the public good?

The bloodlust I'd felt immediately following 9/11 was eventually satisfied. When we found Osama bin Laden, we shot him in the face, took his corpse, and dumped it in the ocean while the president told jokes at the White House Correspondent's Dinner. The president then went on national television and celebrated our great accomplishment: after 10 years, two wars, trillions of dollars, tens of thousands dead, the invention of a flying robot army, and the abandonment of our most basic principles, it seemed we were capable of finding and assassinating a single man living in a third world country.

But this did not mean our "War on Terror" was over. The War On Terror replaced the Cold War in many thematic respects, but with two notable distinctions: the War on Terror would presumably last until terror was defeated (i.e., "never"), and it would be an armed conflict against unseen enemies, determined at will, without consent or even notification.

For the duration of this infinite war, we were to be permanently terrified, and at times of high alert, we were to be *really* terrified. (RED ALERT: SOMETHING MIGHT HAPPEN!!!) The United States began torturing people around the globe, imprisoning them indefinitely without charge or trial, and even assassinating them at will. We strapped electrodes to people's genitals. We drowned them, only to revive them, and drown them again. We set attack dogs loose on them. We deprived them of sleep, we stripped them naked, and we defecated on their religious effects. And we glorified this kind of "necessary evil" in our popular culture, where our movie and television heroes assumed the role of patriotic sadist, along with judge, jury, and executioner.

The President of the United States now personally maintained a "kill list," which he reviewed and amended from time to time. If the president decided that a terrorist needed some killing, a robot would be dispatched to shoot a missile at that person. If women and children happened to be around that person when the robot arrived, well—that was considered acceptable collateral damage.

Under presidents of both political parties, an enormous global surveillance system was built. After the Supreme Court ruled certain surveillance activities unconstitutional, the system was not abandoned or curtailed, but rather expanded exponentially, an activity that the Executive kept secret from the people, and even from members of Congress. This surveillance system wasn't just used to monitor our enemies, but also our allies and our own citizens. In secret partnerships with the government, our telecommunications companies built in "back doors" so the government could easily access our phone records, Internet use, financial records, and our social media pages. All of our correspondence was now permanently "warehoused," in case the government needed to access it at a later date. Members of the Executive Branch denied the existence of such programs—even when asked direct questions, under oath, in public hearings before Congress.

We were assured that there were safeguards. The surveillance system was overseen by a secret court, whose rulings, members, and deliberations could never be revealed to the public, or challenged in any public way. We learned new terms, like "extrajudicial killings," "rendition," "enemy combatants," and "enhanced interrogation techniques." These replaced older and more problematic terms, like "assassinations," "indefinite detentions," "prisoners of war," and "torture."

I told you about that strange moment of opportunity and solidarity after 9/11. I now wonder if our leaders realized there was a different opportunity in the wake of 9/11—the same kind of opportunity that Augustus Caesar must've recognized after the terrifying Roman civil wars and the fall of the Roman Republic. In the aftermath of 9/11, the citizens—myself included—were willing to sacrifice everything, including our most precious possession: we were willing to grant our leaders absolute authority to wield arbitrary power.

We were willing to give them our consent.

CHAPTER 21

WHAT'S BEST FOR EVERYONE?

JEAN-JACQUES ROUSSEAU
The Social Contract

I spent my entire childhood in the same house in the small town of Geneva, Illinois. Today, Geneva is just another suburb of Chicago, but when I was a kid, it was still a farm town. Some people commuted to the city, but most people lived and worked in the town. The population was 9,000. There was a Main Street with lots of independently owned shops. When Pizza Hut tried to open a store on Main Street, the Chamber of Commerce nearly revolted, and it wound up in a pole building down by the train tracks.

Every Sunday morning our family would attend mass, where we saw our neighbors, our friends, and the kids I went to school with. The Priest knew all our names. After church, my dad would drive us to Riley's Drug Store, and we'd each get to pick one candy bar. Mr. Riley knew us. The ladies behind the registers knew us. Everybody knew us, and we knew everybody else. And we didn't just know their names—we knew where they lived, where they worked, and what was going on in their lives.

Farming was still very much a part of the town. One mile west was the end of the known universe, until you hit the Quad Cities three hours down I-80. The rest was farmland. We knew farming families, like the Brichers. Julie Bricher used to take care of us when my parents went on vacation, and sometimes we'd go to their farm.

I got my first job working at the local chocolate shop for Bob

Unteidt, who lived in a rented room three blocks from my house. Then I was hired on by Weldon Johnson, who owned Viking Office Supply. On summer break from college, I worked for the Landbergs out in LaFox, Illinois—literally a one-stop-sign town—where I sold farmers' work boots, overalls, and flannel shirts at Potter's General Store. Potter's General Store had existed on that road for 150 years, and the Landberg family had been in Geneva almost as long. There was an ancient photograph of the founder, Lemuel Milk Potter, hanging in the store. Keith Landberg was one of the city councilmen. So was Weldon Johnson. Later, my little league baseball coach, Kevin Burns, became mayor. I knew Kevin Burns. I ate Jell-o mold at his house.

The people who ran Geneva grew up in Geneva. They raised their families in Geneva. They were part of the town. The prominent families of Geneva had been in town for generations or even centuries. And every summer, the whole town celebrated its Swedish founders with a big carnival. Weldon dressed up like a Viking and stood outside his store selling discount pens.

Geneva wasn't just a town—it was a community. When a tragedy happened—when Chris Malone drowned out at the quarry, or Mike Jones was killed while sledding, or Jennifer Keith died of a brain tumor—the *community* felt it, and the community responded. There were small-town intrigues, scandals, and politics, but everyone cared about the community. People looked out for each other, even in the smallest, most subtle ways. When the football team went to State, school was canceled, the stores closed, and everybody got in their car, drove two hours to Herschell, Illinois, and watched the Vikings play. There was a parade. We had lots of parades.

Geneva was maybe the last place I lived where I saw Rousseau's **general will** in effect. And maybe it's the only kind of place where such a thing *could* exist. I miss it.

What is the general will?

Well, it's pretty confusing, Violet.

Man is born free, but everywhere he is in chains. One thinks himself the master of others, and still remains a greater slave

than they. How did this change come about? I do not know.
What can make it legitimate?

Remember Machiavelli's *The Prince*? Some people think that the ruler is the master of others, and they desire to be the ruler for this reason. They want to be the boss or, for the sake of this discussion, the *sovereign*. They think ruling gives one power. But the truth is that the person in charge (the sovereign) is always under greater restrictions than his "subjects." I learned this the hard way: by being in charge myself. I've served as an executive for three different organizations—in effect, I was the sovereign, or, the person in charge. Naïvely, I believed each time that I would have the power to do what I wanted. In reality, it meant the complete opposite.

First of all, I didn't have unlimited resources, but I had endless objectives, so I had to prioritize my objectives—which invariably meant upsetting people. As the executive, I also had legal obligations that I had to meet, and if I did not meet those obligations, I was responsible. I was bound by obligation to keep these companies financially solvent, so I had to spend a great deal of my time simply managing the books. I was bound by cultural and political circumstances. Yes, I had power, but so did others, even those below me. If I disagreed with an effective or popular subordinate, I had to be careful about how I expressed that disagreement, or else that person might leave, which would either mean I would have to do their job, or I would have to hire someone else to do their job—and not always someone better. So even though I was the sovereign, there were many interests to keep happy if I wanted to keep my job. I had to answer to the board, to the funders, to the members, and I also had to answer to the staff. I had an obligation to the people who worked for me. So I was the "master of others," but I was also "a greater slave than they."

My jobs were quite insignificant in the big picture, but I have learned that when you're in charge of anything, you have to be very careful to hold on to *legitimacy*. What is legitimacy? For me, it meant two things: the *freedom to operate*—the freedom to make decisions for the general good of the community or the organization I was leading—and also *the willingness of others to obey*. My decisions had to satisfy all or most of the constituencies I served. I had to keep the staff motivated, so I couldn't overburden them, or pay them too little. They also needed sufficient autonomy to do their jobs. But I had to keep an eye on the budget as well, and make sure that we earned enough money and didn't spend too much. I also had to keep the board engaged and informed, so that they weren't taken by surprise. But I couldn't enroll them *too* much, or else they would paralyze the decision-making process. I had to give the members what they wanted in the short term, but I also had to keep an eye on the long-term good of the organization and the long-term interests of the people we served. Often something that seems good in the short term can be disastrous in the long term, and vice versa.

As a leader, it is extraordinarily difficult to enact unpopular measures, even if those measures are in everyone's best long-term interests. I knew if I lost the support of one or more of these constituencies (the staff, the board, or the members), I would eventually find myself unemployed. I could only exercise authority to the extent that people agreed to follow me. If my "sovereignty" was deemed illegitimate, then what good were my decisions? If I made unreasonable demands of the staff, for example, they'd just stop doing their work. I could fire them, sure, and replace them with other people—but eventually, those people would stop following me as well.

So how does this apply to the *Social Contract?*

Rousseau's basic thrust is that sovereignty is only legitimate when it exercises the general will. And this concept of the general will is very difficult to get your arms around.

Maybe you would argue, "If you're in charge, and you have all the power, then why don't you just *make* people do what you want? Why don't you use force?"

If I took into account only force, and the effects derived from it, I should say: As long as a people is compelled to obey, and obeys, it does well; as soon as it can shake off the yoke, and shakes it off, it does still better.

Force can't legitimize rule. History is full of examples. Persia tried to maintain authority over the Greek colonies through force. Eventually, the colonies rebelled. Rome tried to exercise power over the barbarians by force. Eventually, the barbarians rebelled. The British maintained power over their American colonies by force. Eventually, there was revolution. When the United States tried to maintain sovereignty by force in Iraq and Afghanistan, the result was guerilla war. Force is never a long-term political solution.

The same is true in business. If you try to be autocratic and despotic as a boss, and coerce people through fear, it will probably work for a while. But the moment the oppressed can stab you in the back, or get another job, they'll do it. And besides, power waxes and wanes.

> *The strongest is never strong enough to be always the master, unless he transforms strength into right, and obedience into duty .... To yield to force is an act of necessity, not of will.*

So might *does not* make right. Force can't make a master legitimate. If that's true, then slavery can't work, either. The moment a slave can run away or free themselves, they will.

> *To renounce liberty is to renounce being a man, to surrender the rights of humanity and even its duties.*

Absolute submission to a ruler is impossible, because we can never really surrender our individual morality to anyone.

> *To remove all liberty from his will is to remove all morality from his acts .... I maintain that a slave made in war, or a conquered people, is under no obligation to a master, except to obey him as far as he is compelled to do so.*

Even if one had the ability to conquer the world through force—and some men *have* had this ability—the people they conquer only obey so long as that individual lives.

> *The man in question, even if he has enslaved half the world, is still only an individual; his interest, apart from that of others, is still a purely private interest. If this same man comes to die, his empire, after him, remains scattered and without unity, as an oak falls and dissolves into a heap of ashes when the fire has consumed it.*

Alexander conquered much of the known world—but after his death, his empire eventually dissolved, because it lacked a ruler with his talents. Genghis Khan once ruled over China, Russia, and Arabia—but after his death, the Mongol empire collapsed. People can be conquered, but they can never be enslaved.

What about majority rule? We love that as Americans, right? Well, no, Rousseau says. Majority rule doesn't work either.

How have a hundred men who wish for a master the right to vote on behalf of ten who do not? The law of majority voting is itself something established by convention, and presupposes unanimity, on one occasion at least.

In order for majority rule to be legitimate, we have to agree unanimously that we will follow the will of the majority. That's not a guarantee. (If a hundred people vote to jump off a cliff, and we're in the minority, are we really bound to jump off the cliff?) When we submit to the will of the majority, we are surrendering our own right to make a decision for ourselves. And we have to agree to that *process* without being coerced by illegitimate force.

So we have the dilemma of legitimate governance:

The problem is to find a form of association which will defend and protect with the whole common force the person and goods of each associate, and in which each, while uniting himself with all, may still obey himself alone, and remain as free as before. This is the fundamental problem of which The Social Contract provides the solution ....

Each of us puts his person and all his power in common under the supreme direction of the general will, and in our corporate capacity, we receive each member as an indivisible part of the whole.

In order to make a government legitimate, we surrender our sovereignty to a system that protects and serves our individual interests by advancing the common good.

What man loses by the social contract is his natural liberty and an unlimited right to everything he tries to get and succeeds

in getting; what he gains is civil liberty and the proprietor-
ship of all he possesses.

We all have different interests, and our interests may conflict with
the general will, or with what's best for the community. For example,
I might own a house, and the town might want to put a road through
it. The town may benefit from the road, but I will suffer from the
loss of my house.

So—is it compromise? Well—no. A decision is not legitimate just
because we satisfy the powerful factions on either side.

> *But when factions arise, and partial associations are formed*
> *at the expense of the great association, the will of each of*
> *these associations becomes general in relation to its members,*
> *while it remains particular in relation to the State: it may*
> *then be said that there are no longer as many votes as there*
> *are men, but only as there are associations …. Lastly, when*
> *one of these associations is so great as to prevail over the*
> *rest, the result is no longer the sum of small differences, but a*
> *single difference …. There should be no partial society within*
> *a state … but if there are partial societies, it is best to have as*
> *many as possible and to prevent them from being unequal, as*
> *was done by Solon, Numa, and Servius.*

The general will is a decision that we abide by, even if we do not
benefit personally from it—and even if we suffer in the short term.
We surrender our sovereignty to a community decision, with the
understanding that in the long term, we, too, will prosper.

In Geneva, Illinois, the general will existed. It was not consensus,
compromise, majority rule, or communism. It was something else;
something unique and rare. The community acted as a whole; the
individuals in the community advanced their own interests by helping
each other, and by advancing policies that served the collective good.
Yes, we paid taxes to subsidize the annual Swedish Days festival,
but the Swedish Days festival brought in visitors from all around
the state to our shops and restaurants. We turned down the jobs
Pizza Hut promised, and the lower prices of its product, so that local
pizza places like Alfono's could stay in business. We were willing to
wait 15 more minutes and pay a dollar more for pizza. When our

high school football team went to the playoffs, we closed our schools
and businesses to recognize the accomplishments of members of our
community.

It was by no means a perfect system—certainly some interests
were more powerful than others—but for the most part, it was a
happy, prosperous, and most importantly, a *virtuous* system. Everybody thought they were treated fairly. Everybody knew that if they
had a real problem, they could go to the community and the community would do its best to address it.

But Geneva was a small town. The larger a political entity
becomes (as you go from town, to city, to state, to federation of
states, to empire), the more difficult it becomes to arrive at the general
will. The *common good* becomes harder and harder to determine,
because the interests of the people in Maine are so different from the
interests of people in Arizona. It also becomes increasingly difficult
to achieve shared sacrifice. The individual interests involved become
too disparate, too divided, and they wield increasingly arbitrary
amounts of power.

Historically, no republic has survived rapid growth without
devolving into despotism. Rousseau describes how governments
degrade naturally in this fashion, and Rome is the perfect example.
In Rome, there was once a great republic, but when the republic
became too large, it also became incapable of governing itself
through the development of the general will. There were too many
powerful interests, and they were too disparate to be reconciled.
So the republic devolved into despotism through the "reforms" of
Julius Caesar and Augustus. And then *that* imperial system itself
devolved over time, until the interests of a handful of individuals
took precedence over the interests of millions. And what happened?
The Roman Empire essentially broke up into smaller political entities, which were more capable of legitimate self-rule.

> *The dissolution of the state may come about in either of two
> ways.*
>
> *First, when the prince ceases to administer the State in
> accordance with the laws, and usurps the common power. A
> remarkable change then occurs: not the government, but the
> State, undergoes contraction: I mean that the great State is
> dissolved, and another is formed within it, composed solely*

of the members of the government, which becomes for the rest of the people merely master and tyrant. So that the moment the government usurps the Sovereignty, the social compact is broken, and all private citizens recover by right their natural liberty, and are forced, but not bound, to obey.

The same thing happens when the members of government severally usurp the power they should exercise solely as a body: this is as great an infraction of the laws, and results in even greater disorders. There are then, so to speak, as many princes as there are magistrates, and the State, no less divided than the government, either perishes or changes its form .... If Sparta and Rome perished, what State can hope to endure for ever?

CHAPTER 22

ARE GODS IMMORTAL?

EDWARD GIBBON

The Decline and Fall of the Roman Empire, Chapters 15–16

———◦◦◦———

The Romans were polytheists, which means they worshipped
many gods. They worshipped ideas, they worshipped great
men who had died, and they worshipped a large pantheon of deities,
demigods, and heroes. The Romans were far more tolerant of other
religions than the Greeks had been (and the Greeks themselves were
pretty tolerant), and certainly they were more tolerant of other faiths
than we are today. When the Romans conquered a people, they generally allowed the conquered people to continue to worship as they
pleased, so long as they paid tribute to Rome and observed certain
standard religious holidays and festivals. This was a major factor in
Roman success, because Rome didn't meddle with the cultures of the
territories it annexed. Instead, Rome assimilated those cultures into
the larger culture. Rome was truly the world's first melting pot.

But there were two religions that proved difficult to assimilate:
Judaism and Christianity. Christianity evolved from the Jewish tradition, but it wasn't the same thing. Early Christians (including Jesus
Christ) were Jews. To the Romans, at least in the beginning, Christianity just seemed to be another sect of Judaism, and not really a
distinct religion.

The Romans didn't even want to crucify Jesus. Throughout
the New Testament, Pontius Pilate, the Roman prefect ultimately
responsible for crucifying Jesus, seems confused as to why the mob

wishes to have Jesus put to death. Pilate actually tries repeatedly to free Jesus before submitting to the will of the people. When he finally does consent to execute Jesus, he does so with great reluctance, and he says to the crowd that "he washes his hands" of guilt for the crime. He then is said to have reported to his superiors that he was forced to put an innocent man to death.

This incident sheds a great deal of light on how the Romans treated early Christians. The Romans remained tolerant of Christianity for a century after the death of Jesus. It was only later that the Romans began to persecute Christians inside the empire. By this time, Christianity had spread beyond Jerusalem and into every corner of the Roman Empire. It had become distinct from Judaism, and in fact, it had spread largely thanks to Roman infrastructure, Roman tolerance, and Roman law, which protected people from unfair persecution.

What made Christianity so successful? Edward Gibbon cites five reasons:

> I. The inflexible, and if we may use the expression, intolerant zeal of the Christians, derived, it is true, from the Jewish religion, but purified from the narrow and unsocial spirit which, instead of inviting, had deterred the Gentiles from embracing the law of Moses. II. The doctrine of a future life, improved by every additional circumstance which could give weight and efficacy to that important truth. III. The miraculous powers ascribed to the primitive Church. IV. The pure and austere morals of the Christians. V. The union and discipline of the Christian republic, which gradually formed an independent and increasing state in the heart of the Roman Empire.

Christians were stubborn, and they were entrepreneurial. They believed in one god, and they would not submit to *idolatry*, the worship of other deities. The Jews were also monotheists in a polytheistic world, but there was a key difference: the Jews occupied a state, while the Christians were stateless. For the most part, one was born Jewish—the Jewish people did not aggressively seek converts beyond their borders. Christians sought converts everywhere, and one could become Christian without much trouble at all.

Monotheism was a difficult concept for a polytheistic world to grasp. Today, we take the idea for granted, but the ancient world had been polytheistic for thousands of years. The Romans thought of Jesus Christ as they would any other god, like those worshipped by, say, the Gauls or the Egyptians. There was room to worship Jesus, so long as there was also room to worship Osiris, Jupiter, Minerva, and every other far-flung pagan deity. Just another god. We're lousy with them! But the Christians didn't see it that way. To Christians, you couldn't worship any other god *but* Jesus; to do so was an act of idolatry.

Monotheism had already been practiced by the Jews, and the Romans found this difficult to understand as well. The Jews were willing to die rather than have a statue of Caligula placed in their temple.

> *The mad attempt of Caligula to place his own statue in the temple of Jerusalem was defeated by the unanimous resolution of a people who dreaded death much less than such an idolatrous profanation. Their attachment to the law of Moses was equal to their detestation of foreign religions.*

To the Romans, this seemed insane. They did not (at first) understand the *intolerance* required by monotheism. Neither Jews nor Christians could make exceptions for other deities. And because the Jews made such a stink about it, the Romans largely left them alone inside the borders of Judaea. As long as they paid their taxes, who really cared?

But while Judaism was able to keep its monotheistic traditions inside its borders, it was never equipped to spread its faith *beyond* its borders.

> *The Jewish religion was admirably fitted for defense, but it was never designed for conquest .... [There was] a national god of Israel, and with the most jealous care [he] separated his favorite people from the rest of mankind .... With the other nations they were forbidden to contract any marriages or alliances; and the prohibition of receiving them into the congregation, which in some cases was perpetual, almost always extended to the third, to the seventh, or even the tenth generation .... The descendants of Abraham were flattered*

> *by the opinion that they alone were the heirs of the covenant,
> and they were apprehensive of diminishing the value of their
> inheritance by sharing it too easily with the strangers of the
> earth.*

Christians, on the other hand, were quite different.

> *It became the most sacred duty of a new convert to diffuse
> among his friends and relations the inestimable blessing
> which he had received, and to warn them against a refusal
> that would be severely punished as a criminal disobedience to
> the will of a benevolent but all-powerful Deity.*

Eventually, the Jewish people rebelled against the Romans, and the
Christians had an out—they could reasonably renounce Judaism
and escape Roman persecution.

Now Christianity began to spread across the Roman Empire. But
to Christians, the other gods worshipped across the Roman Empire
could not simply be ignored. They had to be treated as demons. The
worship of Jupiter, Aesculapius, and other gods had to be fought
against vehemently, as these were "false gods" who were tricking
mankind.

This wasn't easy for Christians to do, because polytheism was
woven into the fabric of Roman society the way monotheism is
woven into ours. Religion wasn't simply practiced in temples one
day a week. Religion was involved in every festival, theatrical performance, and every kind of public amusement. Moreover, most religious observances seemed harmless, and in some cases, virtuous.
This led the Christians to retreat from public life, and to form their
own society.

The Christians were in the right place at the right time, because
by this time, religion had become the object of derision in the Roman
upper classes. Paganism had been so diluted and confused that its
overall moral message was often contradictory or incomprehensible,
whereas Christianity offered a clear, simple message.

> *1. The general system of their mythology was unsupported by
> any solid proofs; and the wisest among the pagans had already
> disclaimed its usurped authority. 2. The description of the*

infernal regions had been abandoned to the fancy of painters and poets, who peopled them with so many phantoms and monsters who dispensed their rewards and punishments with so little equity, that a solemn truth, the most congenial to the human heart, was oppressed and disgraced by the absurd mixture of the wildest fictions. 3. The doctrine of a future state was scarcely considered among the devout polytheists of Greece and Rome as a fundamental article of faith.

Christianity also offered something very attractive to an empire in decline: an everlasting reward. There was also a flip side. If you *didn't* accept Christ, you'd be damned forever. And the reckoning was always right around the corner. God's displeasure was evident in every earthquake, plague, fire, and natural disaster that befell the empire.

The calmest and most intrepid skeptic could not refuse to acknowledge that the destruction of the present system of the world by fire by was itself extremely probable .... [People] considered every disaster that happened to the empire as an infallible symbol of an expiring world.

These were rough times for the Roman Empire. By the 2nd century, there had been military setbacks, plagues, fires, and repeated financial crises that nearly caused the empire to collapse. Then, as now, people thought the world was ending.

On top of all this, the Christians boasted miraculous powers.

The Christian Church, from the time of the apostles and their first disciples, has claimed an uninterrupted succession of miraculous powers, the gift of tongues, of vision, and of prophecy, the power of expelling daemons, of healing the sick, and raising the dead.

Unlike the Jews, the Christians didn't make trouble for the empire— at least not at first. While they would not serve in the military or take part in government, they paid their taxes, and their faith demanded that they conduct themselves according to a strict moral code. This meant they didn't steal, they weren't violent, and they didn't lie.

> *The Christians felt and confessed that such institutions might be necessary for the present system of the world, and they cheerfully submitted to the authority of their Pagan governors.*

As people made donations to the church, there came to be a need for administration, so the Christian Church was founded, but this church was different from other temples and orders: it operated very much like a state. The early Church was noble and pure, and it was populated by wise and judicious rulers selected by a virtuous body politic.

> *A regard for the public tranquility, which would be so frequently have been interrupted by annual or by occasional elections, induced the primitive Christians to constitute an honorable and perpetual magistracy, and to choose one of the wisest and most holy among their presbyters to execute, during his life, the duties of their ecclesiastical governor ... [whose duties included] the administration of the sacraments and discipline of the church, the superintendency of religious ceremonies, which imperceptibly increased in number and variety, the consecration of ecclesiastical ministers, to whom the bishop assigned their respective functions, the management of the public fund, and the determination of all such differences as the faithful were unwilling to expose before the tribunal of an idolatrous judge .... Every society formed within itself a separate republic; and although the most distant of these little states maintained a mutual as well as friendly intercourse of letters and deputations, the Christian world was not yet connected by any supreme authority or legislative assembly .... It was soon established that the bishops of the independent churches should meet in the capital of the province at the stated periods of spring and autumn.*

In the beginning, the Christian Church was very much a franchise model, with each franchise having a common mission. People were free to choose their own bishops and manage their affairs locally, but eventually, a larger network began to emerge to govern them. The power of bishops began to grow, even to the point where their power (while completely cultural) exceeded the power of any local government or law, at least within the Christian community.

While the Roman Church remained the most powerful (and would emerge as the Roman Catholic Church), the other franchises were entrepreneurial and expansionist. They sought to increase the number of their followers, and each follower gave a percentage of their earnings to the church. They gave these donations in the form of cash, because that's the only kind of gift the Romans allowed.

> These oblations, for the most part, were made in money; nor was the society of Christians either desirous or capable of acquiring, to any considerable degree, the encumbrance of landed property. It had been provided by several laws, which were enacted with the same design as our statutes of mortmain, that no real estates should be given or bequeathed to any corporate body without either a special privilege or a particular dispensation from the senate; who were seldom disposed to grant them in favor of a sect, at first the object of their contempt, and at last of their fears and jealousy.

As a result, the Church began to amass huge amounts of liquid cash. And while some bishops abused this sudden windfall, for the most part, the Church acted honorably and wisely with the money. The Christians even started using their resources to help the poor. The Church became an instrument of public welfare unlike any the world had ever seen.

> The whole remainder was the sacred patrimony of the poor. According to the discretion of the bishop, it was distributed to support widows and orphans, the lame, the sick, and the aged of the community .... Such an institution, which paid less regard to the merit than to the distress of the object, very materially conduced to the progress of Christianity.

The citizens of the Roman Empire may simply have been ready for a new religious system, and Christianity fit the bill nicely. The pagan religion was weak, incoherent, and not rigorously defended—but people may simply have an innate desire to believe in something bigger than themselves.

> *The practice of superstition is so congenial to the multitude that, if they are forcibly awakened, they still regret the loss of their pleasing vision. Their love of the marvelous and super-natural, their curiosity with regard to future events, and their strong propensity to extend their hopes and fears beyond the limits of the visible world, were the principal causes which favored the establishment of Polytheism. So urgent on the vulgar is the necessity of believing, that the fall of any system of mythology will most probably be succeeded by the intro-duction of some other mode of superstition.*

Christian texts were translated into Latin, and this common language allowed the Gospel to spread all over the empire. And for a long time, Rome allowed this to happen. By the time they tried to stop it, it was too late.

The ancient world was tolerant of other traditions and religions, but that tolerance had its limits. Rome allowed other religions, but Rome expected that the other religions would also tolerate Roman religious customs. Jews and Christians removed themselves from Roman life, and then they condemned it. In the case of the Jews, this could be managed, because the Jews had their own state. When the Jews broke out in open rebellion against Roman rule, the Romans sent the army in and crushed the rebellion. There were known proce-dures and responses to the rebellion of a rogue province.

But in the case of the Christians, it became far more problematic, because the Christians did *not* have a state. They were everywhere in the Roman Empire. Moreover, Christians shrouded themselves in secrecy, so rumors sprang up about their customs. It was rumored, for example, that Christians drank blood and murdered babies.

> *Malice and prejudice concurred in representing the Chris-tians as a society of atheists, who, by the most daring attack on the religious constitution of the empire, had merited the severest animadversion of the civil magistrate. They had separated themselves (they gloried in the confession) from*

*every mode of superstition which was received in any part
of the globe by the various temper of Polytheism: but it was
not altogether evident what deity, or what form of worship,
they had substituted to the gods and temples of antiquity ....
The pious disobedience of the Christians made their conduct,
or perhaps their designs, appear in a much more serious and
criminal light; and the Roman princes, who might perhaps
have suffered themselves to be disarmed by a ready submission, deeming their honor concerned in the execution of their
commands, sometimes attempted, by rigorous punishments,
to subdue this independent spirit, which boldly acknowl-
edged an authority superior to that of the magistrate.*

Then, in the tenth year of the reign of the Roman Emperor Nero,
a great fire broke out in Rome, and most of the city was destroyed.
Today, the famous story is that Nero "fiddled" while Rome burned
to the ground, but in fact, Nero took extraordinary steps to alleviate
the suffering of the Romans. The imperial gardens were opened up,
temporary shelters were erected, and the government distributed
heavily discounted grain and water to people. But Nero was so hated
by the Romans that they suspected he had deliberately started the
fire. Nero needed a convenient scapegoat, and he found one in the
Christians. He had Christians rounded up, tortured, and killed.

*Some were nailed on crosses; others sewn up in the skins of
wild beasts, and exposed to the fury of dogs; others again,
smeared over with combustible materials, were used as
torches to illuminate the darkness of night.*

Unfortunately for Nero, this strategy backfired. Instead of rousing
public hatred for Christians, people were disgusted by it. It aroused
public sympathy, and people felt that the Christians had been
punished unjustly simply for practicing their faith.

A new policy of tolerance was again instituted. The emperor
Trajan established rules that made it difficult to prosecute people
for being Christian. And then the emperors Hadrian and Antoninus
Pius continued (and increased) Roman tolerance for Christians.
There was still prejudice against Christians, but the official state
didn't do much about it.

It is certain ... that the greatest part of those magistrates who exercised in the provinces the authority of the emperor or the senate, and to whose hands alone the jurisdiction of life and death was entrusted, behaved like men of polished manners and liberal education, who respected the rules of justice, and who were conversant with the precepts of philosophy. They frequently declined the task of persecution, dismissed the charge with contempt, or suggested to the accused Christian some legal evasion by which he might elude the severity of the laws.

Eventually, intolerance would rear its head again, but when it did, the Romans would encounter a very serious problem. The Christians began to *embrace* martyrdom as a way to reach heaven. To Christians, martyrdom was the best thing that could possibly happen. One Christian, Ignatius, proclaimed that if the Romans sentenced him to death, he would provoke the executioner or the wild beasts sent to kill him, in order that he could achieve martyrdom more quickly.

Then came the reign of Diocletian, who was prompted to stamp out the Christians by a man named Galerius. Galerius hated the Christians, and viewed them as a threat to Roman values. Galerius proposed that those who did not offer sacrifice to Rome be burned alive, and that all Christian churches be leveled to the ground. All Christian texts were to be burned.

By the same edict, the property of the church was at once confiscated; and the several parts of which it might consist were either sold to the highest bidder, united to the Imperial domain, bestowed on the cities and corporations, or granted to the solicitations of rapacious courtiers.

Special laws were set up to prosecute Christians, who were tortured and killed in every conceivable way. This was a public relations disaster. Roman bureaucrats balked at enforcing these kinds of horrific policies. Many rulers of Roman provinces—now made up largely of Christians—found these edicts difficult, impossible, or dangerous to carry out. And once again, the Christians bore their suffering in an exemplary fashion.

Galerius eventually reversed his own order, but took the extraordinary measure of explaining himself:

Among the important cares which have occupied our mind for the utility and preservation of the empire, it was our intention to correct and reestablish all things according to the ancient laws and public discipline of the Romans. We were particularly desirous of reclaiming into the way of reason and nature the deluded Christians who had renounced the religion and ceremonies instituted by their fathers, and presumptuously despising the practice of antiquity, had invented extravagant laws and opinions according to the dictates of their fancy, and had collected a various society from the different provinces of our empire.

By then, the Christians were so pervasive and so culturally powerful that when Constantine came to power, he not only instituted a national policy of tolerance, he adopted Christianity as the official religion of Rome. From that day forward, the power of the Church only grew and grew.

The pagan system that preceded Christianity in the West was once equally powerful and prevalent in the social fabric. But at some point, it became degraded to the point of uselessness, and it stopped providing everyone with basic moral ground rules. Judaism and Christianity, for all their faults, informed the political fabric with new values, which had, at least in part, been forged in response to the excesses of the global superpower that was the Roman Empire. The expansionist Church, open to new converts and even some new ideas, spread those values right under the nose of the Romans, until at last, the new values supplanted the old ones.

A new system came along that offered this promise: "Here are the fundamental ground rules *of life*, on which all other *political* rules should follow." New political models and systems had to be created, and new concepts such as "natural rights" followed. And these inventions would evolve into our modern political and economic way of life—all of which find their moral underpinnings in the Mosaic and Christian traditions. As Paganism corroded as a viable belief system, so too did the political and economic models informed by the pagan values.

The point is that religions are impermanent, Violet. Human history is littered with dead gods, and if we trust history, then Christianity will eventually be replaced by another belief system. When the Christian system becomes too corrupt, diluted, or illegitimate, a new belief system will be introduced, and that event will require the collapse or substantial reform of our social, political, and economic models.

Gibbon had some cautionary words for the legitimacy of the Church in subsequent centuries:

> *We shall conclude this chapter by a melancholy truth which obtrudes itself on the reluctant mind .... It must still be acknowledged that the Christians, in the course of their intestine dissensions, have inflicted far greater severities on each other than they had experienced from the zeal of infidels .... The church of Rome defended by violence the empire which she had acquired by fraud; a system of peace and benevolence was soon disgraced by the proscriptions, wars, massacres, and the institution of the holy office.*

CHAPTER 23

WHAT ARE "AMERICAN VALUES"?

VARIOUS, INCLUDING THOMAS JEFFERSON
AND BENJAMIN FRANKLIN,
The Declaration of Independence

———◆◆◆◆■———

When you were two years old you saw *Superman: The Movie* for the first time. You were blown away. After you saw it, you made me rewind "the Lois part" over and over again, so you could watch Superman fly. In that scene, before they take off, Lois Lane interviews Superman, and she asks him why he's here.

"I'm here to fight for Truth, Justice, and the American Way," he says.

Lois Lane, the cynical reporter from the big city, laughs at him. She says every elected official in the country will be after him. Superman replies, "You can't really mean that, Miss Lane," and then, in an oddly earnest moment in an otherwise corny movie, Superman looks at Lois and insists, "I never lie."

I loved Superman when I was a little kid, and I loved that you loved him, too. Your mom thinks I pushed him on you, but I didn't. You discovered Superman all by yourself. You wanted a cape and a supersuit, and you wanted to dress up like Superman for Halloween. And when you put on your costume, you put your hands up like you could fly. There are millions of other kids around the world, Halloween or not, who do the same thing. I did it when I was a kid.

But pause and consider the story of Superman.

Superman starts his life as an immigrant with a funny name ("Kal-El"). He grows up on a farm, raised by ordinary, poor people.

In adolescence, he wonders about his roots, so he spends years in solitary contemplation, studying the classics of his ancestors, the rulers of a vanished ancient civilization. Having reached adulthood, possessed of agrarian values and a reverential understanding of the antique past, he moves to the city, where he becomes a member of the free press. It is here, as an adult, that he first becomes Superman, wearing the garments of his long-dead ancestors.

Superman is now immensely powerful, and he can do literally anything he wants. He can abandon mankind to its own fate and spend his life in the Fortress of Solitude. He can rule the world by force. But instead, he protects the weak and punishes transgressors of the law. He lives a humble life devoted to some very basic, core principles: he fights for truth, justice, and the American Way. Superman helps, but even with his ridiculous might, he obeys the law.

What makes Superman unique is not his limitless power, but rather his remarkable restraint.

Superman is the personification of the America the founding fathers wanted for you, Violet: learned, humble, strong, and absolutely committed to principles. The next few readings deal directly with being an American. And as an American, Violet, you are one of 400 million Supermen in the world. Like Superman, you have accidentally grown up in a unique environment that grants you immense powers and privileges. Consider what you get just for showing up:

1. The most powerful military force ever assembled in the history of mankind.
2. A set of basic rights that (theoretically) cannot be revoked by the government.
3. Access to clean water, public education, and a social safety net
4. A generous life expectancy
5. Access to a powerful system of redress
6. An efficient, intercontinental transportation network
7. One language and currency that carries you from one ocean to another
8. Freedom from invasion and foreign occupation
9. A robust and highly influential cultural infrastructure

10. A dynamic, innovative private sector
11. Social mobility, or at least the freedom to move between classes

What's even more astounding is that the founding fathers believed that all this was possible. They understood the unique promise of America, and they could see far into the future to imagine a very powerful country, unique among nations, as it was founded not by conquest, but by mutual agreement on a core set of principles. This is the idea of **American Exceptionalism**. We are different from other nations, because we are the first nation to be founded on a set of shared principles.

There were plenty of reasons to think the founders were nuts. When they saw all this in the distant future, the colonies were in chaos. There were no "United States." At best, you might call them a loose confederation of British provinces, but they certainly weren't united. Most of them didn't even want to leave the British Empire. Some of them disliked each other. And what was so bad about the British? Sure, they taxed you, but on the other hand, they protected you, they gave you access to the world's markets, and if you just kept your mouth shut and paid your bill, they'd mostly leave you alone.

What idiot would pick a fight with the British Empire? England wasn't exactly a third-rate power in the late 18th century. It was huge and powerful, as dominant in the world as we are today. Wasn't it good to be on their side? The colonies didn't even have an army, let alone a navy. The "country" had no money. There was no way to raise money in any collective fashion. Even if it could raise money, nobody would ever agree on how to spend it, or who should spend it. There was no central political system. It was a mess. So the people who wanted to rebel didn't just have the British to worry about. They had to convince the people living in America.

The Declaration of Independence is a reasoned argument, and its audience is not just the British, but the colonists as well. Today when we use the word *argument*, we imbue it with a lot of negative baggage. But to Enlightenment thinkers like the founders of our country, schooled in classical rhetoric, there was nothing negative about an argument.

When, in the course of human events, it becomes necessary for one people to dissolve the political bonds which have connected them with another, and to assume among the powers of the earth, the separate and equal station to which the laws of nature and of nature's God entitle them, a decent respect to the opinions of mankind requires that they should declare the causes which impel them to the separation.

The Declaration of Independence did not create new laws or operate from a presumption of a law superior to England's—it is grounded quite specifically in *English* Law. The authors make a very large argument, supported by the writings of thinkers like John Locke. Then they use England's own law to indict England. They start out by stating that all men are endowed with certain rights:

We hold these truths to be self-evident, that all men are created equal; that they are endowed by their Creator with certain unalienable rights; that among these are life, liberty, and the pursuit of happiness. That, to secure these rights, governments are instituted among men, deriving their just powers from the consent of the governed; that, whenever any form of government becomes destructive of those ends, it is the right of the people to alter or abolish it, and to institute a new government, laying its foundation on such principles, and organizing its powers in such form, as to them shall seem most likely to effect their safety and their happiness. Prudence, indeed, will dictate that governments long established should not be changed for light and transient causes; and accordingly, all experience hath shown, that mankind are more disposed to suffer, while evils are sufferable, than to right themselves by abolishing the forms to which they are accustomed. But, when a long train of abuses and usurpations, pursuing invariably the same object, evinces a design to reduce them under absolute despotism, it is their right, it is their duty, to throw off such government, and to provide new guards for their future security.

Straight out of John Locke: governments exist solely through the consent of the governed. Governments exist to expand the freedoms of individuals, not abuse them. And when governments fail to protect the rights of their citizens, then it is not just the right, but the obligation of the governed to withdraw their consent, and to set up new governments.

Most of the Declaration of Independence is a catalog of the abuses suffered by the colonies under English rule, but it not a random list of gripes and complaints. The grievances described in the Declaration of Independence were complaints about violations of existing English Law. The founders were not proposing a radical new law, or appealing to some "higher law" or philosophical principle. They provide concrete examples of how the King has repeatedly overstepped his authority under the existing rules of government set forth by parliament.

> He has refused to assent to laws the most wholesome and necessary for the public good. ...
>
> He has dissolved representative houses repeatedly, for opposing, with manly fairness, his invasions on the rights of the people. ...
>
> He has obstructed the administration of justice, by refusing his assent to laws establishing for judiciary powers. ...
>
> He has kept among us, in times of peace, standing armies, without the consent of our legislatures. ...
>
> He has combined, with others, to subject us to a jurisdiction foreign to our Constitution, and unacknowledged by our laws; giving his assent to their acts of pretended legislation:
>
> For quartering large bodies of armed troops among us:
>
> For protecting them by a mock trial, from punishment, for any murders they should commit on the inhabitants of these States:
>
> For cutting off our trade with parts of the world:
>
> For imposing taxes on us without our consent:
>
> For depriving us, in many cases, the benefit of a trial by jury:
>
> For transporting us beyond seas to be tried for pretended offenses. ....

All of these actions were supposed to be illegal. The framers were showing their fellow citizens that the English were not living up to their end of the bargain. Then they remind their audience that solutions have repeatedly been sought inside the system. But all their inquiries have been ignored. So what other conclusion can then be reached but the one they give us?

> *We, therefore, the representatives of the United States of America, in general Congress assembled, appealing to the Supreme Judge of the world for the rectitude of our intentions, do, in the name, and by the authority of the good people of these colonies, solemnly publish and declare, that these united colonies are, and of right ought to be, free and independent states; that they are absolved from all allegiance to the British Crown, and that all political connection between them and the state of Great Britain is, and ought to be, totally dissolved; and that, as free and independent states, they have full power to levy war, conclude peace, contract alliances, establish commerce, and to do all other acts and things which independent states may of right do. And, for support of this declaration, with a firm reliance on the protection of Divine Providence, we mutually pledge to each other our lives, our fortunes, and our sacred honor.*

The Declaration of Independence is the first great statement of American principles, but it reiterates principles that were already celebrated by the British. It sets the line of what we will not tolerate as a people. It was composed by men who spent their childhoods working the soil, their adolescence studying the great works of antiquity, and their adulthoods fighting for justice. It is a document written by Supermen—men who understood nature, humility, reason, and history.

The principles set forth by these men—here, and also in the Constitution and the *Federalist Papers*—are the true wellsprings of American power, Violet. America is not powerful because we have a big army, or because we have a lot of money, or because we have the best universities in the world. We are powerful because our principles enable us to have those things.

Abandon the principles, and we are not exceptional at all.

CHAPTER 24

YOUR RIGHTS*

*SUBJECT TO CHANGE AT ANY TIME.

VARIOUS
The Constitution of the United States

———=>◦◦◦<=———

When the Roman civil wars finally concluded and Augustus
Caesar essentially assumed absolute power as a dictator,
the average Roman citizen was unaware that they were now living
under a tyranny. Inside the Roman Empire, things looked basically
the same as they always had. There was still a senate and a judicial system. Augustus was not even called emperor. He rejected any
title that smacked of tyranny or monarchy, and finally he "humbly"
allowed to be called *princeps,* or "first citizen." This is where we get
the word *prince.*

But despite the appearance of a free republic, Rome was now a
tyranny under the absolute control of Augustus Caesar. If there was
debate in the senate, the outcome was preordained. Augustus determined the composition of the senate. He also controlled the army,
the treasury, the courts of law, and everything else.

Tyranny may have come to Rome, but it didn't look like you'd
expect. In the first century of empire, life was fantastic. The standard of living for the average Roman improved dramatically. Life
was better than it had ever been under the Republic, and it was
certainly better than it had been during the civil wars. Rome entered
its Golden Age, during which time the huge geographic area under
Roman dominion experienced unprecedented peace and prosperity.
In fact, for the average person, life would not be this good again for

thousands of years. It was not until the middle of the 20th century that the living standards of the average American rivaled those of the average Roman citizen living under imperial rule.

Of course, over time, people became aware that things were different. Augustus didn't seem to go away as other elected officials had. He remained in power for 40 years, after which he handed power to his son, Tiberius, who reigned for another 20 years.

On his deathbed, Augustus was said to remark, "Have I played my part well?" He could've meant any number of things, but he may have meant that he'd discovered the proper fiction that would satisfy the republic-loving Romans. Unlike Julius Caesar, Augustus didn't seek the trappings of a monarch. He didn't live extravagantly. He didn't have mistresses all over town, he didn't live in a golden palace, and he definitely didn't want anyone calling him king. He lived a simple life. He might've been the most boring dictator in history.

But he was definitely a dictator, and so were those who followed him for the next 400 years. Some of those dictators, like Trajan, Hadrian, and Marcus Aurelius, were benevolent and competent. Some were fools or figureheads. Some were insane. Some died in office, and others were "removed from power" by various means.

The Roman Republic had expanded for centuries until its transition to empire under Augustus Caesar, after which the Roman Empire entered five centuries of gradual decline, during which the people were entertained by the occasional military coup, assassination, or family betrayal. But before that, life was good. Why rock the boat?

Like the Roman Republic, the American republic began with the expulsion of a king. The last king of Rome had been Tarquin, and the last king of America was King George III. The American colonies revolted against imperial domination by Great Britain. Having won their freedom, the independent colonies united under a fierce commitment to republican values of shared power, civil rights, and limited government. They created a covenant with each other to cement their union; we know that covenant as the Constitution of the United States.

The Constitution did not create a democracy. It created a

republic. And in a republic, the people do not have direct control of the government. Even the most democratic component of the US system of governance—the House of Representatives—is not a truly democratic institution. The House is composed of elected representatives who must be reelected every two years. That was as far as the framers were willing to go in terms of democracy. The people do not actually elect the president (the Electoral College does that). In the original Constitution, the people did not even elect their own senators (state legislators did that). Even today, the American people do not select members of the Supreme Court, the most aristocratic element of our governance structure, in which nine individuals, appointed for life and essentially accountable to no one, are granted absolute authority to interpret the law.

So you don't live in a democracy, Violet. You live in a republic. You live in a system of governance built upon the notion that some people are better suited to govern than others. And make no mistake: the men who founded this country absolutely believed that this was true. They believed some men were better than other men. They were not democratic, but almost universally *aristocratic*. They did *not* believe that "all men were created equal," in the sense that we mean "equal" today. They meant that *white, propertied* men should all be equal *under the law*. Even within this narrow group, they didn't think all men were possessed of the same abilities, intelligence, or character. They didn't mean women. They *certainly* didn't mean the growing slave population in the United States. Many of the men who authored this document owned slaves. Some of the most famous "founding fathers," like Thomas Jefferson, fathered children with their slaves. The men who wrote the Constitution were terrified of "the common people," and (they believed) with good reason. To them, the model government of classical antiquity was not ancient Athens (a true democracy) but ancient Sparta, which was a republic with a mixed regime. Ancient Athens was easily co-opted by demagogues like Alcibiades, who convinced the masses that war and empire were in the best interest of the Athenian state. And democratic Athens was not a peaceful state. It expanded its empire unapologetically through force. At its zenith, the Athenian democracy believed in the dictum "Might makes right," most famously articulated at Melos, where an Athenian general remarked, "The strong take what they can, and the weak suffer what they must."

The framers of the Constitution did not desire an imperial destiny for America. They did not want America to become Athens, Rome, or Great Britain. George Washington, who presided over the Constitutional Convention, famously warned the country against foreign entanglements. (He also warned against political parties and debt—oops!)

The American governance system is a mixed regime, incorporating the best elements of aristocracy (rule by the best), democracy (rule by the most), and monarchy (rule by the one)—but also checking the dark tendencies of each: oligarchy (rule by the few), timocracy (rule by the rich), and tyranny (rule by the one). In this respect, the Constitution is yet another footnote to Plato, who described all these forms and problems in *Republic*.

In order to achieve that balance, the framers made an effort to empower each branch sufficiently to check the other two. They defined them in the following order:

The Legislative Branch is defined in Article I of the Constitution. It is made up of two houses of government: the House of Representatives and the Senate.

The House of Representatives is the most democratic portion of our government. In order to serve as a representative in the House of Representatives, you have to be 25, you have to have been a citizen of the United States for seven years, and you have to reside in the state where you are elected. If elected, you serve for only two years. The authors of the Constitution did this on purpose, in part to weaken the democratic element. The idea was that representatives would constantly have to answer to their constituents, and that people who were too extreme would quickly find themselves out of office. The winds would change frequently. The House is the largest legislative body, and the representation of the house is based on each state's population.

The primary power of the House is financial. We refer to it as "the power of the purse." All spending bills must originate in the House. The House also has the sole power to begin impeachment proceedings against the President of the United States. Importantly, the House may decide to impeach the president, but they don't get to vote on removing the president—that power rests with the Senate.

Originally, the Senate was designed as a purely aristocratic body. There are two senators for each state (regardless of the population).

In order to be a senator, you have to be 30 years old, you have to have been a citizen for nine years, and you have to be an inhabitant of the state where you are elected. If you are elected senator, you serve for six years. The idea behind this was that senators would *not* be answerable to the changing whims of the people, so they would be free to make prudent judgments without fear of immediate reprisal.

The Senate can propose legislation, and it can amend spending bills passed in the House. The Senate must consent to the president's nominees for the Supreme Court, ambassadorships, and other offices.

Together, the House and Senate make up the **Congress,** which has the following joint powers:

- Declare war
- Propose all legislation
- Approve all taxes
- Borrow money
- Remove the president from office (with a two-thirds majority of the Senate)
- Police its own members
- Override a presidential veto (with a two-thirds majority in each house)
- Regulate commerce
- Establish procedures for becoming a citizen
- Coin money
- Establish post offices
- Promote the progress of science and useful arts by providing copyright and patent protection
- Raise and support armies
- Provide and maintain a navy

There are also things Congress *cannot* do:

> *The privilege of the writ of habeas corpus shall not be suspended, unless when in cases of rebellion or invasion the public safety may require it.*

This means the Congress can't detain you without formal charges.

No bill of attainder or ex post facto law shall be passed.

This means that the Congress can't deny someone a trial (bill of attainder), and it can't pass a law that can be retroactively (ex post facto) enforced. So if you do something the Congress doesn't like, they can't just throw you in the clink without a trial. If the Congress then outlaws whatever it is that you did, then they can't then go back and charge you for your old crime under the new law.

No capitation or other direct tax shall be laid, unless in proportion to the census or enumeration hereinbefore directed to be taken.

This says the Congress can't impose a federal income tax. A lot of the people who argued against the Constitution were terrified that the federal government would impose an income tax. "Never fear!" said the Constitution's proponents. "It ain't never gonna happen." It happened. The Sixteenth Amendment overturned this part of the Constitution, and granted powers to Congress to levy income taxes.

The Constitution was written because the initial governing document of the colonies—the Articles of Confederation—was clearly flawed. The most glaring problem with the Articles of Confederation was the lack of an Executive, or a guiding intelligence that could go out and get things done. Large groups of people are not capable of *executing.* They are capable of laying out principles and policies, but they are terrible at practical governance.

So Article II of the Constitution lays out the powers of the **Executive Branch**, which incorporates monarchical elements into the system. For obvious reasons, the men who wrote the Constitution were terrified of monarchy, and they wanted to make sure that Congress was more powerful than the chief executive.

In order to become President of the United States, you must be a natural-born citizen of the United States, you must have resided in the country for 14 years, and you must be 35 years old. The president serves a term of four years. Before accepting the term, the president must take the following oath:

I do solemnly swear (or affirm) that I will faithfully execute the office of President of the United States, and will to the best of my ability preserve, protect, and defend the Constitution of the United States.

The president is commander in chief of the Army and Navy. He can make treaties, provided that two-thirds of the Senate agrees. He (the president is referred to as "he" in the Constitution) appoints judges to the Supreme Court, and every so often he is to provide a speech to Congress in which he assesses the state of the union and makes recommendations to Congress. He can convene both houses of Congress in extraordinary times. He can veto legislation passed by Congress, and the veto can only be overridden by a two-thirds vote in both houses. He can be removed from office for "treason, bribery, or other high crimes and misdemeanors," which basically means he can be removed for any reason the Congress wants, provided that two-thirds of the Senate votes to impeach him.

The president is not elected by the people. Article II sets up the elaborate system of the electoral college, which is a complicated scheme whereby electors from each state assign votes to the candidates based on the popular vote. These electors can, however, follow their own conscience, and act against the will of the people. It hasn't happened, but it could.

Article III of the Constitution is the shortest section, and it lays out the powers of the **Judicial Branch.** This is the most aristocratic element of the Constitution, because judges may be appointed essentially for lifetime terms, and they are given wide latitude to interpret the law as they see fit. They can be impeached, but the process is very difficult. The House may impeach a Supreme Court justice for high crimes, and then the Senate must vote by a two-thirds majority to remove the judge. The Judicial Branch is hampered by the fact that it has no money of its own, nor does it have an army at its disposal.

The Constitution is difficult to amend. It's only been amended 27 times, and 10 of those amendments were ratified immediately after the body of the Constitution was passed. We know the first 10 amendments as the **Bill of Rights;** these amendments are supposed to greatly restrict the power of the federal government. The architects of the Bill of Rights imagined abuses the government might impose on citizens. In general, the remaining amendments were passed after unforeseen abuses had occurred.

The First Amendment is perhaps the most famous:

Congress shall make no law respecting an establishment of religion, or prohibiting the free exercise thereof; or abridging the freedom of speech, or of the press; or the right of the people peaceably to assemble, and to petition the Government for a redress of grievances.

The Second Amendment says that Congress cannot prevent people from owning weapons. Some people think it means that this freedom is unlimited, while others believe that the clause was referring to "well regulated militias" only. The meaning of this clause is hotly debated today.

A well regulated militia being necessary to the security of a free state, the right of the people to keep and bear arms shall not be infringed.

The Third Amendment says that soldiers can't occupy homes during times of peace. This was a common practice under British rule.

The Fourth Amendment says that people can't be subject to unreasonable searches and seizure. The police can't just go through your stuff without probable cause.

The right of the people to be secure in their persons, houses, papers, and effects, against unreasonable searches and seizures, shall not be violated, and no Warrants shall issue, but upon probable cause, supported by Oath or affirmation, and particularly describing the place to be searched, and the persons or things to be seized.

The Fifth Amendment says you can't be tried twice for the same crime. (This is known as *double jeopardy*.)

The Sixth Amendment says that you have a right to a speedy and public trial, by an impartial jury of the state and district where the crime was committed. In theory, people can't be hauled off and held indefinitely without being tried.

In all criminal prosecutions, the accused shall enjoy the right to a speedy and public trial, by an impartial jury of the State and district wherein the crime shall have been committed, which district shall have been previously ascertained by law, and to be informed of the nature and cause of the accusation; to be confronted with the witnesses against him; to have compulsory process for obtaining witnesses in his favor, and to have the Assistance of Counsel for his defense.

The Seventh Amendment says you have the right to a jury trial "in cases where the value of the controversy exceeds twenty dollars."

The Eighth Amendment says that courts cannot make you pay excessive bail, and that you can't be subject to cruel or unusual punishments.

Excessive bail shall not be required, nor excessive fines imposed, nor cruel or unusual punishments inflicted.

The Ninth Amendment says that just because the Constitution may have laid out certain rights of the people doesn't mean that people don't have a particular right if it's not in the Constitution.

The enumeration in the Constitution, of certain rights, shall not be construed to deny or disparage others retained by the people.

The Tenth Amendment says that any powers not expressly delegated to the United States by the Constitution are reserved to the states themselves. For example, in most cases, murder is a state crime, not a federal crime, and states may punish offenders according to their own law.

So, along with the other 17 amendments, which attempt to address various inequities and problems, technically, these are your "rights."

But you don't have a right to your rights, Violet. The Constitution includes one giant asterisk: *none of this applies during wartime.* During wartime, your rights can be suspended indefinitely. You can be imprisoned for life without trial. Your property can be seized without recourse. Even if you're not charged with or even suspected of a crime, the government can read your private correspondence, monitor your phone calls, catalog your political views, and keep track of your financial transactions. The president can even decide to torture or kill you. And, in fact, we know that our government has done all these things—but only during wartime, of course.

Surprise! Officially or unofficially, America has basically been in a perpetual state of war for the last 75 years. Since 1941, when we entered World War II, the United States has been engaged in the following conflicts, among others:

1941–1945	World War II
1947–1991	Cold War
1950–1953	Korean War
1961	Cuban Invasion (Bay of Pigs)
1962	Defense of Thailand
1955–1975	Vietnam War
1965	Invasion of the Dominican Republic
1982	Lebanon deployment
1983	Invasion of Grenada
1983-1989	Honduras
1986	Libyan missile strikes
1990–1991	Persian Gulf War
1993–1995	Bosnian War / Somalia / Haiti
2002–2014	Afghan War
2003–2011	Iraq War
2001–?	"War on Terror"
2015-	President seeks war powers to combat ISIS

You were born during wartime, and as I write this, five years later, you have never known peacetime. I myself have only lived through a brief period of something resembling peacetime, between 1995 and 2001. Since the bombing of Pearl Harbor in 1941, The United States has been at war for 48 of 74 years, or roughly 65 percent of the time. If you count the Cold War, we've been at war for 65 of the last 74 years (90 percent). Since 2001, we've been at war 100% of the time. It's been nearly 15 years now, with no end in sight. World War II lasted as long as high school. The War On Terror has already endured for a generation. Like the Roman and British Empires before it, the United States always seems to find a new war to wage.

Politicians may insist that we're a peaceful nation. Empirically, that is simply not true. The United States has spent most of the last century engaged in armed conflict, and like previous empires, what distinguishes us is our ability and willingness to project over-whelming force to achieve our political objectives. (Because, as the Prussian strategist Clausewitz wrote, "War is the continuation of politics by other means.") The United States maintains the largest military force on the planet. This force dominates the land, the sea, the skies, and even space. Our nation was founded in war, took control of the continent through force, was unified after a civil war, and became an international empire through global conflict. And like Rome, military service in America is a well-trodden path to political power.

Remember when that Roman citizen pleaded with Caesar not to empty the treasury to satiate his army?

Caesar replied that arms and laws each had their own time; "If what I do displeases you, leave the place; war allows no free talking. When I have laid down my arms, and made peace, come back and make what speeches you please. And this I will tell you in diminution of my own just right, as indeed you and all others who have appeared against me and are now in my power may be treated as I please.

I was born during the Vietnam War, and I grew up during the Cold War. You were born during the wars in Iraq and Afghanistan, and you will grow up during the War on Terror. We were born 35 years apart, and yet you and I both heard the same things as children. *There's a strange and foreign enemy who will one day nuke you without warning. They are bad and godless slaves of oppressive ideologies, and their leaders hate you because you are good and free. If we don't stop them, the entire world will quickly be radical-ized against us. You must surrender some of your rights so that we may protect you from this menace.* The odds are very good that we'll be at war when you read this in 2028, and that your children will also be born during wartime. So it goes.

So, yes, there is a Constitution, and it says lots of nice things about your rights, Violet.

And 2,000 years ago, when a Roman citizen's rights were violated, they, too could write a senator or seek redress from the courts. But remember Augustus Caesar's last words, Violet:

"Have I played my part well?"

CHAPTER 25

IS GREED GOOD?

ADAM SMITH

An Inquiry into the Nature and Causes of the Wealth of Nations

———⊃◦◦◦⊂———

I got my first part-time job working for a chocolate shop in Geneva, Illinois. There'd been a chocolate shop on Third Street for a long time, but it had always failed and it was constantly changing hands. It used to be Grandma's Chocolates, but the new guy who owned it renamed it Graham's Chocolates. I didn't get that, since his name was Bob.

Bob was a young, lean man who drove a VW bus. He must've been around 30 at the time. He had a second job as a trombone player in a wedding band. He probably made more money in the wedding band. He certainly kept his night job. But Bob's dream was to be a chocolatier.

I thought you couldn't do much better than a job at the chocolate shop. Who wouldn't want to work in a candy store? I quickly discovered that the chocolate business was a tough racket. Bob would arrive very early in the morning to begin making chocolates, and he often worked until late in the night, unless he had a gig. Bob didn't have "weekends." Weekends were when the store did the most business, and the weekdays were needed to prepare for the weekend.

I boxed chocolates and restocked the cases, but mostly I cleaned the kitchen. Throughout the day, chocolate and caramel would drip down and harden on the tile floor, and about an hour before closing, I would get down on my hands and knees and scrape it off with a plastic edge. The edge quickly became useless with scraped candy, and you'd have to clean it with boiling hot water.

When the floors were done it was time for the dishes. Bob used an enormous copper cauldron to make caramel. It was a beautiful piece of equipment, the color of a new penny, and it looked hand-beaten, with little petals up and down the sides. You could tell the bowl was special to Bob, and he was often telling us to be careful with it. At the time, I thought it was a family heirloom, but looking back, it was probably special because it was the most expensive piece of equipment he owned. The thing weighed a ton, and you couldn't use soap to clean it. You had to use boiling hot water. When you pour boiling hot water into a copper pot full of hardened caramel, it lets off a vent of stench that's one of the worst smells I've ever known. I'd stand over the cauldron as that vent sprayed in my face, filling the cauldron with boiling hot water from a special hose from the kitchen. When it was full of water I could barely manage the weight, but I had to dump the water out, and repeat the process until the bowl was sparkling clean. It was easy to scald yourself every time you emptied it.

The rest of the dishes were just covered in chocolate, marshmallow, and molten sugar. Those you soaked. Marshmallow was the worst.

I was easily the laziest person there. Bob was always working. I think he slept there sometimes. One time in college, when I was home for Christmas break, I happened to be walking by the shop at 1:30 in the morning. The light was on in the shop. Bob was making chocolates in the window. Christmas was an important season in the chocolate business. You sold a lot of chocolate around the holidays. Gotta make hay while the sun shines.

The shop wasn't just about the chocolates. People came there for the charm of the place, with its hardwood floors, its old-timey display cases, the cast-iron tables, and its carefully selected merchandise. Bob mostly worked in the kitchen, and he hired the singer of his wedding band to run the front of the shop. Her name was Beckie. Beckie was pretty, friendly, and funny. Beckie expected you to show up on time. Beckie didn't want your excuses. Beckie agonized over what to put in the various displays. Beckie kept the ledger and totaled the sales every day. Beckie wasn't happy if you dropped a box of truffles.

Bob and Beckie were business partners, and eventually, they

got married. In the beginning, they had nothing. Bob rented a room in somebody's house, and he drove a VW bus that doubled as a mobile storage unit. But over time, the chocolate shop became hugely successful. Twenty-five years later, Bob and Beckie own several stores, and I'm sure they earn a comfortable living. The chocolate shop is a destination in my hometown. People travel from miles around just to see it. Besides the storefront business, Graham's sells chocolates online, and the store supplies specialty chocolates for weddings, corporations, and fancy restaurants. From humble origins, it's become a thriving enterprise that employs many people.

Your mom and I took you there when you were three years old, and you sat at one of the cast-iron tables marveling at a hand-dipped chocolate-covered strawberry.

But if I rewind back to the summer I first started working for Bob, when his success seemed so uncertain, there was something else going on in my town. The previous fall, the stock market crashed, and our neighbors abruptly sold their home and moved. My brother and I spent a lot of our childhood playing in their yard, which was about an acre of wooded lawn surrounding an ornate and enormous 19th-century schoolhouse. Our neighbors seemed to be fabulously rich, and they'd lived there for years. But in a matter of days, they were gone.

The neighbor had been a trader on the Chicago Mercantile Exchange, and he'd lost a fortune in the stock market crash of '87. That crash had followed something called the "Savings and Loan Crisis." A savings and loan association was like a small local credit union. You would deposit your money there, and the S&L would loan money to local businesses and people who needed to buy homes. The S&Ls made modest profits off their loans, and they'd pay depositors interest on their savings accounts. S&Ls counted on the fact that all their depositors would never try to withdraw all their money at once, so they would always have some operating capital to make modest investments and manage withdrawals.

Savings and loans were prevented from speculation until the 1980s, when Congress decided that they should be able to operate just like banks. Banks could buy stocks and speculate on all sorts of things. It wasn't fair that savings and loans couldn't do the same. The argument went that the S&Ls could make more profit if they were allowed to compete, and all this competition would help everyone, including customers. So the S&Ls were *deregulated*, and they began to speculate in the markets.

The problem was, they were playing with house money. Their deposits were insured by the federal government, so if their investments failed, the government would simply bail them out. Economists refer to this problem as **moral hazard,** a situation in which parties are incentivized to take unnecessary risks because they do not bear ultimate responsibility if things go south. Sure enough, the S&Ls took on too much risk, and when their risky investments failed, S&Ls went bankrupt across the country. The government was on the hook to repay depositors. But like any insurance fund, the responsible government agency didn't have enough money to pay everyone back at once. It could handle a few banks failing each year, but not a crisis on this scale.

Our politicians told us to be patient. Eventually, the Invisible Hand of the Market would solve everything. In the meantime, confidence had to be restored. So the government (i.e., the taxpayers) bailed the S&Ls out.

In the 25 or so years since then, as Bob's chocolate business grew, there have been three major financial panics, and each one has been more spectacular than the last. In 2001 we had the dot-com bubble (or the tech bubble), when investors suddenly pulled out of hugely overvalued tech companies. The result was a recession, which worsened after the Enron scandal of 2002, when it was discovered that some of the biggest corporations in the United States were simply fabricating their balance sheets. Finally there was the granddaddy of them all: the Great Recession of 2008, which was the worst financial crisis since the Great Depression. After investors lost confidence in the stock market following the tech collapse and Enron scandals, they began speculating in real estate. Housing prices soared until they became absurd, and then they collapsed. Banks had constructed various betting systems (known as "derivatives") to make even more money off the housing boom, wagering that prices would rise, and insuring one another ("hedging") against prices falling. The government provided incentives for this behavior by keeping interest rates very low, and banks were making so much money that they began to give out huge loans to people who could not afford to pay them back.

So for example, I would take out a mortgage, the bank would cut my mortgage up into pieces and sell those pieces as "investments" to third parties. The third parties would take out insurance against those investments failing, and the insurer would take out insurance as well. It all worked great, so long as housing prices continued to climb. I took out a mortgage at this time. When I went to the bank to get a home loan, I was making $42,000 a year. The bank offered to loan me $400,000—almost 10 times my annual salary. I would never be able to repay that; but the thinking was that I would buy a house and it would quickly appreciate in value. Then I would sell it, pay the bank back, and pocket a tidy profit myself. Everybody would make money. I wound up borrowing much less (and still getting burned), but many others jumped at such opportunities. The bank tried repeatedly to loan me more money. Actually, during this time I received multiple solicitations every day. Everybody wanted to loan me another $50,000 or $100,000.

When housing prices fell, the whole thing fell down like a series of dominoes. People couldn't make their mortgage payments, and they defaulted. Banks turned to their insurers to cover the bad loans, but these insurers didn't have the money. The banks' insurers turned to *their* insurers, and those institutions didn't have the money, either. These last insurers folded, and then the banks' insurers folded, and then the banks folded. It all happened in a matter of days and weeks. Nobody knew who-owned-what or who-owed-who, but everybody understood the magnitude of the problem: it would cost *trillions* of dollars. The entire global financial system collapsed. The stock market lost 50 percent of its value. Millions of people lost their jobs, their homes, and their life savings.

———

Although the phrase *the invisible hand of the market* is often attributed to Adam Smith, the "father of capitalism," Adam Smith never wrote that phrase. He wrote this, in Book 4, Chapter 2 of *The Wealth of Nations*:

> *But the annual revenue of every society is always precisely equal to the exchangeable value of the whole annual produce of its industry, or rather is precisely the same thing with that exchangeable value. As every individual, therefore, endeavors*

as much as he can both to employ his capital in the support of domestic industry, and so to direct that industry that its produce may be of the greatest value; every individual necessarily labors to render the annual revenue of the society as great as he can. He generally, indeed, neither intends to promote the public interest, nor knows how much he is promoting it. By preferring the support of domestic to that of foreign industry, he intends only his own security; and by directing that industry in such a manner as its produce may be of the greatest value, he intends only his own gain, and he is in this, as in many other cases, led by an invisible hand to promote an end which was no part of his intention. Nor is it always the worse for the society that it was no part of it. By pursuing his own interest he frequently promotes that of the society more effectually than when he really intends to promote it.

What he wrote was that when people are free to choose their own work, they will naturally choose work that is the most profitable to them personally, because that means they will enjoy security for themselves and their families. By doing so, the individual, guided by a force he does not understand ("an invisible hand"), also maximizes the wealth of the nation, because he is employed in the optimally profitable labor.

But all wealth—*all of it*—is derived from labor.

The annual labor of every nation is the fund which originally supplies it with all the necessaries and conveniences of life which it annually consumes, and which consist always either in the immediate produce of that labor, or in what is purchased with that produce from other nations.

All wealth is created by work (labor). Wealth can't be derived from complicated financial algorithms. It can only be produced by labor.

Now, some work is more valuable than other work. The more specialized the labor, the higher price that labor commands. If there's more work than can be performed by the supply of labor, then the price of labor will increase. If there's less work than can be performed by the available labor, then the price of labor will fall. And this is not just true of labor, but of any commodity. This is called the **law of supply and demand.**

Supply & Demand (Inverse relationship)		
Supply	High	Low
Demand	Low	High
Price	Falls	Rises

This dynamic creates a natural incentive for both supply and demand to equalize, and when supply is equal to demand, the price of any commodity will reach its "natural" level. This happens all the time in the labor force. For example, in the mid-1990s, demand was extremely high for labor that could develop websites, and website designers commanded large salaries, which then attracted others to pursue those skills. As more people entered the workforce with web design skills, the price of that labor fell.

Labor can create new wealth through innovation, and generally speaking, that innovation is introduced to reduce the amount of work a laborer needs to perform. It is often introduced by the laborer himself:

> *A great part of the machines made use of in those manufacturers in which labor is most subdivided, were originally the inventions of common workmen, who, being each of them employed in some very simple operation, naturally turned their thoughts toward finding out easier and readier methods of performing it.*

It's obvious, when you think about it. If you spend all day doing some menial task, eventually, you're going to figure out a way to make it easier. You're going to create systems and machines that can help perform your labor. Instead of dragging the plow yourself, you get an ox to do it. The ox is stronger than you are, so you invent a bigger plow. Now all the other farmers want your new plow. Somebody starts manufacturing the bigger plows. In the process of manufacturing the plow, new systems and efficiencies are introduced: assembly lines, machines, and inventory management, and these have applications beyond farming. So a great chain of innovation begins with the most basic labor.

Adam Smith did *not* say that the market would invisibly promote justice, or regulate itself fairly. Actually he seemed quite aware that the government would need to play a key role in preventing abuses from occurring and in deterring monopolistic practices. The government would also need to provide certain services (like public education) so the whole of society (including industry) could benefit. Within the market, commodities and labor would find natural prices through supply and demand—if left to their own devices—but the market would not protect children from working in factories, prevent pollution, or thwart monopolies from forming. The market is not magically immune from corruption or excess. Nor is the market a sentient being with emotions. It doesn't "react" to anything. It doesn't "get jittery" or "fear" or "applaud" things people do. Prices rise and fall based on supply and demand, and that's basically it. And even *that* can only occur under conditions of total noninterference. Once you start artificially manipulating the prices of commodities (as all nations do) the marketplace described by Smith no longer functions in its ideal form.

Our country manipulates the price of commodities in countless ways: through taxes, subsidies, tariffs, patents, and even certain monopoly protections. Citizens in the United States don't pay the "natural" cost of oil, any more than we pay the "natural" cost for steel, corn, tires, prescription drugs, cable television, financial services, or even labor itself. In fact, even the currency we use to affix a value to all these things is manipulated. Our market is not at all free, and it really has never been free. Today, when people claim to desire "free market policies," what they usually mean is that they would like preferential treatment for a particular industry, or they would like a certain set of regulations to be eliminated (such as those that prevented S&Ls from reckless speculation). They are certainly not advocating for a true "free market," in which businesses are all treated the same and all are allowed to fail. But if the market were actually free, and if people were allowed to pursue that work which was most profitable to them, then Smith argues that they would naturally create national wealth through their individual labor.

Wealth is good for a nation. We want to create wealth, but not simply for the sake of its acquisition. The wealth of nations serves a larger purpose.

> *Among the savage nations of hunters and fishers, every individual who is able to work, is more or less employed in useful labor, and endeavors to provide as well as he can, the necessaries and conveniences of life, for himself or each of his family or tribe as are either too old, or too young, or too infirm to go a hunting and fishing. Such nations, however, are so miserably poor that, from mere want, they are frequently reduced, or, at least, think themselves reduced, to the necessity sometimes of directly destroying, and sometimes of abandoning their infants, their old people, and those afflicted with lingering diseases, to perish with hunger, or to be devoured by wild beasts. Among the civilized and thriving nations, on the contrary, though a great number of people do not labor at all, many of whom consume the produce of ten times, frequently of a hundred times more labor than the greater part of those who work; yet the produce of the whole labor of the society is so great that all are often abundantly supplied, and a workman, even of the lowest and poorest order, if he is frugal and industrious, may enjoy a greater share of the necessaries and conveniences of life than it is possible for any savage to acquire.*

People in wealthy, industrial societies have it much better than those living in poor, developing countries. It may be fashionable to romanticize "the simple life," but in industrial societies, people live longer and have more leisure time. Most importantly, there is sufficient abundance in the society to *provide for the needy:* for children, the elderly, and the infirm.

Smith states quite clearly: that's why capitalism is desirable as a system. Capitalism is not "every man for himself," and capitalism is not about one person "winning all the marbles." Nor is it about exploiting people or stealing from them for the purpose of acquiring more wealth. Nor is any wealth actually created through exploitation or theft— existing wealth is merely transferred from one hand to another.

When Bob took over the chocolate store, he put every dime he had back into his business. He worked hard to improve it. And slowly, over time, that work produced great wealth. He created jobs, and those workers used their wages to purchase goods and services, which produced more jobs. Bob bought commodities to produce his product: cocoa, sugar, milk, and butter. Through labor, he transformed those raw materials into a refined product, which commanded a price beyond the sum of the cost of the materials and labor it took to produce them. The difference was Bob's profit, which he used to expand his business, to invest in innovations that would allow him to expand further, and also to do things like buy a home and support his family.

Had Bob failed, the government would not have bailed him out. Bob assumed all the risk, but he only enjoyed some of the reward. Many other people were rewarded as Bob built his business. The man literally shared his wealth. He had no choice. There was the woman who'd previously owned the chocolate shop, who sold her property to him. There were his employees, like me, who earned money from his risk. There were the businesses that benefited when we spent the money we earned at the chocolate shop. There were those who sold Bob the raw materials he needed to make his chocolates. There were neighboring businesses that benefited from the tourists visiting his store. There was the town of Geneva, which earned tax revenue from Bob and his employees. And there was the nation, which acquired taxpayers and highly skilled laborers, those trained by Bob through the expansion of his business.

But the real prospect of failure was essential to the creation of Bob's wealth. After all, if success were guaranteed, why wouldn't everyone own a chocolate store? If everyone owned a chocolate store, then the value of Bob's product would fall. There would be more supply and less demand. But since Bob's chocolates (the product of labor and raw commodities) were rare, they commanded a premium in the marketplace. The price of Bob's chocolates was partially determined by the commodities he used, but it also reflected the value of his highly skilled labor (and Beckie's skilled labor, as well). Anyone could go out and buy cocoa and butter, but not everyone could refine those raw materials into such a valuable commodity. Labor added the true value.

Today, Bob could be called a wealthy man.

And in all these financial crises of the last 25 years—the S&L

crisis, the dot-com bubble, the Enron Scandal, and the Great Recession—everyone lost a lot of money, but no *wealth* was actually destroyed. The truth is, it had never existed. What people lost was the *illusion* of wealth. That wealth didn't exist, and it had never really existed, because nobody had actually worked for it.

There are no shortcuts to financial prosperity, Violet. If you want wealth, then follow your passion, because your passion is the only thing that will enable you to take risks, be patient, and work your ass off.

CHAPTER 26

DOES CAPITALISM WORK?

KARL MARX AND FRIEDRICH ENGELS
Manifesto of the Communist Party

A fter I worked in the chocolate shop for a couple years, I got a job working for Weldon Johnson at Viking Office Supply. Viking Office Supply sold to most of the local businesses, and it also sold to the school system and City Hall. It was a thriving enterprise. Weldon wasn't rich, but he made a good living. He drove a convertible and he had a hot tub. Every summer he had a cookout for his employees. This was the grand finale to the city's Swedish Days festival, which Weldon helped organize and sponsor. During Swedish Days a carnival would come to town, all the shops would be open until midnight, and people came from all over Illinois to visit historic Geneva. Weldon would dress up like a Viking and amuse the tourists. He named his business after the high school mascot, the Viking. The man actually looked like a Viking. He was a big, burly man with a bushy red beard. He even invested in a very nice horned helmet and a sword. He went to all the football games, and you could spot him in the stands because he'd wear the helmet.

Weldon was an important man in Geneva. (Actually, his nickname was "Mr. Geneva"). He was a city councilman, and a generous donor to the high school and the church. He also employed a lot of people. In addition to me and a bunch of other high school kids, his entire family worked at the store. They had good jobs, with salaries and benefits. When Viking Office Supply had a good year, they had a good year.

Weldon had powerful incentives to contribute to the community. He needed to make connections through the local chamber of commerce, the school board, and the city. So he sat on boards and participated in the city's governance. His family had a genuine desire to be good citizens, because they actually lived in the community where their business was located. The Johnson kids went to Geneva schools, and Fran and Weldon were devout Catholics. I saw them every week at St. Peter's Church. Whenever a soccer team needed sponsoring, or the band needed new instruments, Viking Office Supply was there. Weldon was proud of that, and he also understood that what was good for his community was also good for his business.

Weldon and his family worked very hard. He was very big on customer service, and on offering the best prices he could. If you found a better price somewhere else, you could deal with Weldon. He'd even take a loss, if it meant keeping a good customer happy.

There used to be stores like Viking Office Supply in towns across America. On Saturdays, my dad used to take us to run errands—to the bank, the drug store, the hardware store, and so on—and every place was different. I knew all the people who worked at these places. They called us all by name. The owners worked behind the counter, and their families worked at the stores. I went to school with their children, many of whom began working in the shops long before it was technically legal. They'd grown up with the business—some of them actually lived in apartments above the shops. One of my best friends, Tim Landberg, grew up like that—stocking shelves, managing inventory, and making deals. That kid could sell anything to anyone, and it wasn't what he said, but the way he could listen to people, and make them feel listened to. It's a unique skill. Maybe the most useful skill. You learn it growing up in a shop.

There was a time in America when you could make a good living running one of those shops. You could buy a house, you could support a family, and you could employ people in the community. You could be your own boss, and you could build something.

Those days are gone. Viking Office Supply finally closed the year you were born, after 33 years in business. It held out longer than I believed possible. In the end, it couldn't compete with the big-box office supply stores. Office Depot, OfficeMax, and Staples were simply too huge, and they purchased their supplies on a scale that Weldon could never match. For every box of pens Weldon bought, those stores bought 100,000. They could sell their pens for a lower price than Weldon could even buy them for, and for most customers, that's the only thing that mattered.

One day, a big-box store moved into town, and it quickly replaced about four office supply shops in the area. Each of those smaller office supply shops had an owner like Weldon, and each of them employed family members, and offered them decent salaries and benefits. The big box only needed one Weldon, and it certainly wasn't going to share profits with that person. And it didn't need to pay all those other people down the chain, either. It didn't exist to support families. It existed to keep prices as low as possible and to deliver maximum return to investors. Employees were expensive. The less the big box spent on health care and salaries, the better. So they replaced those full-time, salaried jobs with lower-paying, part-time jobs without benefits—jobs that paid even less than I made as a high school kid working after school for Weldon. It's hard to believe, but more than 20 years ago, I made $6.50 an hour at Viking Office Supply. Today the minimum wage is $7.25 an hour. Adjusting for inflation, most part-time workers today make 35 percent less than I did when I was 16 years old.

Viking Office Supply wasn't alone. Around the same time, exactly the same thing happened to bookstores, hardware stores, and coffee shops. When I was a kid, all of those kinds of small stores still existed in Geneva, and also in neighboring towns like St. Charles and Batavia. Small towns across the country had them, too. But gradually chains like Borders, Barnes & Noble, Home Depot, and Starbucks became dominant.

Adam Smith and Karl Marx would both agree that this was simply capitalism at work. All of these new "super businesses" had lowered the cost of production, reduced the cost of labor, and discovered a more efficient way to deliver products to people. In theory, consumers benefited from this. The average consumer now spent much less on office supplies, books, coffee, food, and clothes, so in theory, that person had more disposable income to invest or to do whatever they wanted with it. As a result, their standard of living improved. Marx and Smith would both agree that the capitalist system is enormously efficient at creating abundance.

In the *Communist Manifesto,* Marx and Engels want to know the end of the American Office Supply story.

First let's consider all the people who actually make the actual office supplies—the pens, the paper, and the rest of it: the manufacturers and suppliers. When there were hundreds of independent office supply stores, there were also hundreds of suppliers spread out around the country. Most of them made good livings, but nobody was "super-rich." But as these three big chains begin to emerge as the only buyers for office supply products, their suppliers *also* begin to merge with one another. They are forced to consolidate in order to stay alive. Big chains purchase supplies in volumes that no individual supplier can manage, and they also demand such enormous discounts that suppliers must create efficiencies themselves, and thereby lower the cost of production. Gradually small companies merge with each other, or are bought out by larger companies. Management is consolidated throughout the supply chain in order to increase efficiency and reduce the cost of products.

At this point, there is still some competition in the market. The three remaining big-box chains have outcompeted thousands of Viking Office Supply stores around the country. But now the three that remain are duking it out with one another, and each one seeks a competitive advantage. That competitive advantage gets harder and harder to find, until even the slightest edge can make the difference. These businesses are all based on the same model: they must drive prices as low as humanly possible. Each of the remaining three office supply behemoths puts pressure on the other two. If one company can lower the price of pens by $.01, the other two would be forced to do the same, even if they can't afford to. Because they're operating on such a massive scale, that single penny price difference can add up to millions and millions of dollars.

Eventually, one of those three chains decides to either buy the suppliers outright, or start manufacturing their own pens, their own paper, and the rest of it. This is called *vertical integration.* Better to control all parts of the supply chain. By "getting rid of the middle man," you can increase efficiency and decrease the number of employees in management positions. Instead of multiple owners of various pen, paper, and pencil companies, you just pay one guy to run all the supply production. Then you buy all the distribution trucks, you buy the factories, and you consolidate everything in one gigantic office supply monolith.

Then, after consolidating the suppliers under one roof, it becomes apparent that even after vertically integrating and automating tasks as much as possible, the supply chain is *still* too expensive. Why make pens in Illinois, where there's a minimum wage and all these expensive environmental standards? The chain can make these same pens in Mexico, or China, and even when shipping is factored in, they'd cost 50 percent less to produce.

Production is moved to *emerging markets*, and now even those supplier jobs, which were already more scarce than they were before, suddenly vanish. Poof: they're gone, and they're never coming back. These formerly prosperous suppliers join all the former owners of small office supply stores among the ranks of the unemployed.

Meanwhile, in those emerging markets, there is enormous poverty and a huge surplus of labor, so wages for workers are reduced all the way down to subsistence levels. You don't have to put up with laws and standards, either. Governments need your corporation to provide the thinnest veil of social stability, so they bow to your every demand. A hundred people fight for each available job, and that job barely pays enough to survive. And that one guy who gets the job? He'll do *anything* to keep it. He'll work 20 hours a day, in hazardous conditions, without health care, without retirement. All he cares about is surviving *today*, and feeding his family *today*. He has no other options.

But even *these* workers are too expensive. Eventually a machine is created that can perform the work of thousands of workers. The machine costs a lot to produce—at first. But it's not an ongoing cost. Once it's in place, the only cost is maintenance. And the machines can work 24 hours a day, seven days a week, in very cold or very hot warehouses.

The physical stores where consumers buy products are also too expensive. It would be cheaper to get rid of them, and simply sell directly to the consumer, and have machines produce, pack, and ship everything directly to them. The only costs left pertain to management and basic upkeep.

At a certain point, it becomes obvious that the only way to win in this competition is for the two smaller competitors to consolidate. If they do that, they can double their market share, and slash their management expenses even further by eliminating duplication. Yes: they'll fire half the people from each side (or everyone on one side) but the current management will all receive generous buyouts. Those individuals will be okay. But here again, those few remaining prosperous middle managers now join the former owners and suppliers among the ranks of the unemployed. And however generous the buyouts might be, the children of these managers will now have fewer opportunities to join the rich. Over time, wealth erodes.

Two of the remaining three office supply chains merge, leaving only two companies. Both are vertically integrated, both have pushed production to its lowest possible cost. But one is twice as large as the other, and it operates much more efficiently. At this point, the bigger company engages in a short price war, taking temporary losses to drive its competition out of business. The smaller chain is easily dominated, and eventually, there is one winner: MegaMaxSuperOffice, which has a monopoly on all office products across the entire world. It makes everything, it sells everything, and nobody has any choice. The market is now effectively closed to competition, unless you know how to make paper and pens in your basement. Even then you might not be allowed access to the raw materials you need (MegaMaxSuperOffice controls those, too). Even if you could make the raw materials, you'll never be able to produce office supplies on the same scale. The remaining suppliers certainly aren't going to sell to you. MegaMaxSuperOffice either owns them all, or it can sufficiently pressure them to deny other potential customers.

As Marx writes, at each step in this long process more and more wealth is concentrated in fewer and fewer hands, as the **means of production** are consolidated. In the beginning stage, when there was Viking Office Supply and a thousand other stores like it, there were thousands of Weldons, and thousands of suppliers, all making decent livings. Nobody was especially rich, but everyone was doing fairly well. Wealth was dispersed among a substantial middle class.

In the second stage, with three big chains, there are still hundreds of people doing well in middle management. Much fewer than there were before, yes, but still—the middle class still exists. It's smaller, and it's under more pressure—but it's there. There are the executives at all the companies, followed by the management teams, followed by the store managers, and there are three sets of CEOs, corporate vice presidents, managers, accountants, lawyers, and so on.

But in the final stage, the office supply middle class has vanished. There are only two classes: an extremely small upper class (the owners, or shareholders) and a huge and growing underclass (everyone else). All the people who previously were doing well—including small business owners like Weldon, the suppliers, and even the former CEOs of the huge chains—have joined the workers in the ranks of the underclass. Even the corporate vice presidents, lawyers, and accountants find themselves in stiff competition for very few jobs, so the price that labor commands drops precipitously as well. Only a handful of people make living wages anymore, and eventually there's only one person making a fortune: a SuperWeldon, the sole proprietor of MegaMaxSuperOffice, who has replaced hundreds and thousands of workers down the line. There are still some workers below Super-Weldon, but as few as humanly possible, and they are paid as little as possible. Eventually their wages are suppressed so much that they live on the edge of starvation.

And yet, ironically, there is remarkable abundance. There are so many pens and so much paper being produced, and at such a low cost, that it's absurd. The world will never want for more pens, papers, or binder clips.

But even at these insanely low prices, who is left to buy them?

———

The Communist Manifesto argues that the emergence of industrialized free-market capitalism is the beginning of the end of the liberal tradition, which produced various modes of economic and political control. It is the also the end of the West's philosophical underpinnings, which have only been invented as a means to serve the ruling classes.

> *In the earlier epochs of history we find almost everywhere a complicated arrangement of society into various orders, a manifold gradation of social rank. In ancient Rome we have patricians, knights, plebeians, slaves; in the Middle Ages, feudal lords, vassals, guild-masters, journeymen, apprentices, serfs; in almost all of these classes, again, subordinate gradations.*
>
> *The modern bourgeois society that has sprouted from the*

ruins of feudal society has not done away with class antago-
nisms. It has but established new classes, new conditions of
oppression, new forms of struggle in place of the old ones.

Our epoch, the epoch of the bourgeoisie, possesses,
however, this distinctive feature: it has simplified the class
antagonisms. Society as a whole is more and more splitting
up into two great hostile camps, into two great classes directly
facing each other—bourgeoisie and proletariat.

The **bourgeoisie** is the ruling class. It is the class that controls all the capital, all the property, and most importantly, the means of production. The **proletariat** is the class of workers, all of whom labor for the benefit of the bourgeoisie.

According to Marx and Engels, modern industrialized capitalism inevitably produces two classes whose interests are naturally at odds. The bourgeoisie's interest is to reduce the living standard of the proletariat as much as possible, while at the same time squeezing more and more productivity out of them. As time goes on, the proletariat gets larger and larger and larger, while at the same time it grows ever more miserable. The bourgeoisie becomes smaller and smaller, and ever more wealthy and more powerful—but *also* more miserable. And in the end, the imbalance is so great, and so many are disaffected, that the system simply becomes absurd. And just like preceding social systems such as feudalism, the capitalist system collapses, and the bourgeoisie class disappears with it.

Now there is only one class: the proletariat. The workers. Everyone is proletariat. The proletariat seizes control of the means of production, and the concept of private property vanishes. Everybody owns everything. People have everything they need, because there is enormous productive power in the hands of all, and that productive power is used for the benefit of everyone.

In this future, education undergoes radical change as liberal values are cast aside. The idea of the family, for example, disappears. The idea of inequality is absurd. Notions of "justice" and "individuality" and "freedom" do not exist, because they are not necessary; in fact, these ideas themselves were merely tools of oppression. According to Marx and Engels, political systems (like democracy) were only mechanisms to enforce the will of the ruling class. There will be no religion. There will be no state, really. There will just be everyone living cooperatively and harmoniously in a communist system.

The Communist Manifesto does not dispute the logic of Adam Smith's *The Wealth of Nations*. Actually, it agrees with it completely. It simply extends Smith's theories to (what Marx and Engels believe to be) their logical conclusion.

First, Marx argues, free-market capitalism leads to an explosion in the productive powers of the world.

> *Modern industry has established the world market, for which the discovery of America paved the way. This market has given an immense development to commerce, to navigation, to communications by land. This development has, in turn, reacted on extension of industry; and in proportion as industry, commerce, navigation, railways extended, in the same proportion the bourgeoisie developed, increased its capital, and pushed into the background every class handed down from the Middle Ages .... The Bourgeoisie during its rule of scarce one hundred years has created more massive and more colossal productive forces than have all preceding generations together .... It has been the first to show what man's activity can bring about. It has accomplished wonders far surpassing the Egyptian pyramids, Roman aqueducts, and Gothic cathedrals; it has conducted expeditions that put in the shade all former migrations of nations and crusades.*

As capitalism gets going, the bourgeoisie begins to consolidate industries. Consolidation, Marx and Engels argue, is the natural tendency of capitalism. Corporations become bigger and bigger as they gobble each other up. They soon become untethered from the state, and they begin to concentrate property and wealth in the hands of a very few. Meanwhile, industry becomes and more automated, and jobs become increasingly scarce. Workers compete with each other for fewer and fewer jobs, resulting in ever lower wages. Society is politically organized around the interests of the ruling class.

Eventually, overproduction becomes a threat to the bourgeoisie. They are producing more goods than society needs, and they cannot sell them to impoverished workers, so they open up new markets in order to sell products. In these markets, the same political systems are established to serve the interests of the bourgeoisie. Whole nations are exploited.

> *It is enough to mention the commercial crises that by their periodical return put the existence of the entire bourgeois society on trial, each time more threateningly. In these crises, a great part not only of the existing products, but also of the previously created productive forces, are periodically destroyed. In these crises, there breaks out an epidemic that, in earlier epochs, would have seemed an absurdity—the epidemic of overproduction. Society suddenly finds itself put back into a state of momentary barbarism ... because there is too much civilization, too much means of subsistence, too much industry, too much commerce ....*
>
> *And how does the bourgeoisie get over these crises? On the one hand by enforced destruction of a mass of productive forces; on the other, by the conquest of new markets and by the more thorough exploitation of the old ones.*

Just as Smith argued, labor is a commodity. So *people* are commodities, and they trade themselves for less and less, until they are essentially reduced to slavery.

At first, there may exist a middle class, like our small group of independent shop-owners, for example. But as industries are centralized and conglomerates grow larger and larger, these shopkeepers cannot compete with their gargantuan competitors. They are either bought out by the bourgeoisie or they are forced out of the class entirely, and they find themselves joining the ranks of the proletariat. Fewer and fewer people control more and more of the wealth.

> *The lower strata of the middle class—the small tradespeople, shopkeepers, and retired tradesmen generally, the handicraftsmen and peasants—all these sink gradually into the proletariat, partly because their diminutive capital does not suffice for the scale on which modern industry is carried on and swamped in competition with the large capitalists, partly because their specialized skill is rendered worthless by new methods of production.*

Marx and Engels argue that this process is a zero-sum game. In the beginning stages, workers unite with one another and are occasionally victorious in winning concessions from the bourgeoisie, but that period is only temporary. If concessions are granted, they are usually granted because of some competing interest in the ruling class.

> *Finally, in times when the class struggle nears the decisive hour, the process of dissolution going on within the ruling class, in fact within the whole range of old society, assumes such a violent, glaring character that a small section of the ruling class cuts itself adrift and joins the revolutionary class, the class that holds the future in its hands.*

The ruling class cannot even maintain a standard of living inside the proletariat that would qualify as slavery.

> *It is unfit to rule because it is incompetent to assure an existence to its slave within his slavery, because it cannot help letting him sink into such a state that it has to feed him, instead of being fed by him. Society can no longer live under the bourgeoisie, in other words, its existence is no longer compatible with society .... What the bourgeoisie, therefore, produces above all are its own gravediggers. Its fall and the victory of the proletariat are equally inevitable.*

According to Marx and Engels, the concept of *private property* itself is the problem.

> *The distinguishing feature of Communism is not the abolition of property generally, but the abolition of bourgeois property .... In this sense the theory of the Communists may be summed up in the single sentence: abolition of private property.*

And with the abolition of private property comes the abolition of all the ideas and concepts used to support private property, such as those proposed by John Locke, Adam Smith, and the framers of our

Constitution. Gone are ideas of individualism, the liberal conception of freedom, of individual rights, and justice.

But don't wrangle with us so long as you apply to our intended abolition of bourgeois property the standard of your bourgeois notions of freedom, culture, law, etc. Your very ideas are but the outgrowth of the conditions of your bourgeois production and bourgeois property, just as your jurisprudence is but the will of your class made into a law for all, a will whose essential character and direction are determined by the economic conditions of existence of your class.

Does it require deep intuition to comprehend that man's ideas, views, and conceptions—in one word, man's consciousness—changes with every change in the conditions of his materials existence, in his social relations and in his social life?

What else does the history of ideas prove than that intellectual production changes its character in proportion as material production is changed? The ruling ideas of each age have ever been the ideas of its ruling class .... When the ancient world was in its last throes the ancient religions were overcome by Christianity. When Christian ideas succumbed in the 18th century to rationalist ideas, feudal society fought its death battle with the then revolutionary bourgeoisie. The ideas of religious liberty and freedom of conscience merely gave expression to the sway of free competition within the domain of knowledge.

And, since we're coming to the end, Violet, guess who shows up again? Plato.

"Undoubtedly," it will be said ... "There are ... eternal truths such as freedom, justice, etc., that are common to all states of society." But Communism abolishes eternal truths, it abolishes all religion and all morality, instead of constituting them on a new basis; it, therefore, acts in contradiction to all past historical experience.

What does this accusation reduce itself to? The history of all past society has consisted in the development of class antagonisms, antagonisms that assumed different forms at different epochs.

But whatever form they may have taken, one fact is common to all past ages, viz., the exploitation of one part of society by another. No wonder then, that the social consciousness of past ages, despite all the multiplicity and variety it displays, moves within certain common forms, or general ideas, which cannot completely vanish except with the total disappearance of class antagonisms.

The Communist revolution is the most radical rupture with traditional property relations; no wonder that its development involves the most radical rupture with traditional ideas.

What will transpire during this Communist revolution? Marx and Engels lay out 10 steps that will emerge in the advanced countries:

1. Abolition of private property
2. A heavily progressive income tax
3. Abolition of inheritance
4. Confiscation of property of all emigrants or rebels
5. Centralization of credit in the hands of the state
6. Centralization of transportation systems in the hands of the state
7. Common, central industrial and agricultural planning
8. Equal obligation of all to work
9. Combination of manufacturing and agriculture
10. Free public education (though radically different from our liberal education)

According to Marx and Engels, the inequality produced by capitalism will lead to its demise. Eventually, inequality will become so absurd as to be clearly unsustainable. Even the people on top of the pyramid will find it absurd.

At last, everyone will be equal.

The United States is the richest, most powerful country on Earth. Simply by being American, even a "poor" American, you are better off than *billions* of people. But in the United States, where modern capitalism has had the longest and most successful tenure, wealth has begun to concentrate in the manner Marx and Engels predicted. As of 2015, we had reached a point far beyond the inequality experienced during the heyday of the Roman Empire or the Gilded Age of the robber barons. According to research by UC Berkeley professor Emmanuel Saenz, cited by the PEW Research Center in January 2014, US income inequality is the worst it's been since 1928. The rich are getting richer, and the poor are getting poorer. A November 2012 study by Edward N. Wolff, published in the *National Bureau of Economic Research*, found that the richest 20 percent of Americans possessed nearly 90 percent of the total national wealth. A 2013 report by the AP found that not only was poverty increasing among Americans, but that four out of five American adults will eventually struggle with joblessness, near poverty, or reliance on public assistance. At the same time, the pay at the top of the scale has risen exponentially. In 1974, when I was born, a typical CEO took home about 50 times the salary of his average worker. According to the AFL-CIO, CEOs today earn 380 times the salary of their average worker. And perhaps most ominously, in 2014, Oxfam published a report that the richest 85 people in the world control wealth that is equal to the combined wealth of the world's poorest 3.5 billion.

Adam Smith argues that while capitalism does produce inequality, the benefits to society are tremendous, as even the poorest receive the benefit of an increased standard of living. When capitalism is working, the cost of goods and services is suppressed to its lowest natural level, so even if people make less money, they can afford more goods and services. Over time, you *should* make more money, but even if you don't, your money will go further. This buying power is only supposed to improve over time.

Well, let's see if it's been true over the last 20 years. Here are just some very basic price comparisons between when I graduated college (1996) and say, 2013, (the most recent year the comprehensive information is readily available). In these 17 years, the official inflation rate was 48 percent. Even adjusting for inflation, prices should be lower now, right?

	1996	2013	% Change
My college education (University of Illinois)	$10,732	$46,584	434%
My first home	$114,090	$257,000	225%
Gallon of gas	$1.23	$3.58	291%
Gallon of milk	$2.56	$3.52	138%
Family health insurance premium	$4,954	$15,745	318%

I guess milk is a little cheaper. Hooray.

Well—maybe we're earning 300–400 percent more than we did in 1996?

	1996	2012	% Change
Median household income	$35,492	$51,017	44%

US Bureau of Labor Statistics

Nope. Actually, adjusted for inflation, we're earning 6 percent *less* than we were 17 years ago—even as prices for most modern essentials have doubled, tripled, or even quadrupled.

The good news is that this trend cannot continue indefinitely. The bad news is, it might end with a complete upheaval of our economic system. Capitalism is not the first, second, or fifteenth economic paradigm human beings have tried. It will not be the last.

When transitions in economic paradigms have occurred in the past, the transition wasn't exactly as quick, smooth, and easy as Marx and Engels predict. People didn't just wake up one day and say, "Well, I guess that's it for feudalism. Let's all sit down and have a pleasant, civil dialogue about private property and the free market." People got their heads chopped off. Lands were seized by force. The world was thrown into long periods of chaos and revolution.

I worry for your generation—not because you are incapable of innovation, or because you lack the industriousness of previous generations. You simply find yourself living in an era beset by enormous structural challenges. Capitalism began and thrived under a very different set of demographic, economic, and technological assumptions.

When John Locke was writing about private property and labor, kings and queens were giving away hundreds of acres of land to anyone who would agree to work it. If we believe that modern humans evolved around 200,000 years ago, then the societies Locke wrote about operated under (basically) the same demographic assumptions that had existed for 199,800 years: simply put, there weren't enough people to do all the work. That was before the population explosion made possible by the industrial revolution. It took human beings roughly 1,998 centuries of our existence as a species to achieve a global population of one billion. In the next two centuries, the global population shot up to seven billion.

Things have changed. Not only are there more people, but thanks to modern advances in medicine and agriculture, those people are living much, much longer than they used to. Technological progress also means these individuals are several times more productive than say, a 17th-century field hand with an ox and plow. For the most part, that 17th-century worker was performing labor the same way it had been performed for 10,000 years. Yes, that 17th-century worker might have had slightly better instruments and improved techniques, but he didn't have a 10-ton, combustion-powered, robot-driven plow running around his field. Planes didn't dust his crops with advanced pesticides. Irrigation water couldn't be piped thousands of miles and distributed instantly, and in precisely the right amounts, with the press of a button.

But, just as Marx and Engels predicted, these innovations came with costs. As machines have become increasingly sophisticated, they have replaced vast swaths of the labor force by automating tasks that previously required human hands. As computers become more capable, they will render more and more occupations obsolete, and at higher and higher skill levels. We are undergoing this transition now, Violet. There are already factories, warehouses, and farms that operate with very few (or no) human workers. In the next decade, companies will begin to replace millions of truck drivers with fleets of self-driving automobiles. Financial transactions are now conducted with cold ruthlessness by computers, on massive scales, and on timescales too infinitesimal for human beings to replicate. Only a few days after you came home from the hospital, on May 6, 2010, the algorithms used by these machines led to a 1,000-point drop in the stock market, which occurred so quickly that human traders could not understand what was happening. In your lifetime, machines may even replace the most highly skilled workers, such as doctors. IBM has developed a computer called "Watson" that first became famous by soundly defeating game show champions on *Jeopardy*. That same system is now diagnosing illness in patients—and doing so far more effectively, efficiently, and accurately than human doctors. Already—today—machines are producing our food, managing our finances, manufacturing our products, driving our cars, fighting our wars, and treating our illnesses. Just 20 years ago, human hands were required to perform 100 percent of this labor. Not anymore.

There's even a term for this: **technological unemployment.** Marx predicted this phenomenon, and he experienced a rudimentary form of it firsthand. He lived during a time of increased automation and productivity, which saw many menial tasks automated by machines in factories. Fundamentally, as both Adam Smith and John Locke posited, capitalism is a system based on the **cost of labor.** Most of the central assumptions of our political system—including ideas like private property, limited government, and even individual rights—rely upon the assumption that all labor has some cost.

If the cost of even the most highly skilled labor drops to virtually nothing, how can the system be sustained?

I fear that you are living in the age of abundance and inequality described so ominously in *The Communist Manifesto*, and that this age may very well signal the decline of our economic and political systems. Nobody knows what will (or can) replace those systems. Somehow, I don't think it will be the utopian (or perhaps dystopian) Communist vision described in the *Communist Manifesto*. Whatever comes after capitalism and the republic, the transition will be difficult, and, if history is any guide, it could even be violent.

So what's going to happen? I don't know. I don't think Marx and Engels knew, either. Even if they are proven right about the end of capitalism, it doesn't seem that their suggested replacement system has worked out so well in practice. Marx and Engels' reduction of individualism seems to me to be fatally flawed. Denigrating people like Socrates, Aristotle, Jesus, and John Locke as mouthpieces for the "Establishment" doesn't really make much sense. Most of these guys weren't cheerleaders for the ruling class, and a couple of them were put to death for challenging the establishment. History is filled with examples of great individuals who change the world with their singular contributions. I think the world would look a lot different without people like Socrates, Abraham Lincoln, or Steve Jobs. These individuals could never emerge under the rigid, conformist dogma suggested in the *Communist Manifesto*. Ironically, it is quite a Communist sentiment to say "We're all created equal." Capitalists living in a republic don't believe that at all—we believe in the supremacy of the individual; we celebrate differences, and we encourage inequality. Our economic and political systems are *based* on inequality—on the idea that each individual is unique, and even that some are better suited to rule than others. That idea seems validated by a lot of historical evidence—both in our country and in Communist countries as well.

But you don't have to be a Communist to appreciate the *Communist Manifesto*, because it reminds us that nothing is permanent, Violet. Our republic is temporary. Capitalism is temporary. I am temporary, and so are you. One day the sun will expire and the cosmos will collapse. There is really no such thing as "Virginia," where you were born, there is no such thing as a dollar, and in the end, private property is an invention, too.

We have experimented with kings and economic systems, with liberty and tyranny, with every conceivable model to improve our lives. Some experiments have been more successful than others. But there is always a better way to do things, and you will have a hand in finding a better way for all of us.

Maybe that is why your soul fought your way into this world, and why you possess those qualities I found so strange when you weighed just three pounds and couldn't breathe: toughness, persistence, and most importantly, cheerfulness. These are not your only gifts, Violet, but they are the traits that I saw in you from the moment you arrived in this world, and I believe they are inherent to your soul. And you are so fortunate, because in the end, these qualities are far more important assets than degrees, or money, or power. Life will test you; it will try to strip your soul, but I know you will prevail. Be tough, Violet. Persist. And above all else, be cheerful.

Since the day you were born, I have strived every day to be more like you, Violet, and to follow the example your spirit sets.

BIBLIOGRAPHY

All source books except *The Confessions* and the Bible are part of the *Great Books of the Western World* series, Robert Maynard Hutchins, Editor in Chief (Chicago: University of Chicago, 1952).

Plato, *Apology*, trans. Benjamin Jowett. (Volume 7, 200–212.)

Plato, *Crito*, trans. Benjamin Jowett. (Volume 7, 213–219.)

Aristophanes, *Clouds*, trans. Benjamin Bickley Rogers. (Volume 5, 488–506.)

Aristophanes, *Lysistrata,* trans. Benjamin Bickley Rogers. (Volume 5, 583–599.)

Plato, *Republic,* trans. Benjamin Jowett. (Volume 7, 295–441.)

Aristotle, *Politics,* trans. W.D. Ross. (Volume 9, 455–455.)

Aristotle, *Nicomachean Ethics,* trans. W.D. Ross. (Volume 9, 339–348.)

Plutarch, *The Life of Lycurgus,* trans. Dryden. (Volume 14, 32–47.)

Plutarch, *The Life of Numa Pompilius,* trans. Dryden. (Volume 14, 49–60.)

Plutarch, *The Life of Alexander,* trans. Dryden. (Volume 14, 540–576.)

Plutarch, *The Life of Julius Caesar,* trans. Dryden. (Volume 14, 577–603.)

St. Matthew, The Gospel of Jesus Christ (Holy Bible, Revised Standard Version, American Bible Society, New York, 1952), 835–866.

St. Luke, The Acts of the Apostles (Holy Bible, Revised Standard Version, American Bible Society, New York, 1952), 947–976.

St. Augustine, *The Confessions,* trans. Gary Wills. (New York: Penguin Publishing Group, 2002), 1–182.

Machiavelli, Niccolò, *The Prince,* trans. W.K. Marriott. (Volume 23, 1–38.)

Rabelais, Francois, *Gargantua,* trans. Sir Thomas Urquhart. (Volume 24, 1–67.)

De Montaigne, Michel Eyquem, *Of Custom, and That We Should Not Easily Change a Law Received,* trans. Charles Cotton. (Volume 25, 42–50.)

De Montaigne, Michel Eyquem, *Of Pedantry,* trans. Charles Cotton. (Volume 25, 55–61.)

De Montaigne, Michel Eyquem, *Of The Education of Children,* trans. Charles Cotton. (Volume 25, 62–79.)

De Montaigne, Michel Eyquem, *That it is Folly to Measure Truth and Error by Our Own Capacity,* trans. Charles Cotton. (Volume 25, 80–81.)

De Montaigne, Michel Eyquem, *Of Cannibals,* trans. Charles Cotton. (Volume 25, 91–97.)

De Montaigne, Michel Eyquem, *That the Relish of Good and Evil Depends in Great Measure Upon the Opinion we Have of Them,* trans. Charles Cotton. (Volume 25, 115–124.)

De Montaigne, Michel Eyquem, *Upon Some Verses of Virgil,* trans. Charles Cotton. (Volume 25, 406–433.)

Shakespeare, William. *Hamlet,* edited by William George Clarke and Aldis Wright. (Volume 27, 29–72.)

Locke, John. *Concerning Civil Government, Second Essay.* (Volume 35, 25–84.)

Rousseau, Jean Jacques. *The Social Contract,* trans. G.D.H. Cole. (Volume 38, 387–439.)

Gibbon, Edward, *The Decline and Fall of the Roman Empire,* Chapters 15–16. (Volume 40, 179–233.)

Various, The Declaration of Independence. (Volume 43, 1–4.)

Various, The Constitution of the United States of America. (Volume 43, 11–21.)

Hamilton, Alexander, James Madison, and John Jay. *The Federalist*. (Volume 43, 29–53, 62–66, 103–105, 153–156, 162–165, 205–216.)

Smith, Adam. *An Inquiry into the Nature and Causes of the Wealth of Nations*. (Volume 39, 1–41.)

Marx, Karl, and Friedrich Engels. *Manifesto of the Communist Party,* trans. Samuel Moore. (Volume 50, 415–434.)

Pew Research Center. "5 Facts about Economic Inequality." http://www.pewresearch.org/fact-tank/2014/01/07/5-facts-about-economic-inequality/

National Bureau of Economic Research. Edward N. Wolff, "The Asset Price Meltdown and the Wealth of the Middle Class." http://www.nber.org/papers/w18559

 **MATT BURRIESCI** is the author of *Nonprofit* (New Issues Press, 2015) and his stories have appeared in numerous literary magazines. He began his career at the Tony Award-winning Chicago Shakespeare Theater on Navy Pier, and later served as Executive Director for both the Association of Writers and Writing Programs (AWP) and the PEN/Faulkner Foundation. During his tenure at AWP, he helped build the largest literary conference in North America, and he served as a national advocate for literature and the humanities. In his work as a consultant, he has interviewed dozens of global leaders in healthcare, scientific research, and higher education. He lives in Alexandria, Virginia, with his wife Erin and their children, Violet and Henry. (Sorry, Henry, the next one's for you, buddy!)